NEW
YORK
WORLD
CITY

$12.50.89

Report of the Twentieth Century Fund
Task Force on the Future of
New York City

NEW YORK WORLD CITY

Background Paper by
Masha Sinnreich

Oelgeschlager, Gunn & Hain, Publishers, Inc.
Cambridge, Massachusetts

Library of Congress Cataloging in Publication Data

Twentieth Century Fund. Task Force on the Future of New York City.
New York—world city.

Includes bibliographic references.
1. New York (City)—Economic policy. 2. Fiscal policy—New York (City)
I. Sinnreich, Masha. II. Title.
HC108.N7T86   1980   330.9'747'1   79-25129
ISBN 0-89946-009-7
ISBN 0-89946-008-9 pbk.

Printed in the United States of America.

Paperbound International Standard Book Number: 0-89946-008-9

Clothbound International Standard Book Number: 0-89946-009-7

Library of Congress Catalog Card Number: 79-25129

Contents

Foreword *M.J. Rossant*   xi

Task Force Members   xv

Report of the Task Force   1

    Recovering from the Fall   4
    Striking a Balance   7
    The City's Strengths   7
    Toward the World City   9
    Serving New Yorkers   13
    Promoting the Private Sector   16
    Maintaining the City   20
    Reviving Neighborhoods   22
    National Obligation   28
    Meeting the Challenge   30

Dissent *Andrew J. Biemiller*   33

Background Paper *Masha Sinnreich*   35

Chapter 1   Introduction   37

Chapter 2   New York's Changing Economy   47

Dispersion   48
New York in Decline   53
Declining Metropolis, Declining Core   54
Dispersive Trends and Structural Change   54
New York's Export Base: A Detailed Look   55

Chapter 3   Changing Demographics   61

Migration Patterns   62
Overall Trends   65
Fiscal Implications of Migration Patterns   66
Economic Mobility of City Residents   72
Housing in New York   75

Chapter 4   City Fiscal Policies   79

The National Context   80
New York's Budget Trends   81
The Fiscal Crisis   96
New York since the Fiscal Crisis   109

Chapter 5   New York in 1990   115

Macroeconomic Trends   116
Microeconomic Trends   119
Trends in Locational Preferences   120

Chapter 6   Policy Options   139

The Basis for Making Choices   141
The Choices Available   144

Notes   165

Appendix: Capital Construction Needs of New York City
            in the 1977-86 Period   *David A. Grossman*   175

Preface   177

Chapter A1   Introduction   179

Capital Construction in the Past Decade   179
Problems Facing the Infrastructure   181
Rising Construction Costs   182

Chapter A2   Infrastructure Priorities and Needs   185

  Mass Transit   186
  Streets and Highways   191
  Water Supply and Distribution   196
  Electricity   201
  Education   208
  Other Construction Needs   213

Chapter A3   Comparing Needs and Resources   219

  City Capital Budget   220
  State and Federal Aid   222
  State and Federal Projects   223
  Public Authority Projects   223
  Privately Financed Projects   224
  The Needs-Resources Gap in the 1977-86 Period   224
  Suggestions for Next Steps   227

Notes   229

Foreword

Some years ago, or so the story goes, a left-wing European journalist on his first New York assignment was looking out over Manhattan at dusk from a vantage point high up in the United Nations building. Watching the streams of cars snaking along the highway fronting the East River, the bustling traffic on the streets, the bridges and skyscrapers so aglow with lights that their reflection lit the darkening sky, he said, "I see the past and it works." Apocryphal or not, that paraphrase of Lincoln Steffen's celebrated observation about the Soviet Union seemed appropriate during and immediately after New York's publicized fiscal crisis. For the city was not only on the brink of bankruptcy but not working very well. The city had seen its best days, and its future was bleak.

It was during the darkest days of the fiscal crisis that the Twentieth Century Fund decided to focus on the longer-run future of the city. Our interest in its fate was neither detached nor sudden. Although founded in Massachusetts, for over fifty years the Fund has made its home in New York, and it has been a property owner for over twenty years. In 1967, the Fund became the first foundation to make an annual payment to the city for the municipal services rendered it free of charge, a move followed, although in different form, by the Ford Foundation. Unfortunately, few others have followed suit, but the Fund continues its practice; this year, because of inflation, it will be making a payment two and a half times its original gift. Furthermore, New York has also loomed large in our program of public policy research on urban issues.

We were impelled to concentrate our attention on the future by the knowledge that many different groups were studying the immediate and prospective financial difficulties of the city. At the time we began, almost no one was engaged in examining what would happen to the city over the next decade. It may have been an act of faith on our part to assume that the city would somehow survive longer than that; more, it was a realization that a city as big and as rich in resources, human and material, as New York, could not become a wasteland.

The first phase of our study was carried out by the Fund staff, which was given the assignment of reviewing the city's past and determining what options, if any, were available for the future. This task involved several members at various stages, but the chief responsibility fell on Masha Sinnreich, who wrote the background paper that accompanies the report of the Fund's independent Task Force. Her work is, I think, a clear and concise analytical account of the changing role of New York, with special emphasis on the city's particular strengths and weaknesses.

Once the background paper was in hand, we assembled the Task Force, deciding at the outset to invite both New Yorkers and non-New Yorkers, in order to assure a broad rather than a narrow perspective, based in part upon our experience with a previous Task Force on the city that was made up solely of New Yorkers. As it turned out, all members of the Task Force, both outsiders and natives, took the view that New York City has much in common with other aging cities in the nation, but nevertheless stands separate and apart. Without excusing or absolving the city for its excesses, the Task Force held that its special role made it deserving of some special treatment by the national government.

But the most important work of the Task Force was in formulating a vision of what New York City can be. That vision, which is spelled out in the report, is neither idealistic nor impractical. On the contrary, it builds on the ingredients and assets already present and takes into account political and social realities. The forging of a cohesive vision, which places its greatest emphasis on creating opportunities for people and is aimed at improving the city as a job market and as a place to live, is intended to make policymakers and the public think about a workable future for the city. The more it provokes discussion and debate, and there were lively debates on the

Task Force over its own plans, the firmer the city's longer term prospects.

I must pay tribute to Judge Charles Breitel and his colleagues on the Task Force who devoted so much concern and thought to their assignment and attained such a large measure of agreement. The Fund is indebted to all of them for their dedicated hard work and for their good humor and enthusiasm, which, despite many disputes in the course of prolonged discussions, never flagged. We also are grateful to all of those who contributed to the work of the Task Force, particularly those who appeared as guest witnesses at its meetings. The Task Force, of course, arrived at its recommendations independently, with all individual clarifications and dissent noted in its report.

M. J. Rossant, *Director*
The Twentieth Century Fund
November 1979

Task Force Members

Charles D. Breitel, chairman,
formerly chief judge, State of New York; counsel, Proskauer Rose Goetz & Mendelsohn

Peter A. A. Berle,
attorney, Berle, Butzel, Kass and Case

Andrew J. Biemiller,
formerly congressman from Wisconsin; recently retired legislative director, AFL-CIO

José A. Cabranes,
general counsel, Yale University

Peter F. Flaherty,
formerly mayor, Pittsburgh; formerly deputy attorney general, Carter administration

Gaylord Freeman,
honorary chairman, The First National Bank of Chicago

Theodore C. Jackson,
executive vice-president, Bowery Savings Bank

Robert Lekachman,
distinguished professor of economics, Herbert H. Lehman College and Graduate Center of the City University of New York

Stephen May,
formerly mayor, Rochester, New York; chairman, State Board of Elections

J. David Moxley,
northeast regional partner, Touche Ross and Company

John R. Petty,
president, Marine Midland Bank

John S. Samuels 3d,
chairman of the board, Carbomin International

Ellen S. Straus,
president, Straus Communications

Julien J. Studley,
president, J. J. Studley, Inc.

Jacqueline Grennan Wexler,
formerly president, Hunter College

Charles W. Whalen, Jr.,
president, New Directions

Report of the Task Force

We have a vision for New York City—and for New Yorkers. We believe it essential to begin planning the New York of the future while the city is still making its slow and painful way back to fiscal solvency.

Although the exigencies of the city's continuing financial difficulties have shortened still further the traditionally short time horizons of the elected officials—city, state, and federal—who are seeking to restore the city's credit, we have deliberately looked beyond the current crisis to concentrate on the longer term outlook that has been virtually ignored. There is no denying the gravity of the city's fiscal condition, but our assessment of the city's basic assets has convinced us that the long-run future of New York is potentially bright.

Thus, our vision for the city is one of thriving neighborhoods where diverse communities of New Yorkers can live in relative security; it is a vision of a city increasingly oriented toward white-collar employment while maintaining a variety of essentially small-scale manufacturing enterprises; and it is a vision of New York as the true world capital, the principal marketplace and cultural center for the world.

We believe that our vision is attainable, provided that the solutions for the city's short-term financial problems work and provided that public policy succeeds in promoting and fostering those formidable resources of the city that hold the most promise for the future.

RECOVERING FROM THE FALL

Five years after the onset of its fiscal crisis, New York City appears surprisingly robust. The revival of economic activity is most visible in Manhattan, where real estate has been booming. Rents for office space and sales of luxury cooperatives in prime locations are at all-time highs, and scores of new buildings are under construction. The city is host to record numbers of tourists, who crowd its shops, its restaurants, its theaters, its galleries, its museums. It is profiting from the production of new films, the recording of disco rhythms, and burgeoning foreign investment in banks, boutiques, real estate, and auction houses. Manhattan, however, cannot be the savior of the city, and the resurgence has not been confined solely to its commercial precincts. On the contrary, once-dingy neighborhoods in the outlying boroughs are being revived by communities of immigrants, many of whom have exhibited an aptitude for individual entrepreneurship, and by community activists, who demonstrate a determination to improve the areas in which they live.

The Task Force, made up of New Yorkers and non-New Yorkers, who have had the assignment of deliberating over the future of the city, is impressed by the vigor of the recent revival. It contains the seeds that, if properly nurtured, may well assure a true renaissance for the city. But the most significant force in this revival, the one that no financial accounting can either measure or assess, is people.

New York City, in our view, is not Manhattan alone or the larger area delineated by the borders of its outlying boroughs; it also embraces the surrounding suburban areas. Within this metropolitan region live 16 million people—rich and poor, native and foreign-born—comprising the nation's, and perhaps the world's, greatest concentration of initiative, knowledge, skills, financial acumen, and cultural creativity. Moreover, New York's polyglot population is not only remarkably cosmopolitan and tolerant but also highly motivated, resilient, and resourceful. Once New Yorkers became aware of the magnitude of the fiscal crisis—a crisis that made New York a symbol of urban profligacy and squalor—their acceptance of sacrifice and their enterprising spirit confounded those who were predicting that the city was a lost cause.

The city's revival has been aided by outside forces—the strength and duration of the rise in national economic activity, the growth in international trade and investment, the declining dollar, and political instability abroad. These forces, all beyond the city's control, are, of course, reversible. Obviously, the economic health of New York will be affected by adverse short-term developments and the critical international energy problem, which is likely to endure. Yet the municipal administration can strengthen the city's defenses by a determined effort to preserve and to protect New York's still formidable attributes—its people, its port, its remaining industry, its cultural riches, and its financial and business resources.

The Task Force believes that these assets present New York with the opportunity to become a true world capital. One major reason the city is currently thriving is because it is a magnet for foreigners and foreign investment. Looking ahead to the next decade, **we are convinced that the city, by building on its present strengths as a great international metropolis, can become the global marketplace for business, finance, communications, the professions, and the arts.**

Whatever the short-term uncertainties, the essential ingredients are already present. Traditionally, New York has been the "gateway" to foreigners. It still is. Foreigners, whether immigrants or visitors, feel more at home in New York than in any other American city. Attracted by its cosmopolitan culture, its vibrant bustle, its creative tempo, they regard it as more hospitable and politically stable than metropolitan centers in Europe or Asia.

Moreover, an increasingly interdependent world has brought about a steady rise in global trade and investment. The nominal dollar value of world trade has increased fivefold over the past ten years; many corporations, domestic and foreign, have achieved multinational status; and capital markets have become internationalized. New York, which has benefited from these trends—two-thirds of all foreign enterprises set up shop here since 1961, one-fifth since 1974—is superbly placed to achieve preeminence as the international center for trade, banking, investment, and tourism, provided that government recognizes this potential and formulates effective policies to encourage it.

In envisioning New York as the future world capital, the Task Force is thinking in terms of an international business, financial, and cultural center rather than a political center. After all, when New York was recognized in the nineteenth century as the nation's leading city, it was the seat of neither the state nor the federal government. We believe that New York can achieve similar status in the world at large. International recognition of the city's leadership does not imply, now or in the future, American hegemony in the world. Nor are we suggesting that the United Nations, which makes its headquarters in New York and which is a welcome presence of international significance, will be transformed into a world government. Rather, we believe that New York can claim global leadership in the private sector because of its ability to attract the most ambitious, competitive, and creative people from the rest of the nation—and from the world at large.

The size and scope of New York's international activities are already far greater than those of other cities, here and abroad. Foreigners, even more than Americans, appreciate the depth of the city's human resources—technical, professional, intellectual—and the ceaseless striving for innovation and quality that distinguish New York and New Yorkers. The Task Force believes that these assets can be expanded and enhanced.

In giving substance to our vision for the city, our guiding principle has been to build on the city's existing strengths. We are convinced that developing and stimulating what the city already possesses in such impressive depth is far more likely to prove productive than attempts to recapture the past or ventures to attain the unattainable. Accordingly, the Task Force urges that the municipal administration coordinate its efforts with those of private businesses and civic organizations to take action to:

- **Begin an active and sustained effort to promote the city's international and white-collar sectors, areas that will benefit most from a continued growth in world trade and investment.**

- **Preserve the city's existing industrial base.** The manufacturing sector, though smaller than it had been, is still vital to the city's future. Instead of massive industrial park development or a costly and risky campaign to induce companies to return or to locate here, we strongly favor measures to retain—and promote the expansion of—manufacturing enterprises that are already located in and employing residents of the city.

- **Strengthen and protect the city's existing neighborhoods.** Because New York's most important resource is its people, we believe that the city should maintain and improve family life in New York by concentrating on renovating and refurbishing livable neighborhoods rather than by building new communities in abandoned areas. **If people are to be served, public policy must concentrate on people, not places.**

In essence, the Task Force's proposed strategy for the future is to strengthen the city's position by making the most of its advantages. It is a strategy of mutual reinforcement. By retaining the city's commercial and industrial base, by educating and training its residents to compete in a city that is a global marketplace, by making residential neighborhoods more attractive, New York can provide a great variety of employment opportunities for all of its people and, at the same time, better the quality of their lives.

STRIKING A BALANCE

The first step in achieving our vision of New York as the world capital is strengthening the city's still precarious financial condition. Despite the recent recovery in local business activity, as well as the reductions made by the municipal administration in manpower and services following the onset of the fiscal crisis, the city's operating budget continues to run at a substantial deficit. These deficits, moreover, are projected for future years even without taking into account the wage increases for the municipal labor force that are likely to be negotiated when the present contracts run out next year. Since the federal loan guarantees are scheduled to expire in June 1982, the city must do more than it has been doing to balance its revenues and expenditures.

In its own deliberations, the Task Force neither ignored nor minimized the need for the city administration to make further progress in restoring its finances. But as a number of other groups, public and private, including state and federal overseers as well as civic associations of different shadings, have been preoccupied with seeking solutions to the city's deficit, we have assumed that insolvency will be averted, which is essential if the city is to have a secure future. In treating the fiscal problem, however, we must caution against measures that are so draconian as to widen the gap between the privileged and underprivileged in the city, or so short sighted as to harm the city's longer term prospects for economic growth.

Whatever steps are taken short term, we recognize that the resources available for long-term development will be scarce. This awareness has shaped our view that building on the foundation of the city's strengths should be the basis of public policy. We are convinced that more can be accomplished for the city's residents by a series of small and relatively inexpensive measures than by expensive and grandiose plans designed to resurrect what has not worked.

THE CITY'S STRENGTHS

New York City has already emerged as a center of world trade. Just as the development of railroads a century ago led to the development of national corporations, most of which chose head-quarters in New York, the expansion in global trade and investment and the industrialization of such Third World countries as Korea, Mexico, and Taiwan have helped to stimulate the growth of vast multinational financial and nonfinancial enterprises, most of which have chosen to locate their American operations in New York. New York and other aging cities have lost manufacturing plants to the Sunbelt and foreign competition, but the city has gained—and is in a position to gain more—from continued internationalization. It is now in a position to serve world business as it once served national business.

New York holds many attractions for foreign firms bent on expanding in the United States and for American firms doing business abroad. It has the nation's largest port and airports that are far more convenient for domestic and international travel than those of any other American city. It is the headquarters of four of the five largest American banks, the major stock exchanges, three of the five largest insurance companies, the biggest international investment banking firms and nonbank financial companies, as well as 136 foreign bank branches or agencies.

The city also has an abundance of international law firms—the number of international lawyers in New York has nearly quadrupled in the last twenty years—major accounting firms, advertising agencies, architectural firms, business consulting firms, and publishing companies. Its universities, its private schools, its medical research centers, and its libraries and museums are renowned for their excellence. New York has a vast array of diverse cultural attractions—from theater on Broadway to off-off Broadway, from chamber music to symphonies, from internationally acclaimed ballet companies to folk dance, from free concerts in the parks to expensive discotheques. To be sure, the city can no longer claim a monopoly of the nation's cultural and professional talent, but no other city has so much in such depth. And because it retains its commitment to quality, it still attracts the aspiring and the enterprising from all over the world—in law and medicine, in the theater and fashion, in advertising and journalism, in business and finance.

New York's greatest strength as an international marketplace lies in its core companies—the 1400 foreign firms whose North American headquarters or sales offices are located here, and most of the roster of *Fortune*'s 500 largest domestic firms with either their corporate headquarters or their international headquarters in the city. Together, these core companies stimulate demand for the firms—legal and financial, consulting and communication—servicing national and international corporations, and which, according to the most recent estimates, provide employment for over 300,000 workers. The corporate service sector, in turn, has a spin-off effect on tourism and the local firms—in office equipment, printing, secretarial, maintenance, and messenger services—that are its suppliers and that account for approximately another 135,000 jobs.

The entire complex of internationally oriented firms, services, and cultural institutions is closely linked. While comprising many different industries, the firms that are part of the complex were attracted to the city by the presence of all the others. New York would not be an international financial center if it were not a communications and information center; tourism would be a minor industry without the presence of foreign and domestic corporate headquarters and the city's cultural institutions. Both the visual and the performing arts depend in large measure on the support of the city's sophisticated foreign community and its corporate headquarters-corporate service sector. Continued development in all these areas will bring substantial benefits to New York and to all the people working in it.

TOWARD THE WORLD CITY

New York is not Chicago or St. Louis or San Francisco writ large. As the center for international trade, finance, and culture, it is both a great marketplace and a pacesetter in terms of ideas, business opportunities, fashion, and standards of quality for the rest of the nation. More than any other American city, New York represents the United States to the world. Its unique significance merits special assistance, and a more effective targeting of such assistance, from the federal government.

This Task Force is aware that the national mood of fiscal conservatism, intensified by inflation, and the magnitude of the energy crisis preclude a marked increase in federal aid to the nation's ailing cities. But because the nation as a whole has so much to gain from universal recognition of New York as the world capital, there are a number of measures that the federal government could—and should—adopt to achieve this objective.

We recommend that the federal government contribute to the costs of the protection of official personnel of the United Nations and the foreign missions associated with it. Although the presence of representatives of foreign governments is one of New York's attractions as the world city, from which it derives tangible and intangible benefits, they are a federal rather than a municipal responsibility. As it is, the city renders municipal services free of charge to the tax-exempt properties of foreign governments, providing them with police and fire protection, garbage collection, and water supply. These costs should be offset by the federal government.

The federal government can also make regulatory changes that would draw capital into the city's financial markets. We endorse the proposal to allow domestic offshore banking facilities in New York and urge that the Federal Reserve Board modify its present regulations to enable such facilities to operate here.

We also recommend the elimination of the withholding tax on foreign portfolio investment. The withholding tax now diverts an estimated $7 billion a year in foreign investment from the U.S. bond market (which is preferred because of its greater depth, breadth, and liquidity) to dollar-denominated Eurobonds issued in the international market. Elimination of the tax would bring a portion of the Eurobond market to New York.

Increased federal assistance, direct or indirect, to New York City calls for a different federal-city relationship from the one that has traditionally prevailed. In the past, successive municipal administrations were obsessed with home rule, insisting on autonomy in their operations. This autonomy has a good deal to do with the city's undoing. When the city's fiscal difficulties were publicized around the world, foreigners were perplexed over how New York of all places could come so close to bankruptcy and why the federal government was so reluctant to provide assistance to the nation's biggest and most important city, the second largest government employer in the United States. The notion of fiscal autonomy, particularly for a city of New York's present and prospective international importance, may well merit reexamination once the short-term crisis, and its federal and state overseers, is dealt with. The objective must be an efficient and effective government for the city, not an excess of home rule.

New York must also change its relationships with local governments in the metropolitan region, of which it is the anchor. The region can only grow and prosper if New York can take full advantage of the growth of world trade and investment. Because the region stands or falls with New York, the city administration and the local governments surrounding it must work together, not apart. In particular, the region's congressional representatives must be more cohesive. With New York State's anticipated loss of congressional seats after 1980, obtaining federal aid will depend increasingly on the effective cooperation of the region's congressional delegation. In addition, there must be greater coordination among local government units on plans for recruiting and retaining businesses. Coordination also is essential among the independent agencies now competing with overlapping and conflicting development plans within the region, which, if continued, can only prove detrimental to the entire area.

It also is time for a new and more harmonious relationship between the city and its surrounding suburbs. The suburbs rely on New York to provide employment for many of their residents, and New York depends on the suburbs to provide housing for many of its most valuable public and private employees. Despite this critical linkage, they have failed to make common cause.

Yet the world capital must continue to attract skilled professionals and middle management personnel to New York. To some extent, that problem may be ameliorated with the rapid rise in the number of two-career families seeking to live close to their places of work. Certainly, New York, more than most cities, has great appeal for young working couples because of the variety of opportunities that are available. But the fact must be faced that corporations and corporate service firms have encountered problems with many white-collar workers, especially those with young children, who will come here only if they have the amenities of suburban living. If there were no attractive and accessible suburbs surrounding New York, corporations would find it impossible to recruit enough managerial and professional personnel to work in the city, and many other employment sectors, including the municipal government, would be seriously handicapped. The surrounding suburbs are an asset to the city and must be treated as such. **The Task Force therefore recommends that the city administration join with suburban governments to lobby for improved public transportation for suburban commuters and to explore other means of making New York a more attractive work place for many of the people it needs.**

Even more important than federal and regional help, however, is the city's own role in promoting and encouraging international business. **The Task Force recommends that the municipal administration show a responsiveness to the problems encountered by foreign enterprise, which we believe can best be accomplished by the creation of a special office reporting to the Deputy Mayor for Economic Development.** In addition, the Deputy Mayor should establish a monitoring system over the entire corporate head-quarters-corporate service sector to anticipate problems while they can still be resolved.

The official fostering of a hospitable and responsive environment is more important than reducing taxes (or profferring tax incentives) to foreign enterprises. Rather than special treatment, an evenhanded, nondiscriminatory approach will do the most to improve the city's business climate and facilitate its role as a global center. **Thus, the city's administration should make known to foreigners, whether corporations or individuals, that they have the assurance of doing business under the same laws and regulations that apply to everyone else.**

Mounting an elaborate campaign to recruit foreign businesses is unnecessary. The main task of enhancing New York's appeal must be accomplished here rather than outside the city's borders. **If the city demonstrates a sense of fair play toward business, then the best recruiters for the city will be the executives of the domestic and foreign firms now working in the city.**

Under current economic conditions, the Task Force believes that special incentives are not now needed to attract or maintain business in the city. **If incentives are needed at a later date, we urge that they be provided sparingly and selectively.** The municipal administration should avoid proffering incentives that cause overbuilding in already crowded districts and should withhold incentives altogether when it is evident that new construction would take place without them.

It is axiomatic that the continued free flow of capital across national boundaries is essential to New York's role as a global marketplace. But because decisions on international loans, to corporations as well as to governments, are often subject to political influence or governmental controls, the locus of power is in Washington rather than New York. The city's influence over domestic money and credit policies was lost to Washington long ago. With the proliferation of federal agencies engaged in regulating corporations, Washington has also gained an increasing share of domestic service activity. **It is the view of the Task Force that the concentration of power over international financial activity should not be entirely located in Washington and that the financial marketplace in New York should retain its acknowledged capacity to serve in a decision-making capacity.** Accordingly, we recommend the relocation of the **World Bank and International Monetary Fund, which are agencies of the United Nations, to New York City.** Such a move would reestablish, symbolically at least, their ties to the United Nations. It also would provide better coordination of public and private participation in international financial markets.

New York's original preeminence was based primarily on its strategic location and its accessibility. That accessibility is no less important today. **The city must improve mass transit access to its airports; in particular, the long-planned rail link to Kennedy Airport should be completed.** If the city is to be the hub of worldwide business activity, it is essential that businessmen can get in and out of New York. Once here, they ought to be able to get around the business districts without difficulty. Easing midtown congestion calls for numerous imaginative and, frequently, unglamorous improvements. We endorse Mayor Koch's action prohibiting private automobiles on certain midtown streets and urge extension of this experiment—perhaps even the addition of shopping-and-entertainment malls that are closed entirely to vehicular traffic. We also favor experiments to ease traffic congestion through the use of vans, small shuttle buses, or other intermediate-sized vehicles. What the city needs is convenient and rapid movement of people—residents, commuters, businessmen, and tourists—that does not make traffic an ordeal.

SERVING NEW YORKERS

Our proposed strategy to develop New York as the world capital addresses, directly and practically, the pressing problem of the city's poor, including many migrants from the South and Puerto Rico and, more recently, from Central and South America and Asia. These New Yorkers must have jobs and opportunities for advancement. Obviously, many of the new jobs that will be generated by a global capital will go to the most ambitious and skilled, from all over the nation, as well as from other countries. Yet there is no conflict between the needs of the city's residents for good jobs and the needs of corporations for employees. Indeed, if the city administration accepts our vision of the world city, it will devote more of its resources to training and equipping the city's population to compete more effectively in the future world marketplace.

The greatest need of the corporate service sector is an adequate supply of competent labor. Of necessity, it employs a large number of people in many different jobs, ranging from messengers to bartenders, from typists to computer programmers, from margin clerks to bank presidents. It also provides a very large number of job opportunities to minority groups. At present, about 15 percent of employees in corporate service firms and 18 percent of employees in ancillary firms are black, compared to 13 percent in manufacturing (figures for other minorities are unavailable).

Because many of the minority-group employees in this sector hold low-level jobs, the Task Force urges private firms to restructure their employee training systems. Lower level workers must be given the opportunity to win more responsible and higher paying jobs. By actively encouraging such progression, the private sector can make a significant contribution toward maintaining the city's tradition of social mobility while assuring itself a continuing supply of skilled workers. Corporations are intimately familiar with their own manpower needs, and many have already instituted programs on their own. Since company-operated training programs are likely to be more efficient in providing new employment opportunities than city-operated manpower training programs, the city administration ought to yield to and stimulate private initiative in the setting up of training programs.

However, most businesses, whether new or established, will still rely on the marketplace for labor. As a consequence, they depend on the city's schools to supply nonprofessional employees as well as skilled employees, while recruiting high-level executives and professionals from the national market. The city's schools, including the city university system (CUNY), must produce enough qualified employees to help keep white-collar service and service-related businesses in New York. Accordingly, we propose measures to make education more effective and more relevant to the world of work.

The transition from school to work requires more attention by educators and employers, who, in education as in manpower training, must learn to work together. There have already been some useful moves in this direction, such as the adoption of individual schools by corporations, and corporate participation in tutoring programs. We think that high school work-study programs should be expanded, and that schools, local communities, and business firms should cooperate to fund part-time and summer jobs. A cooperative working relationship between corporations and the school system—including CUNY, the Board of Education, and the teachers' union—could supervise these programs and come up with other innovative projects to aid both pupils and business. Accordingly, the Task Force recommends that a special liaison office be established within the Board of Education to coordinate the activity of the private and public sectors.

If New York is to have a promising future, the primary and secondary schools along with CUNY must improve their performance while recognizing the special needs of the city's economy, particularly its growing international orientation. Much of the perceived deterioration of the quality of public higher education is frequently ascribed to inadequate preparation in the lower grades. Although the Task Force has not sought to determine the validity of this contention, we are agreed that a program of competency testing should be instituted early in the educational process, rather than at graduation from high school, when it is too late to salvage those students who have failed to measure up or to make accurate judgments about the reasons for their deficiencies. Such competency standards should be used as much for measuring the effectiveness of instruction as for gauging the progress of students. It is our view that competency must be the major objective of the city's educational system in the interest of pupils, their parents, their teachers, and the city itself.

We also recommend that high school and college curricula place greater emphasis on vocational programs in white-collar areas— finance, business administration, communications, computer technology, hotel management—that will be needed in the world city. In addition, we urge the establishment of special language schools, both at the high school and college levels, to promote proficiency in foreign languages by the expanding cadre of young people needed to work for and with foreign businesses.

As for public higher education, CUNY has modified its open admissions policy, which had prompted questions about the devaluation of its degrees.* We endorse an approach that maintains high academic standards for entrance to CUNY's senior colleges and that permits movement from one track to another for those who demonstrate an aptitude for high levels of postsecondary education. This approach has the merit of providing manpower and vocational training to some students while offering the academic disciplines to those intent on entering the professions. The Task Force believes that preserving the integrity and rigor of the academic programs in CUNY's senior colleges is of special concern to all of its students who seek to be prepared for the full range of opportunities.

Mr. Lekachman comments:
The sudden introduction of the open admissions program to the City University did indeed generate much turmoil and confusion. No doubt the program distressed alumni and alumnae who cherished memories (not always entirely accurate) of City College or Hunter as elite institutions. I believe that the questions that, as the report accurately notes, were raised by the public in the wake of open admissions have now been satisfactorily resolved. Let me cite as one piece of evidence Barron's profile of Lehman College, my own campus, which is not one of the more popular senior colleges. Barron's "in-depth study" praised Lehman as offering students "the double advantage of a high-caliber urban institution in a relaxed, informal environment." It noted approvingly that "Lehman College provides the standard array of liberal arts and science majors as well as excellent career-oriented specializations." And much more. Now the serious implication is this: the unique conjuncture of circumstance and talent that graduated such distinguished alumni as Daniel Bell, Irving Kristol, Irving Howe, and Nathan Glazer is unlikely to recur. It is a healthy development for New York that the City University is graduating a steady stream of competent accountants, business managers, hotel administrators, nurses, medical technicians, and men and women who go on to legal, medical, and academic careers.

Because of our commitment to facilitating the entry of young New Yorkers into the increasingly dominant white-collar sectors of the city's economy, **we recommend an expansion of vocational training courses in CUNY's two-year community colleges, even if doing so requires the scaling down of CUNY's graduate programs.** In light of the current—and prospective—national excess of scholars with advanced degrees, and the wide availability of graduate programs in other institutions in the city, a diversion of state funding from CUNY's graduate program to its community colleges would meet the needs of both the city's residents and its economy, provided that tuition assistance grants are made available to capable students to enable them to pursue graduate training at private or other public institutions.*

PROMOTING THE PRIVATE SECTOR

The world city strategy relies on the dynamism of the private sector. But not all the city's businesses and residents can be expected to prosper from the growth of the international marketplace in New York. Despite our conviction that the city would be best served by strengthening its attractions as a world center, we recognize that the city has not been—and is not now—a competitive environment for many industries, especially manufacturing industries, housing, and neighborhood services, and that its lack of competitiveness has caused severe hardships for many of the city's residents. If New York is to continue to perform its historic function as a place where successive waves of immigrants can become assimilated into a modern urban economy and find opportunities for advancement, an activist approach toward protecting industries and neighborhoods is needed. If these existing neighborhoods and industries are lost, much of the diversity that is one of the city's most precious assets will be lost.

*Ms. Wexler comments:
I also strongly endorse an admissions policy that maintains high academic standards for the senior colleges of CUNY. I support the concern of the Task Force that vocational training be strengthened in the community colleges. However, I believe that there is an internal inconsistency in a call for "preserving the integrity and rigor of the academic programs in CUNY's senior colleges" with an assumption that such colleges in the public sector can recruit and nurture appropriate faculty without graduate programs. The irony is compounded by the suggestion that public dollars be provided for tuition assistance grants to students in private sector graduate programs. Such a strategy would strip the public senior colleges in New York City of any important research orientation.

Over the last decade, there has been an exodus of jobs and people from the city; an estimated 550,000 jobs have disappeared and approximately 750,000 people have departed. Yet until the 1974-75 recession, New York's postwar experience had been less disastrous than that of many other large American cities. Because New York has a balanced economy, especially its wide range of white-collar occupations and consumer goods industries, it has proved more resistant to recession than heavy manufacturing areas. As a result, the city has not suffered the severe losses experienced by cities tied to dying industries.

We believe that the city administration should take steps to maintain the balance in the city's private sector, especially now that the rise in the national economy, the most prolonged peacetime advance on record, has apparently ended. Whether the ensuing recession proves to be major or mild, it could have a severe impact on New York if there is a renewed exodus of industry. Thus, the city **must devote its attention to preserving and protecting its existing manufacturing sector if it is to avoid a repetition of the devastating effects of the 1974-75 recession.**

Even local industries that have suffered job losses over the last decade should not be written off. The once moribund film industry, for example, has revived dramatically with city help over the last two years—forty feature-length films were produced in New York in 1978. Conceivably, other such industrial revivals may take place, providing many new jobs, and the city should be prepared to smooth their path.

Slowing the exodus of the city's blue-collar jobs in the immediate future can also ease the long-term transition to the white-collar city serving global markets. Even if the existing white-collar sector were capable of picking up the slack created by the loss of manufacturing, the city's present labor force cannot adjust quickly or painlessly to such shifts. Longshoremen do not become bank tellers overnight, and unemployed garment cutters do not immediately become computer operators. A mismatch of skills and jobs may bring a swelling in unemployment and welfare rolls. Hence, policy measures that slow, even temporarily, the departure of manufacturing and other blue-collar employers will prevent a great deal of human suffering and public spending.

The Task Force believes that stability in the city's job market and its neighborhoods makes for social stability. Every year, thousands of newcomers arrive in New York in quest of opportunities to improve their lot; other thousands of teenagers leave school to enter the labor force. Many, though by no means all, are ill equipped to compete in the city's white-collar economy. Frustrations caused by the shrinking blue-collar job market and by the rapid disinvestment in poor neighborhoods breed social pathology, crime, and political tension.

In our view, the world capital is not an enclave. It must give all of New York's inhabitants a chance to share in the dream of a better life for themselves and their children. Large numbers of city residents now have no such chance. Unless they are given real opportunities to make their own way, the city could be subject to dangerous polarization. This Task Force, therefore, strongly recommends that the city administration commit itself to improving the current living conditions and future prospects for those New Yorkers who have not been absorbed into the economic mainstream.

The pressing need is for jobs. Jobs, of course, depend mainly on a thriving private sector, which is made up of the commercial and manufacturing enterprises currently operating in the city. It is our firm conviction that retaining and expanding the present private sector is a far surer bet, in terms of the benefits to the city and its residents, than frittering away its resources in a dubious effort to attract new business and new people.

In emphasizing retention rather than recruitment, and in keeping with our belief that evenhandedness in the treatment of the private sector is vital, we urge the city administration to pursue fair and equitable tax policies. Thus, we favor maintaining a limit—or cap—on real estate taxes rather than bestowing tax abatements on new construction projects that might well be built in any case.

If abatements are continued, or if they are reintroduced to stimulate construction, we recommend that the city explore ways and means of sharing directly in the profits that result from such subsidized investment. Under current arrangements, the only way in which the city gains from its tax abatement policy is through the gradual increase in taxes as the abatement is reduced. It has been argued that the city also gains from the increased income and sales taxes of those employed or doing business with the corporate recipient of the subsidy. But the extent, if any, of such benefits is doubtful because in a boom period few projects are likely to be abandoned in the absence of an abatement.

As we see it, the city should share in the revenues above a specified level for projects that receive tax abatements, using as a yardstick the average tax burden for similar properties that do not have abatements, thereby assuring a more equitable sharing of the tax burdens.

The Task Force urges the city administration to make greater efforts to attract the participation of business and labor leaders in municipal affairs. The anonymity of New York, which has its attractions, inhibits the kinds of civic participation that characterize the business communities in other American cities. Yet New York sorely needs all the help it can get from those with a sizable stake in the city's well being. Ways must be found, as they were when the fiscal crisis first took hold, to enlist the services—formally and informally—of private executives.

Many agencies—federal, state, city, and the bistate Port Authority of New York and New Jersey—have plans for economic development in and around the city. Perhaps the most ambitious and comprehensive are those of the Port Authority, which is prepared to assume responsibility for economic development of the entire region. There is much that is imaginative and useful in the Port Authority's plans, but we believe that it should place primary emphasis on its original mandate—the provision of sound port (including airport) facilities— and beware of dissipating its effectiveness by taking on too much.

Because the future of New York is closely tied to that of the rest of the metropolitan region, **we call upon all local governments within the region to cooperate in reducing the costs of doing business for local enterprises.** Regional cooperation is absolutely essential if the effects of adverse federal regulations are to be modified or eliminated and if the flow of funds from federal programs is to be increased. Only regional cooperation can assure the kind of rational planning that will provide the services and utilities necessary to keep manufacturers from going elsewhere. Accordingly, we endorse the creation of the Energy Corporation of the Northeast (ENCONO), the proposed entity for promoting energy development in the region.

The Task Force also favors the Port Authority's proposal to use resource recovery plants to generate electricity for industrial use in the region, although we advise building one or two plants on an experimental basis before there is a commitment to a full-scale development program. **We believe that it would be preferable to direct the savings in energy costs derived from the program to existing manufacturing plants in their present locations, rather than tying reduced-rate electricity solely to industrial park development.**

We oppose the use of public resources for the development of large-scale industrial parks. Experience with them in other areas has shown that they fail to yield enough jobs in return for the substantial amounts invested in them. Smaller, vest-pocket industrial parks, which can take advantage of existing infrastructure while providing space for manufacturing plants needing room for expansion, have a far better record of cost effectiveness. **Consequently, we endorse the**

proposal to fund and develop such vest-pocket industrial parks as more in keeping with the city's requirements.*

MAINTAINING THE CITY

Preserving the city's manufacturing sector requires some measures to reduce the cost of bringing goods in and out of the city. However, this Task Force opposes large and speculative new transportation projects, especially Westway, whose costs far outweigh its possible benefits. The city should promote more modest measures—measures that are known to provide a reasonable benefit-cost ratio based upon a thorough analysis of pertinent factors—to take advantage of the city's natural assets, especially its port and its existing transportation network. Instead of Westway, we favor the construction of a simple, easy-to-maintain replacement of the now moribund West Side Highway and recommend that a portion of the port facilities that now lie idle should be made into public parks, while the remainder should be reserved for refurbishment. In addition, we recommend improving rail access to the city, particularly to the port facilities.

We do not believe that the city's economic development program should focus on large new projects, no matter how enticing they may seem. The city will achieve more by better maintenance of its infrastructure. One of New York City's great advantages is that its basic infrastructure is already in place. Its streets are full of potholes; its transit system is dirty and noisy; its bridges are rusting; but these and other facilities are not only extensive, they also work. Moreover, each increase in the price of energy enhances the value of the city's existing infrastructure. The major job now is to keep that infrastructure in good repair.

For many years, city administrations have allowed the roads, bridges, subways, sewers, water mains, and other basic facilities to deteriorate, sometimes dangerously, frequently stretching replacement cycles hundreds of years longer than the facilities could endure.

Messrs. Cabranes and May comment:
We regret the reluctance of the Task Force to more affirmatively encourage the growth and development of manufacturing and other sectors of the economy that employ blue-collar workers, as suggested by (among others) the Port Authority of New York and New Jersey.

Messrs. Biemiller, Flaherty, and Lekachman wish to associate themselves with this comment.

Only in the last year, with federal help, has the city begun a planned program of repair and reconstruction. Although infrastructure repair may not seem directly related to economic development, the facilities in their present state impose substantial costs on all those living and working in the city and lessen the city's appeal as a place in which to live and work. Moreover, there is always a potential threat of a serious infrastructure failure—a cutoff of the water supply or a collapsed bridge—that could have an immediate and catastrophic effect on the city's economy.

Thus, the Task Force recommends that for the next decade the city give priority to its new infrastructure replacement program. After the federally guaranteed loans run out in 1982, there may be difficulty in raising funds for this program. Accordingly, the city should give consideration to the possibility of instituting user fees and issuing revenue bonds wherever feasible—bridges and water supply being the two most likely examples—for maintenance funds are going to be even more difficult to raise since they can no longer be borrowed. (Although they must be kept separate for accounting purposes, maintenance and construction funds are different in degree rather than in kind.) **We recommend that the city make adequate provision for maintenance and establish a program that integrates planning for maintenance and replacement.**

Our recommendation that maintenance and replacement of the city's existing facilities be given priority reflects our concern about their dangerous state of disrepair and our skepticism about urban renewal policies that have entailed replacement through demolition of perfectly good existing structures by massive new projects. It is time to redress the imbalance. Accordingly, we recommend that the federal government, which has accelerated urban blight and suburban sprawl for the last generation by funding new projects rather than promoting rehabilitation of existing structures, now contribute to the maintenance of infrastructure. Several bills now before Congress propose the establishment of agencies which would, through grants and loans (some of them at low interest rates), enable distressed localities to repair and rehabilitate their infrastructure. **We support the establishment of such a program either by the U.S. Treasury or by the proposed independent National Bank for Community Conservation. The important issue, in our view, is targeting federal aid to this purpose.**

The major exceptions to our emphasis on restoring existing infrastructure are the construction of the new Convention Center, whose planning is far advanced and whose function may be competitively useful (provided its costs are carefully controlled), and the necessity of building a third water tunnel for the city. A third tunnel has long been needed and now must be regarded as essential in the event of a stoppage in one of the two existing tunnels. It might have been more sensible to build an overland pipeline in the first place, but now that the first stage of the tunnel, which parallels the existing water tunnels, is 90 percent excavated, there is no reason not to complete it. We believe, however, that the proposed Queens-Brooklyn loop of the tunnel can be postponed and that the costs of the first stage should not be inflated by over-engineering a structure that, after all, amounts to reserve capacity for emergency purposes. The Hudson River flood-skimming project, which would take water from the Hudson when the water level is high and treat it so that it could be added to the city's reservoirs as insurance against drought, is often linked to the project to build a third water tunnel. The Task Force believes that an open-ended commitment to the maintenance of the flood-skimming facility is unwarranted in the absence of firm cost estimates.

REVIVING NEIGHBORHOODS

Of all the objectives we have set for the city, perhaps the most difficult to achieve is improving the quality of life. Over the last fifteen years, there has been no shortage of ideas and new policy ventures, but the results have been disappointing. Some neighborhoods have declined, others have stayed the same, and still others have been rebuilt, all with little apparent relation to the overall thrust of local, state, or federal policies. This Task Force is reluctant to advocate sweeping changes that promise more than they can deliver. Nevertheless, we believe that the city government can make a difference by providing advice, encouragement, and funding for neighborhood revival—especially if the necessary ingredients of citizen participation and sheer luck are forthcoming.

Several recent developments have influenced our views of neighborhood policy. First, the number of households in the city fell by about 130,000 from 1970 to 1978. Second, while the number of welfare recipients has remained fairly constant throughout the 1970s, they are no longer concentrated in a small number of isolated ghetto areas. Third, the city has been taking over property through the in rem process so rapidly that it will soon own most occupied low-income housing. Taken together, these findings depict a city that has already lost large numbers of its middle class, that has witnessed the movement of the poor into neighborhoods recently occupied by the middle class, and that has a housing stock originally built for a large, relatively high-income population whose landlords can no longer afford its maintenance with the rents they collect from a smaller, poorer population. Conceivably, the combination of foreign immigration (legal and illegal), higher energy prices, and changing marital and child-rearing patterns could raise the number of households again before the end of the 1980s. But we see no evidence that these forces have yet begun to outweigh the forces driving so many middle-class New Yorkers out of the city. Accordingly, despite the heartening rehabilitation of neighborhoods in such areas as lower Manhattan and sections of Brooklyn, **public policymakers should assume that the decline in households will continue, at least for the immediate future.***

As long as the number of households—and their average income—continues to fall, it is unwise to attempt to rebuild *all* of the city as if its population were still intact. At this late date, **we believe that it makes more sense to accept the verdict of the residents themselves that certain areas are unsalvageable. Accordingly, the city's funds and energies should be concentrated on those marginal neighborhoods where the residents seem determined to stay.**

We urge the city administration to maintain and improve basic municipal services—police, fire, sanitation, parks, health care—**in marginal neighborhoods, especially those adjacent to abandoned areas, because a strong city presence can persuade residents that their community has a future and is not being written off.** All too frequently, the suspicion that the municipal government, as well as the private sector, has given up on a neighborhood is all that it takes to spur crime and to accelerate abandonment. However, the provision of municipal services and facilities is not only increasingly costly but also increasingly ineffective in areas that have been virtually depopulated and no longer possess the vital signs of community life. **It is our view that the city administration must be willing to close facilities or reduce services if they are in excess of the needs of the remaining population.**

*Mr. Lekachman comments:
We ought not assume, at least before the 1980 census of population has been taken, released, and competently evaluated, that the population of the five boroughs is shrinking. It is quite possible that, as Herman Badillo among others has been maintaining, an accurate count of undocumented aliens would yield a figure substantial enough to represent an actual increase in population. This is a critical matter in endorsing, however cautiously as our Report now does, a policy of neighborhood shrinkage and public service reduction or even withdrawal. As an individual, I reject any inference of this nature from the Report.

The perverse momentum of the abandonment process reduces the city's housing stock in a fashion that is painful for residents of the affected buildings and neighborhoods, ruinous to landlords, and burdensome to the city. Abandonment and deterioration do not weed out the oldest and least desirable buildings across the city, but spread throughout neighborhoods, destroying much potentially sound housing. Abandoned buildings attract addicts, derelicts, and criminals, making life dangerous and unpleasant for residents of nearby buildings, which—whatever their physical condition—are themselves gradually vacated and eventually abandoned.

This Task Force does not believe that, with the city's population still falling, the effects of the last decade of abandonment can be totally reversed. Massive rebuilding in an attempt to restore the South Bronx to its earlier population levels would invite a repetition of the abandonment process in other areas of the city. While we urge the city to take action to halt the spread of abandonment, we do not condone what is for the moment a quixotic effort to undo the damage of the past. We are confident that, in time, these now-blighted areas that are close to the central city and have adequate infrastructure may once again become valuable. **If and when renewal becomes a realistic prospect for those areas, we think that the city should aid the private sector in redeveloping them for job-creating enterprises.**

Scaling down municipal services for blocks of land that have had severe population losses must not, in our view, mean totally abandoning their residents. We think that most of the city's population has demonstrated a clear preference for the more vital areas. Consolidation will make service delivery easier, and by keeping both buildings and neighborhoods occupied, the threat of further abandonment will be reduced.

Housing in all neighborhoods, of course, must be available on a nondiscriminatory basis, **and the city could play a constructive role by working to create balanced neighborhoods that are diverse economically as well as racially.**

The Task Force opposes building new housing with city funds. Private financing is already available for owner-occupied housing and luxury rental buildings; public subsidy or financing of new luxury housing represents a diversion of public funds and energies. We are aware that rental housing for lower- and middle-income tenants cannot easily obtain financing, but in this sector, we think that public policy should be directed to the rehabilitation of existing buildings rather than to the construction of new buildings. In the event that more federal financing becomes available, we favor its use for well-planned low-rise housing for low-income families. For the foreseeable future, however, the Task Force recommends that the city administration focus on measures to encourage rehabilitation, to lower operating costs for rental buildings, and to unblock the flow of available funds for housing.*

Unfortunately, delays in planning result in the temporary or permanent loss of much of the federal money available for rehabilitation. For example, only 45 percent of available Community Development funds were being spent as of December 1978. The city should be spending all such funds since they constitute the bulk of available funds for rehabilitation. At the same time, we urge that the city improve the system used to pay rehabilitation contractors, a system that has caused needless delays. At present, many reputable firms refuse to work for the city because of the city's poor payment record.

We recommend more frequent assessment of real property so that apartment buildings in rapidly changing neighborhoods are not subject to either severe overassessment or underassessment (unreasonably high real estate taxes could make the difference between an economically run building and one that is abandoned). In addition, the program of tax abatements for renovation and repair of multi-family dwellings should be maintained and expanded.

The Task Force believes that the goal in restoring existing buildings should be to do as much moderate renovation as possible, leaving sound structures intact. Current practices seem to encourage "gut" rehabilitation, which is more expensive—and not always strictly necessary. Thus, we recommend that the city revise its standards to allow less costly renovation.

*Messrs. Cabranes and May comment:
We are concerned, also, that inadequate treatment is accorded to the possible development of city areas that have been abandoned by substantial numbers (or in some cases, virtually all) of its inhabitants, such as parts of Brooklyn or the South Bronx.

While we generally endorse the Task Force's conclusions regarding housing, we fear it puts too much faith in costly and time-consuming rehabilitation as the only means of providing housing for residents who cannot fend for themselves on the open market. We feel there is still need for publicly sponsored, well-planned, low-rise public housing for low-income New Yorkers and are pleased that the Task Force has at least held this option open.

Mr. Flaherty wishes to associate himself with the comments in Messrs. Cabranes and May's first paragraph above. He also comments:
I support the overall aim of the Task Force for neighborhood preservation. However, I would not oppose the use of some city funds for new housing starts, particularly where such funding is combined with available federal and state funds for housing for the elderly and low-income families.

We urge that ways be found to close up buildings legally rather than illegally. Owners should be able to shut down buildings that cannot be successfully operated because they are not fully occupied. Buildings then could be sealed before they have deteriorated, and tenants from partly occupied buildings could be moved into more economically sound buildings, thus reducing the costs of providing low-income housing.

The Task Force believes that it is better to keep buildings operating in the hands of private landlords as long as possible, in part because many tenants are reluctant to pay rent to the city, which has all too often become the unwilling landlord of last resort. In addition, we recommend that the city transfer management responsibilities in its existing in rem buildings to tenants or community groups that are able—and willing—to take them over. A potentially promising program is the Department of Housing and Urban Development's Neighborhood Co-op Experiment, which combines private renovation of low-income housing with community management and tenant ownership. If it proves successful, it should be expanded. Another program, carried out by the Morrisania Project in the Bronx, has trained the hard-core unemployed to maintain and repair housing; this program, which has reduced the cost of providing standard housing and has taught marketable skills, might well be adopted by other communities in the city.

We are impressed by community self-help efforts that have improved many neighborhoods in the city. An important and inexpensive way of bettering the quality of life in the city and building community involvement and pride is the expansion of the municipal administration's program of support to community development corporations, neighborhood housing services, tenant management, homesteading, and block associations.

Neighborhoods with solid apartment buildings might be resuscitated if the city took steps to facilitate co-oping. Co-ops have, in recent years, come to be thought of primarily as a rich man's game, a device by which the well-to-do gain tax advantages. Historically, though, cooperative housing was initiated in Europe as a means of providing better housing for people with modest incomes. The Task Force believes that that original goal can—and should—be resuscitated. Through creation of a public or quasi-public agency to assist tenants in the legal and financial aspects, co-oping could be made much more widely available, and at more advantageous terms to tenants than is currently the case. The Task Force believes that Mitchell-Lama housing could be made more profitable and more attractive to moderate-income families if tenant-owners were permitted to share in the capital appreciation of their apartments. There might be less resistance to needed increases in maintenance costs if owners could look forward to the prospect of deriving potential capital gains upon relocation. In addition, we suggest that corporations—or consortia of corporations—could participate in the process by buying large sites, either on unused land or in existing but deteriorating neighborhoods, and developing them for housing.

The gradual phasing out of rent control and rent stabilization is a useful but inadequate means of increasing the funds available to maintain apartment buildings. As we see it, partial or total elimination of rent regulations will have the greatest effect on moderate-priced housing, where many building owners are not receiving enough rental income to maintain buildings properly—and where many tenants can pay somewhat more than they are now paying. Deregulation probably would not have a significant short-term impact on building abandonment since many of the tenants of buildings being abandoned lack incomes sufficient to pay even the presently allowable rents. Nor is deregulation likely to influence luxury housing, where rents are already high and supply is fast increasing.

Because many tenants cannot afford to pay market rents—or even regulated rents—for standard housing, renovated buildings often deteriorate if they keep their original tenants. Such buildings can be maintained only by displacing their original tenants with tenants capable of paying higher rents. Neither of these results is desirable. Accordingly, we recommend that more Section 8 federal housing subsidies, which are rent supplements granted to owners of rental units occupied by low-income families, be made available to city-sponsored rehabilitation projects to assure their proper maintenance without the displacement of residents.

The Task Force urges strict enforcement of antiredlining laws which, together with the lifting of state usury ceilings, could provide a steadier flow of mortgage money into marginal neighborhoods. We also endorse the recent revision of the state FAIR insurance plan (the plan provides insurance protection for high-risk neighborhoods that are not covered by private plans), which has moved toward equalization of the regular and FAIR rates, making the FAIR rates less burdensome for residents and neighborhood businesses.

Apart from the rehabilitation and restoration of housing, it is important to strengthen local retail centers, which are a source of neighborhood stability, as well as jobs. The commercial regeneration already taking place in pockets of the outer boroughs should be promoted by an increase in city funding for commercial strip improvement projects.

Recent immigrants to the city, who have set up many new small

retail enterprises to serve newly created ethnic communities, have
played a prominent part in neighborhood revitalization. Much of
their activity represents a relatively unsophisticated form of economic development, consisting mostly of family-run enterprises, labor
intensive and minute in scale. But it has provided income and
employment outside established commercial channels for rising
numbers of new immigrants. These pockets of small entrepreneurial
activity have developed in the virtual absence of governmental aid or
policy to abet it. It demonstrates that small-scale independent
entrepreneurship, which has been a city tradition, still offers opportunities and is as vital to the continuation of strong, self-sufficient
neighborhoods today as it was in the past. Further expansion can
help the outer boroughs regain a substantial measure of stability and
prosperity.

We also believe that the outer boroughs could be the sites of
hotels, motels, and even more modest tourist facilities that would
cater to families who, unlike high-income businessmen and tourists,
cannot afford to stay in Manhattan. Manhattan's many cultural and
entertainment attractions would still be accessible, but at a much
more reasonable total cost. The construction and operation of such
facilities in the outer boroughs would not only be cheaper than
comparable facilities in Manhattan but would offer a great many jobs
to residents of the surrounding neighborhoods.

The Task Force recommends that the rebuilding of neighborhoods
be further strengthened by enhancing the status and accountability
of community planning boards. One reform, already mandated by
the New York City charter, makes the organizational boundaries of
certain service delivery systems coterminous with local community
boards. We urge that this reform be implemented as quickly as
possible. Obviously, some services must be coordinated on a citywide
basis, and the allocations of funds to particular neighborhoods must
be determined by citywide elected officials. But within a given
allocation, individual communities should have a maximum voice in
determining their own priorities. Enhancing community participation
and control will make possible more effective use of city resources
while strengthening neighborhood ties. Other local institutions—
religious, fraternal, business, and civic—should take increased responsibility in their communities. They could, for example, assume
leadership in the sponsoring of street fairs, neighborhood competi-
tions, and participatory events that foster community spirit.

NATIONAL OBLIGATION

As the nation's gateway, New York has historically been the
city where immigrants became Americans and where the poor were

helped until they could make it on their own. This New York brand of liberalism has even been said to have triumphed in the national arena in the form of the New Deal, which recognized that welfare was not solely a local or state responsibility. Time and experience have made it painfully apparent that neither money nor legislation can eradicate poverty, discrimination, and crime. Yet even with its extremely limited resources, the city cannot abandon its belief that those who cannot find jobs should not be left to fend for themselves. Once again, the federal government has to assume responsibility for what is a national obligation.

At a minimum, we believe that the federal government should maintain, under vigilant scrutiny, the Comprehensive Employment and Training Act (CETA) program at a high level of funding because the program provides valuable jobs and training when restricted to those who are not now equipped to compete in the private sector. **But we do not support keeping open unneeded facilities with either federal or city funds merely to provide make-work jobs.**

The Task Force acknowledges that there is little likelihood of major increases in federal or state contributions to the city's large welfare population in the immediate future. Yet sooner or later, the federal government must take over the welfare burden from states and municipalities. **In a highly mobile society, where people are subject to economic dislocations and displacement by national and international developments, welfare is not properly a local problem.**

New York City, moreover, remains the port of entry for many foreign immigrants, legal and illegal. While immigration policy and enforcement are viewed as federal concerns, their effects bear disproportionately on New York. It is our view that **the federal government must recognize its responsibility by assuming the costs of welfare, with full and adequate funding and with benefit levels that take account of regional differences in living costs.** We are apprehensive about a federal takeover that provides only a minimum federal benefit. The prospect is that this floor would be a ceiling in many states, but those with traditionally higher payment levels, such as New York, would have to provide added benefits. We prefer a gradual increase in the share of existing state benefit levels paid by the federal government, on the ground that this is a surer route to higher federal contributions.*

Mr. Lekachman comments:
However unpropitious the immediate political prospect, we ought to press continually for complete federalization of Aid to Families of Dependent Children (AFDC) and medicaid. This is a matter of general equity, not of special pleading on the part of New Yorkers.

Messrs. May and Cabranes wish to associate themselves with Mr. Lekachman's comment.

MEETING THE CHALLENGE

The people of New York City have always responded to challenge. In the past, though, they could count on the secular advance of the world's mightiest industrial economy and New York's own internal growth for the resources needed to cope with successive waves of immigration, with economic and technological change, as well as with the painful spasms of cyclical business contractions. Even in the Great Depression, when its credit was impaired, Wall Street was a boulevard of broken dreams, and racketeering was rife, the city, led by the indomitable Fiorello La Guardia, managed to pull itself together, rising to new heights during the war and in the early postwar years. In those days of seemingly unlimited resources, the city could afford to be extravagant and wasteful, confident that the future would somehow take care of itself.

Now, with resources scarce, the city no longer has the luxury of choice. Constrained by state and federal fiscal overseers, it has made some commendable progress in the unaccustomed exercise of re-trenchment. But achieving a balanced budget may well require further reductions in municipal services and facilities. Such stringent retrenchment limits the city's options.

One option is to ignore the future entirely, which has been the prevailing course since the fiscal crisis; concentrating on paring the budget and restoring the city's credit, of course, inevitably means unplanned but definite shrinkage. A second option is to adopt a policy of planned shrinkage, reducing the size of the city until it is at a level consistent with the resources likely to be available. A third option is to devote a limited amount of manpower and money to future economic development while taking advantage, in ad hoc fashion, of whatever programs or plans state and federal agencies are willing to finance. Finally, there is the option of deciding what future best suits the city, and then pursuing policies—again with limited manpower and money (money least of all)—to attain it.

The Task Force has chosen this last course. In our view, the dual strategy of promoting New York as the world capital and preserving and protecting its neighborhoods is the most practical and rewarding future for the city. It builds on the city's acknowledged strengths. It lends support to the most dynamic and exhilarating area in the private sector. And it offers the greatest opportunities for the greatest number of New Yorkers.

We do not suggest that adopting this dual strategy will solve all of the problems afflicting the city. We are aware that this dual strategy, in contrast to a shrinkage policy, whether planned or unplanned, is based in part on faith in the city and its people. That faith is not simply a product of New York's recent resurgence. In fact, we are concerned about the vulnerability of the local economy, which may experience a fresh drain of businesses and jobs with a national--or international—recession. But we believe in the pride of New Yorkers and their determination to help sustain the city, provided that they have clear challenges to which they can respond.

In our view, the strategy of building a world capital and strong neighborhoods in New York presents such a challenge. It also provides a framework for making hard choices. We accept the need for fiscal retrenchment, but we do not believe that retrenchment alone will solve the city's problems because such an approach is tantamount to urban euthanasia; no matter how humanely implemented, it would snuff out all prospects of a revival in city life. Instead, the Task Force approach is to propose directing the city's efforts to what the city can do best—serving international markets as the world capital, and providing livable neighborhoods and economic opportunities for its residents. In pursuing this strategy, public policy must be shaped to eliminate and trim those spending programs that do not serve these dual objectives.

The city will need the help of the state, the region, and the federal government. Even so, New York faces difficult times. Its population, even with a continued influx of legal and illegal immigrants, will probably decline further; blue-collar jobs will inevitably become fewer; and municipal government must continue to reduce its services. The entire northeast quadrant of the nation will lag behind the rest of the nation in jobs and population and new investment.

But there is no doubt that the city today is throbbing with the vitality of life and renewal. It is already a more important financial center than London; a richer cultural center than Paris, Rome, or Tokyo; and the headquarters of more major corporations than Chicago, Los Angeles, Houston, Pittsburgh, and Atlanta combined. New York is a metaphor for change and response to change. What it loses in one field, it gains in others. As the domestic securities market decentralizes, it is profiting from internationalization of financial markets. As it has witnessed the dispersal of manufacturing, it has gained in tourism. Since the city cannot recapture its past, it must begin planning its future now.

This Task Force believes that the real choice is between doing some things well rather than everything poorly. We believe that our vision of the future challenges New Yorkers to do what they can do best for New York.

Dissent

Andrew J. Biemiller

Apart from some minor reservations, I find much good in the sections of the Report dealing with education, the infrastructure, neighborhood development, welfare, CETA, and so forth. However, assessing the important role of trade unions in this process has been neglected. As far as the Report is concerned, save for two slight references, one would not know there is a vital labor movement in New York. One reason for La Guardia's success was his close collaboration with the unions. This Report does not even give the unions proper credit for helping to bail out the city during its financial crisis by heavy investment of pension funds.

So I regret that I cannot endorse the Report.

The treatment of blue-collar workers is cavalier, to say the least. The Report fails to emphasize the need for blue-collar and rank-and-file white-collar jobs for people. It concerns itself primarily with the problems of bankers and financiers.

I cannot subscribe to the proposal to allow domestic offshore banking facilities in New York and to eliminate the withholding tax on foreign portfolio investment. The sole effect of these proposals would be to allow foreign entities to evade American taxes. Furthermore, they would not create any significant number of jobs. The Report itself states that foreign banks and other foreign entities should not be the recipients of special favors or incentives. I do not wish to be party to setting up New York as a competitor with the financial and banking practices of the Bahamas or the Netherland Antilles.

I differ strongly with the Report on the proposal to transfer the World Bank and the International Monetary Fund (IMF) to New York. The Bank and the IMF have to deal constantly with the U.S. Treasury and State Department, as well as with embassies of foreign nations.

I further disagree with the kudos heaped on multinational corporations. American labor has suffered from the overseas manufacturing activities of American multinationals, which, as reported by the Senate Subcommittee on Multinationals, have cost hundreds of thousands of Americans their jobs.

A sound American economy must have a solid industrial base. As Dr. Peggy Musgrave and others have pointed out, the economic collapse of England stems from its unfavorable balance of trade during the entire twentieth century. The English economy was kept alive by financial returns from overseas investments as far back as the decade before World War I. Such payments may give the illusion of a healthy balance of trade, but they benefit only the investing and financial groups, not the workers. We should not go through the same process.

I must conclude that the Report does not pay proper attention to the concerns of human beings because it is concerned primarily with the problems of effete financial groups.

Background Paper

Masha Sinnreich

Chapter 1

Introduction

Manhattan has been compelled to expand skyward because of the absence of any other direction in which to grow. This, more than any other thing, is responsible for its physical majesty. It is to the nation what the white church spire is to the village—the visible symbol of aspiration and faith, the white plume saying the way is up.

E.B. White, *Here Is New York*,
Harper & Brothers, 1949

When E.B. White wrote his paean to New York City a generation ago, faith in the future of the city and the nation was boundless. The city's skyline is now loftier and more dazzling than ever, but prophecies of New York's decline (and after the city, the nation) all but drown out those who believe that the way is still up. While the new towers rising in Manhattan add to the city's physical majesty, they no longer mask the spreading wastelands that were once solid neighborhoods or the decay that has worn down New York's streets and parks and schools. Only an incurable optimist, who steadfastly ignored the city's blight and its precarious financial condition, could predict that the city would once again become a symbol of progress.

There are few such optimists: Edward I. Koch, the present mayor of New York, is perhaps the most prominent. He sees the new building boom as proof that the city is recovering from its celebrated fiscal crisis. He also has pointed out that the city has arrested the decline in its economy and that the exodus of its population has slowed. Over the last year or two, other signs have appeared that things may be looking up: tourism, hotel occupancy, and theater attendance are on the rise; office space and luxury apartments are in short supply; and the federal government has finally provided long-term loan guarantees. To a large extent, though, the recovery has been confined to Manhattan—the nation's cultural, fashion, financial, and communications center—and has been stimulated by the strength of the national economy and promoted by rigorous public relations efforts, featuring forms of boosterism that New Yorkers formerly eschewed. As a result, this so-called recovery has something of a temporary and make-believe air about it.

The case for the city's continued decline does not involve wishful thinking. Despite federal—and state—assistance, New York remains a long way from balancing its budget. It has not even kept pace with the national economic recovery, let alone regaining the 600,000 jobs or the 500,000 residents lost in the last ten years. Many of the city's remaining residents are unable to support themselves. One in eleven New Yorkers of working age is unemployed; one in eight depends on public assistance. And although new buildings are under construction, the city's physical deterioration is continuing—indeed, it is more rapid than ever before.

The seeds of New York City's decline had been sown in the 1950s and 1960s, when, to all outward appearances, it was still growing. But the "go-go" years on Wall Street, the real estate boom that accompanied them, and the rise in public employment obscured significant shifts in the city's population and in its economy. The decline became apparent in 1969, but five years passed before the crisis erupted in headlines around the world. Now, four more years later, the city remains in crisis.

New York City is also undergoing a crisis in the older sense of the word: it has reached a turning point. Decisions made now by the city's leadership will have far-reaching effects. The financial and spiritual distress of the last few years seems to have brought home to New Yorkers the need for change; they accept the facts that business cannot go on as usual and that the city must respond effectively to changes in its circumstances. But time and money have been wasted because the city's political leaders have so far failed to take advantage of this will to adapt. They have continued to offer business as usual, only less of it.

The city administration should be making basic, long-run choices, revising the old and invalid assumptions concerning the scope of city government activities, the allocation of the tax burden, and the responsibility of the city government to promote private-sector interests. Once the broad outlines of policy are clear, narrower issues will become less divisive and less difficult. If city officials continue to function on an ad hoc basis, however, they will lose the opportunity to make basic choices as new political and economic patterns fill decisionmaking vacuums. The purpose of this paper is to provide background information as a basis for sound choices regarding the course that the city will take in the future.

* * *

It is easy to understand why most New Yorkers—not only the politicians, but also the average citizens—have been reluctant to acknowledge change. Until relatively recently, New York set the pace for the nation, offering a wealth of intellectual and economic opportunities to the ambitious and enterprising. Without being the center of government (the great metropolises of Europe are supported because they are the seats of government), New York has always managed to attract those with great wealth and talent, including many who made their fortunes elsewhere but wanted the status and the publicity that only New York could confer. If it is not the world's capital, it is, with its huge and cosmopolitan concentration of all races and creeds, the closest thing to it. But it developed because it had great natural advantages that are no longer so evident.

New York owes its existence to its harbor, which is one of the most magnificent in the world. It is neither too deep nor too shallow, and it has an extensive usable shoreline as well as waterways leading to the interior. The European mercantile nations readily acknowledged its virtues. The harbor was first mapped in 1570; by 1615, the Dutch had installed a storehouse, a fort, and some huts at the southern tip of Manhattan. This site offered a flat, inviting terrain at the confluence of two navigable rivers, one of which almost never froze; it was to become the focal point for the city's development.

New Amsterdam quickly became a thriving port city. By 1664, when the English seized it and renamed it New York, it had about 10,000 settlers. Most of the original Dutch settlers stayed on, but they frequently clashed with the British. When anti-British sentiment began to spread throughout the colonies in the mid-eighteenth century, New York, then a city of 24,000 English and Dutch inhabitants, became a center of resistance to royal authority.

With the growth of the United States, New York's port became even more important. Because the rivers flowing into the harbor made the interior of the country accessible, New York became a center of international trade, shipping raw materials from the West and finished goods from Europe and the eastern seaboard. The Erie Canal, built in 1825, and the first railroads, built soon thereafter parallel to the waterways running east and west, greatly enhanced the value of the city's location.

At first, the merchants using the port financed and insured their own shipping or relied on European bankers. But by the end of the eighteenth century, business activity in North America was great enough to sustain independent financial institutions. Commercial banks (such as Hamilton's Bank of New York), the National Bank of the United States, insurance companies, and securities markets, attracted by the city's volume of trade and by its political importance (it was the state capital until 1797 and the nation's capital in 1789-90), began to establish themselves in New York. Early financial institutions were located in lower Manhattan both because much of their business involved shipping and because the port was the main source of news. Out of this beginning, New York became the nation's financial center.

During the early nineteenth century, New York also became an important wholesaling center. This trade is said to have begun after the War of 1812, when the British dumped in Manhattan surplus goods they had accumulated during the war years; it is more probable that it developed as a natural offshoot of port activity. Early wholesale markets, like the first financial institutions, were located as close as possible to the port.

The British colonial administrators had discouraged manufacturing, but the new federal government and the growth of local markets encouraged it. At the same time, the Industrial Revolution brought manufacturing out of cottages and small workshops and into factories built, for the most part, in populous areas. Because of its port, New York was better equipped than any other American city to engage in manufacturing. It shipped and received goods along the Hudson and East rivers (on whose banks most of the early manufacturing plants located); it also attracted labor from Europe, where land was scarce and the agricultural and industrial revolutions made labor a surplus commodity. But in the United States, land was in virtually limitless supply, and labor was scarce and expensive. Throughout the nineteenth century, millions of immigrants, most of them unskilled, left the turmoil and poverty of Europe to start new lives in America. More than two-thirds of them landed in New York, and many of them stayed there.

New York's growth during the nineteenth century was extra-ordinary. From a small town at the turn of the century, it grew to 630,000 by 1855, to nearly 2 million by 1897, and to 3.4 million with the 1898 incorporation of the outer boroughs (Brooklyn, Queens, and Staten Island). Most of this growth was fueled by the manufacturing sector. However, the city was not suitable for all types of industry: it lacked access to natural resources and power, so it never had the heavy industry that characterizes the Great Lakes region; from the beginning, it specialized in labor-intensive manu-facturing.

After the Civil War, the railroads, which had originally served existing population centers, began to extend their lines into uninhab-ited territory in the hope that settlers would follow. From this point on, New York's geographic advantages lost some of their value. Although the Port of New York continued to be the busiest seaport in the country (it still is today), industry no longer had to rely on rivers or seaports for domestic distribution. Manufacturing plants and wholesalers could locate anywhere along the railroad lines, and the Hudson River now appeared to be a barrier rather than an aid to transportation. The railroads triggered a process of decentralization and suburbanization of employment that has affected New York and almost every other metropolitan region in this country. Suburban-ization is often considered a postwar phenomenon, but it has actually been in progress for more than a century. During the Depression and war years, it experienced a hiatus, but it accelerated after the war to compensate for the enforced halt. (Postwar suburbanization, of course, was stimulated by the skyrocketing demand for single-family housing as well as by the earlier industry-preference consideration.)

With the expansion of the railway system and, half a century later, the construction of highways that made truck transport economical, New York's chief asset was no longer its navigable waters but its huge and compact mass of labor, industry, and business. Although this agglomeration had originally been built upon the port, it soon acquired a life of its own. The businesses that left Manhattan for the outer boroughs and surrounding counties were those to which inland transportation was more important; those that depended on com-munications and easy access to suppliers or customers stayed in the center of the city.

For example, in wholesaling, the firms whose business consisted mainly of distributing to retailers in the local markets (liquor, groceries) moved away from the center; those firms whose business consisted of selling nonstandardized goods (textiles, furs) to buyers from national markets regrouped around Manhattan's railroad ter-minals. In manufacturing, plants producing standardized goods (machinery) moved away from the center; businesses producing non-standardized goods (apparel, books), with unpredictable demands for materials and insufficient resources to stockpile, remained in the center, mainly in the lofts of Manhattan. The momentum provided by national growth kept New York's manufacturing industries growing in absolute terms until 1947. But as national markets became larger and more predictable, relatively fewer industries needed the linkages provided by the central city.

The very advances in transportation and communications that diminished New York's attractiveness as a plant site made possible the establishment of national corporations. Railroads, highways, telegraph, and telephone enabled the heads of complex, multiplant companies to manage their enterprises from a single location. In the late nineteenth century, when the great trusts were formed, whole industries—sometimes including dozens of companies—merged horizontally and vertically to form giant corporations. Many of these corporations chose to locate their headquarters in New York City, where they could have easy access to financial institutions. In particular, J. P. Morgan's "money trust" on Wall Street handled the complex financial arrangements surrounding many of the mergers, as well as exercising control over many of the newly formed companies. By 1900, sixty-nine of the nation's one hundred eight-five largest corporations had headquarters in New York.

The railroad companies and large trusts opened their first central offices close to the port and the money markets. By the first decade of the twentieth century, like many other businesses, they had moved up to the Grand Central Station area, where they were soon joined by many commercial banks. This move symbolized the growing independence of the white-collar sector from port activities. Unlike manufacturing enterprises, corporate headquarters were not large employers, at least not until the 1920s. Office work consists largely of record-keeping; throughout the nineteenth century, most business record-keeping was, at best, casual.

Even before World War I, but more markedly after it, New York began to play still another role in the nation's economic life: when the number of corporate headquarters had reached a critical mass, Manhattan became host to a variety of business services. Advertisers, consultants of all types, corporate lawyers, and accountants settled in midtown Manhattan, close to their customers, and brought with them their own suppliers, including legal printers and commercial artists. The transformation of the New York Stock Exchange from a professional to a public market and the advent of nationwide radio and then television networks, which were located in New York, afforded national coverage to city developments and made national celebrities of the city's business and political leaders, especially Fiorello La Guardia, the much publicized reform mayor from 1934 to 1945.

Since World War II, the nation's population has grown, and incomes have risen spectacularly; as a result, much of the population can now afford and expects to partake of space and leisure activities. In addition, the building of the national highway system, the introduction of air conditioning, the shift to a petroleum-based economy, and other developments have combined to open up the South and West. Manufacturing plants have dispersed across the country, and regional centers have grown large enough to support their own regional headquarters and finance and business service sectors, diminishing the central importance of New York except in the most specialized fields.

These changes, taken together, are comparable in significance to the expansion of the railway system a century ago. Before 1945, the population of New York grew faster than that of the rest of the nation; since 1945, it has lagged far behind, while the population of the Southeast and Southwest has grown dramatically. Since 1969, there has been an absolute decline in population and economic activity.

Apart from its various economic roles in national life, New York has always played a special social and cultural role, also strongly influenced by its strategic location. Since 1664, when the English settled alongside the Dutch, New York has had a heterogeneous population. Millions of immigrants, mostly poor and unskilled, have made the city their home, and the story of their assimilation into American life—often painful, but on the whole successful—is known to all Americans. Throughout its history (the 1930-45 period is the only exception), New York has assumed the responsibility of transforming the "huddled masses" into American citizens, giving them the skills and opportunity to enter the mainstream of American life, often sending them or their children to other parts of the country when the job was done. From 1945 to about 1970, much of the immigration was internal, consisting of southern blacks and Puerto Ricans, but foreign immigration still exceeds 75,000 per year. This flux has continually altered the physical face of the city, with most neighborhoods going through several cycles of deterioration and rebuilding.

In addition, a disproportionate amount of the best, the most innovative, and the most sophisticated cultural and intellectual activity in America takes place in New York. That New York is the home of artistic endeavors unique in range and quality is acknowledged throughout the world. Less of a commonplace is the development of a New York consciousness, shaping and enhancing creativity in many fields. The "New York intellectuals," the "New York poets," "the New York school" of artists, and other groups flourishing at various times have played a special role in the national culture. Irving Howe has come close to pinpointing it in his observation that New York writers "think of themselves as deeply cut off from the society in which they live while nevertheless tied to it by bonds of criticism."[1]

Southern writers also have been alienated, and other regions have produced regional styles, but they are traceable, in large part, to adversity and isolation. New York, with its large and wealthy audiences, publishing houses, and mass media, is anything but adverse to the arts. The tensions of multiethnic life in the city, the ability to draw on numerous foreign cultures, and the difficulty of communicating a cosmopolitan experience to the more homogeneous population outside the city are the elements that have helped spur creativity and a feeling of separateness. These conditions have not changed; indeed, they may have become intensified by local perceptions of the national response to the city's fiscal plight.

Some of New York's long-time residents, who remember the city's happier days with affection and pride, long to recreate them and to restore the city's lost glory. But the history of New York is not a tale of consistency or passivity. The city's glory has been, in fact, its success in responding to successive waves of immigration and new political, economic, and technological developments. Although stability may be attractive to those who benefit from the current arrangements, it is not really a desirable goal for the city. Efforts to preserve employment patterns, residential patterns, or fiscal arrangements that have "always" existed may hamper the city's adjustment to changing conditions. Once change is recognized as normal instead of pathological, the city can address its real problems—providing a decent living for all its residents and social and economic mobility for as many as possible.

Accepting the inevitability of change does not mean acquiescing in whatever fate befalls the city. Rather, it means making the best of New York's comparative advantages and equipping the city to compete for business over the next few decades. Since these comparative advantages are in part the result of past developments, managing change also implies building on rather than breaking with the past.

The critical elements of the city's history are easier to identify than are the technological, economic, demographic, and political developments that will shape New York's future. Yet it is essential to make an educated guess about the future and to act on the presumption that the guess is correct.

Over the past three hundred years, the city's leaders have made a series of astute judgments that eased adjustment to change and that enhanced the capacity of the city to serve its residents. As early as 1683, the city corporation owned and was developing all wharves, docks, ferries, waters, and other vital assets. The uptown development initiated by Tweed in the 1860s, the building of the subways and, perhaps especially, the elevated train from the port to the railway station in 1870, the incorporation of the three outer boroughs in 1898, the formation of the Port Authority in 1921, the renovation and coordination of waterfront activity, and the building of Floyd Bennett Field in 1931 are but a few examples of this activism. Some of these investments have been more successful than others, but on the whole, New York's policy of being early to take advantage of new developments paid off.

In the past, the city was in a growing phase that provided a healthy margin for error. Today, of course, the margin for error is slim, and false illusions about growth could prove disastrous. The fact that change has taken the form of decline instead of growth also creates political difficulties; when few benefits are available to trade, it is hard to form political coalitions.

Yet anticipating and guiding change, which was a signal feature of New York's growth, is not less vital today than it was in the past. A realistic assessment of the city's strengths and weaknesses must replace the romantic rhetoric and modest actions that have been resorted to since the crisis first erupted. No political reward may accrue to facing up to and dealing with decline, especially when it affects the lives of so many New Yorkers, but the willingness to adjust to change will ultimately serve the city better than denying and resisting it.

Chapter 2

New York's Changing Economy

Economic activity in New York City has changed markedly since World War II. The city was once primarily a blue-collar town, with hundreds of small- and medium-sized manufacturing operations quartered in Manhattan's lofts and in plants across the river in Brooklyn and Queens. Over half of these manufacturing jobs have been lost, probably forever, while many new jobs became available in local government and in the white-collar and service sectors. Lofts in Manhattan have gradually been abandoned or converted to other uses, while new office buildings have risen in the Wall Street and midtown districts. Some firms in the city still produce toys and hats and jewelry, but entire industries (brewing, for example) and major producers (of typewriters, office safes, biscuits, and cigars) have long since closed their doors.

The city's population is smaller and is spread out more evenly than in the past. Small shops, as well as large department stores and local services, have followed their customers out of old neighborhoods and into Queens, Staten Island, and the suburbs. Although commuters and tourists who confine themselves only to midtown Manhattan continue to experience noise and congestion, the city as a whole is less crowded than it was only a few years ago. The city has lost almost 500,000 people in the 1970s; all the boroughs except Staten

Island, which has grown from 295,400 to 336,800 in the same period, have shared in the loss.

Until 1969, the city's economy grew steadily, although slowly; since then, it has declined rapidly. There are nearly 300,000 fewer jobs today than there were in 1950. This shift was in large part a result of national rather than local factors—changes in technology, in demand, in relative costs, in the attractiveness of different locations, and in the rate of national growth. New York prospered in the early and middle stages of the nation's growth. It is not nearly so healthy today, when national growth has slowed and when previously undeveloped areas of the country are beginning to catch up.

DISPERSION

During the last century, New York's chief economic asset was its density. Markets, workers, suppliers, up-to-date information—all were readily available within a very small area. This was important to all industry, but especially to small businesses, which are not in control of their environment and must be able to respond quickly to changes in the marketplace. (The classic example is the dress manufacturer, who, when fashion changes from buttons to buckles, must have a buckle factory nearby.) For this reason, New York has always been, far more than most major cities, a center for small business. But in the years since World War II, density has become less and less valuable to American industry. Nonagricultural enterprises, which were once heavily concentrated geographically, have become more evenly dispersed across the country, with manufacturing leading the way. In most cases, of course, businesses have not physically moved. But when New York enterprises go out of business or even fail to grow and Jacksonville's businesses thrive, the net effect is the same. The traditional industrial belt, the Northeast and the Great Lakes region, employed 68 percent of the nation's manufacturing workers in 1947 but only 51 percent by 1975.[1] The nine largest manufacturing centers, which employed 36 percent of the nation's manufacturing workers in 1952, employed only 27 percent in 1975.[2] This nationwide trend has had a major effect on New York, where dispersion began early and has persisted.

Although there is no question that dispersion has occurred, a lively dispute continues over what caused it. Some observers claim that the federal government initiated the policies that were mainly responsible for the shift in the way American industry chose to locate itself; others contend that government policies merely reinforced—and perhaps accelerated—the inevitable. While the evidence that would resolve this dispute is not yet in, both government and private decisions can be safely said to have contributed to dispersion—and the cooperation of both sectors would be necessary to slow it down. Any attempt to project continued dispersion must be based on an evaluation of major developments that promoted it in the past.

Availability of Labor

At one time, only large metropolitan areas could provide the labor required for most manufacturers. This is no longer true. Manufacturers no longer need huge labor pools[3] because of technological advances and changes in the nature of industrial activity. But this change affected areas like Detroit and Pittsburgh more than New York, which never had giant manufacturing plants. New York has been hurt more by the fact that it has become easy for manufacturers to open plants in out-of-the-way places and find workers. Now that driving to work is the norm (automobile ownership grew from 40 million in 1950 to 110 million in 1975[4]), businesses can recruit workers from wide areas. They also took advantage of the enormous postwar growth of the American population, of women going to work in large numbers, and of the millions of displaced farm workers. Many areas that were once too thinly populated to support much industry would, even without migration, have reached the "critical mass" essential to attract employers.

But people have, in fact, become more willing to migrate as previously undeveloped areas began to appear more attractive as places in which to live. For instance, air conditioning, an expensive and almost unattainable luxury in 1945, had by 1974 been installed in 67 percent of southern homes.[5] As a consequence, the South is now considered as more inhabitable and its climate preferable to that of the North. Meanwhile, between 1950 and 1976, real median family income nearly doubled,[6] providing a large percentage of the population financial access to suburban living. With income increasing and favorable federal mortgage and tax policies, home-ownership also nearly doubled.[7] Many families sought open spaces for low-density housing and recreation, and these advantages were easier to find and were cheaper away from large cities.

Access to Suppliers and Markets

When railways, a small highway network, and local roads were the only means of overland transportation, enormous areas of the United States were virtually virgin territory. The construction of 340,000 miles of federally funded highways[8] and 44,000 miles of oil pipelines between 1950 and 1975[9] opened up a vast expanse for development. At the same time, the small enterprise characteristic of New York became a less common form of doing business. Because ownership of American industry is increasingly concentrated (from 1947 to 1972, the proportion of manufacturing plants belonging to multiunit companies rose from 17 percent to 28 percent[10]), many plants can rely on parent corporations for the business and financial services and supplies that independent plants seek in cities.

Finally, the migration out of the cities was not only a movement of workers but of consumers. Consumer-oriented businesses now have less reason to locate in large, older metropolitan areas; they tend to follow their markets to sunnier climates.

Availability of Land

While new land was becoming available in the South and West, factories began to run out of room to expand where they were. New technologies called for the conversion of plant operations from multistory to horizontal structures. Given zoning restrictions, existing intensive land development, and even the size of city blocks, many plants could not find suitable urban locations for such structures at any cost. Site assembly and clearing became so expensive and time consuming that many companies found it easier to move long distances than to stay where they were.

Relative Costs

Certain costs—notably land and labor—had always been lower in less-developed regions simply because those regions were less developed. Although these costs have risen, they still have not caught up with those in the older regions. Land and labor are thus not only more easily available but are also cheaper in the South and West. Often, they are less regulated as well: unions, zoning ordinances, and other environmental regulations are less in evidence than they are in the cities of the Northeast. In addition, state and local taxes and energy costs are generally lower in less-developed areas than in the older metropolitan areas. New York in particular has one of the highest tax burdens and extremely high energy costs.

Growth of Industries Preferring the South

The federal government has had a long-standing policy of awarding contracts to plants in areas where costs are low. To some extent, this is an explicit economic development policy; it is also supported by those concerned with efficiency in government. As federal contracts have become more important, they have effectively relocated a great deal of manufacturing employment. Moreover, industry has increased its use of petroleum (both as a fuel and as a raw material) relative to its use of coal. Such industries as plastics, which require large supplies of oil, have moved into the Gulf states, where petroleum is cheaper, just as the steel industry once located itself near the midwestern coalfields.

Dispersion of Nonmanufacturing Employment

Although manufacturing accounts for only about a quarter of the nation's nonagricultural employment, it has been the leading sector in the dispersion of all employment, doing so much faster than business in general. Manufacturing's position as the largest export sector[11] enables it to draw other business with it.

Table 2-1. Share of Fourteen Industrial States

	1952	1975
Manufacturing employment	65%	51%
Nonmanufacturing employment	47%	42%
Total employment	53%	44%

Source: Bureau of Labor Statistics, *Employment and Earnings.*

In today's advanced economy, self-sufficient farms or villages are not practical. If it is to have money to import necessities, a community needs to produce something of value to the outside world. City dwellers cannot live entirely by "taking in each other's washing" and still buy food, fuel, and other externally produced items. However, the export base that supports most cities is not usually large. Most employment serves the local population. Trade, services, construction, local government, and even local manufacturing (bakeries, newspapers, and so forth) need to be near their markets and thus follow the export sector wherever it goes.

Some export sectors (agriculture, mining, and, to a lesser extent, transportation) remain bound by geography, but most are subject to some of the same forces that are dispersing manufacturing. For example, the federal government, a large export industry, chooses its locations in part because of their access to labor; while it once favored heavily populated areas, it is now able to set up large regional offices and military bases in remote places. Specialized business and financial services (those that are not provided internally) and some types of wholesaling have been moving from national to regional centers, which, due to the general population growth, are now large enough to support headquarters-service complexes. Thus, while the manufacturing sector has been first in the migration to the Sunbelt, other export sectors have also been subject to some of the same pressures, and together they have drawn people and local-sector businesses out of the cities.

Intrametropolitan Dispersion

The growth of suburban commuting, which came into its own after World War II, encouraged dispersion of employment within metropolitan areas. As workers moved farther and farther from their jobs, they spent more of their incomes outside the city, sometimes even outside the metropolitan area, on housing and neighborhood services. Downtown commercial and residential areas in many large cities began to decay, while those in the suburbs flourished.

At the same time, of course, the export sectors—manufacturing, headquarters offices, and so forth—continued to move to the suburbs as they had been doing since the late nineteenth century. The appeal of the suburbs and the newer areas as industrial locations was more than the older cities could withstand. Only the high growth rates of the postwar era sustained them, but when growth slowed down in the 1970s, many were hurt severely.

The Shift to Services

This already complicated picture is further clouded by simultaneous structural changes that took place as the American economy moved into its so-called postindustrial phase. Today, most workers are engaged not in the production of goods but in the provision of services. Nationwide, the proportion of nonagricultural workers employed in mining, construction, manufacturing, transportation, and public utilities fell from 53 percent in 1945 to 35 percent in 1975,[12] while, in the same period, the proportion of workers employed in trade, finance, services, and government rose from 47 percent to 65 percent.[13] Some of this change can be attributed to shifting international trade patterns; we now import many manufactured goods from abroad and export many services. But most of the change is due to the rise in the American standard of living. Because financial prosperity has become relatively widespread, people have been devoting a higher proportion of income to personal services (the bare necessities of life are for the most part goods rather than services) and local government.

These structural changes in turn have had regional effects; for example, established manufacturing centers have lost more than the average number of jobs. In addition, service industries, more than goods-producing industries, tend to supply local rather than national markets, which means that regional markets are more self-sufficient than they used to be and less dependent on national centers like New York.

NEW YORK IN DECLINE

These forces have been felt in New York, which initially managed to withstand their impact more successfully than did other aging American cities. Payroll employment[14] in the city remained fairly stable at about 3.5 million from 1950 until the mid-1960s. Then, it rose to 3.8 million in the late 1960s, when cities in the Northeast and Mideast were losing workers. This upsurge proved deceptive. In 1969, the decline set in, with employment falling precipitously until it stabilized at about 3.2 million in 1977.[15] Although changes in the absolute level of economic activity have been erratic, the loss of the city's share of national employment—its relative decline—was fairly steady between 1950, when it represented 7 percent of the nation's nonagricultural employment, and 1977, when it reached 3.8 percent. In other words, most of the fluctuations in New York City's employment seem to have been due to changes in the national rate of economic growth, rather than to changes in New York's competitive position. An exception was the period from 1966 to 1972, when the boom and subsequent bust in employment were somewhat larger than the national business cycle. This unusual cyclical swing can be attributed to the 1960s boom on Wall Street, the buildup in local government employment and government-financed construction, and the Vietnam war.

Like World War II, the Vietnam war induced feverish economic activity in its peak years and tied up labor and capital for both industry and housing. Much of the growth during the late 1960s was achieved by more intensive use of existing resources: the ratio of output to capacity in manufacturing reached very high levels, and the labor market was very tight.[16] After the troop withdrawal began in 1969 and defense production slowed down, the national economy entered a recession, during which obsolete plants in the city began to close down. When, in 1971, industry began to meet capital construction needs, new plants were built, for the most part, not in New York or the other older cities, but in lower cost areas. Thus, in effect, the war checked the underlying dispersion in the late 1960s and sped it up in the early 1970s, a repetition of the experience of 1940-45 and 1945-50.

DECLINING METROPOLIS, DECLINING CORE

If, from 1953 to 1976, payroll employment in New York City had kept pace with the nation as a whole, it would have grown to 5.51 million in 1977 instead of declining to 3.2 million. Of the potential 2.31 million jobs foregone, about 1.47 million were attributable to the decline in the New York metropolitan region as a whole (from 10.8 percent of U.S. employment in 1953 to 7.9 percent in 1976).[17] Thus, even if it had no competition from its suburbs, the city would hardly have grown at all. But as they had been doing since the late nineteenth century, the suburbs accounted for a disproportionate share of metropolitan growth. From 1953 to 1976, the suburban counties in the New York region increased their share of the region's employment from 35 percent to 48 percent.[18]

DISPERSIVE TRENDS AND STRUCTURAL CHANGE

It is simplistic to equate New York's decline with that of other cities. As discussed above, structural change in the national economy has reshaped numerous local economies. Obviously, a city specializing in an activity that is becoming more important nationally is less likely than the average city to decline, and conversely. But New York had—and has—an extremely diversified economy with a large number of specialties. Not all these specialties can be growth industries, nor are all of them likely to be depressed simultaneously. It would be surprising if New York were doing much better or worse than the average large city. In fact, if each sector of New York's economy had matched that sector of the national economy from 1965 to 1975, New York's employment growth would have exceeded national growth by nearly 2 percent,[19] showing that its industrial mix is actually slightly favorable. To put it another way, the structure of New York's economy (which now is oriented slightly more than the rest of the nation toward services, a growing sector) actually gives it an advantage, although only a very small one. In a comparison of employment changes from 1951 to 1971 in the nine major metropolitan areas in the Northeast,[20] Rochester and Boston, which specialize in high technology products, fared the best, and Buffalo and Pittsburgh, which specialize in ferrous metal production, fared the worst. The New York region, with its diversified economy, ranked sixth out of nine, with its relative loss slightly above the average of the nine regions.

In short, New York's decline is about average for a large northeastern city and thus can probably be attributed mainly to the forces creating dispersion that have affected all of them. Its diversity protects it from the sort of severe losses that Pittsburgh has had and, at the same time, keeps it from running counter to national trends, as Rochester has done. New York City cannot regain its lost share of the U.S. economy without either a major structural change in its economy or a reversal of the nationwide dispersive trend. Neither event is likely.

NEW YORK'S EXPORT BASE: A DETAILED LOOK

Although New York has been subject to all the ills of urban America, it is, economically speaking, a very unusual city. Because of its size, density, and history, it comes closer than any other American city to being a national and even an international capital. A large portion of its export activity serves national or international markets, rather than regional ones, and these activities tend to be of the most specialized nature. New York is the locus of more, and farther reaching, organizational, financing, and marketing decisions than any other American city.

New York's areas of specialization roughly approximate what can best be described as its "export base." The city has always been more suitable for light manufacturing than for heavy manufacturing, and it still retains some export functions in the former category. Among these, several industries have high location quotients:[21] watch and clock making; apparel, especially luxury items and hats; knit textiles; printing and publishing, especially periodicals and commercial printing; leather goods, especially handbags; jewelry and silverware; toys; office and art supplies; and soaps and cosmetics. These industries nearly all produce consumer goods, specifically small, nonstandardized items. They are particularly well suited to New York because of the city's unusual cost structure. Space is expensive in New York, which has more than twice the population density of any other city in the United States. The industries locating here are among the least capital intensive of all industries; that is, the amount of plant and equipment (and hence, space) per worker is very low.

Consolidated Edison, the utility serving the city, charges the highest electric rates in the country, partly because New York is at the end of the fuel pipelines (it is more dependent on oil than most other populous cities), partly because high population density necessitates strict environmental standards, and partly because excess capacity is required to meet the extreme swings in demand. New York's industrial specialties are low consumers of energy.

Transportation costs are high in New York, and rail and highway access to the city's manufacturing plants (many of which are still located in the extremely dense and congested central business district) is poor. Accordingly, all of the items in whose production New York specializes are small finished products of high value compared to their weight and bulk; transportation costs are a minimal part of the total costs of such items. Printing appears to be an exception to this rule; it is more capital intensive than other specialties, and some printed products are quite heavy compared to their value. But from 1965 to 1975, the location quotient of printing in New York dropped considerably; moreover, the remaining heavy concentration of printing is not directly an export industry but an adjunct to New York's highly labor-intensive publishing, legal, and advertising businesses. Transportation costs for such printing are negligible because the distances that printed products must travel are close to zero.

Labor costs are somewhat more complex. The industries located in New York typically have low wage scales, but the wages paid by these industries in New York are higher than elsewhere. For example, in 1976, New York's apparel workers earned about 25 percent more than the national average, and New York's printers earned 42 percent more than printers in other cities. But New York cannot generally be considered an expensive labor market. Production workers in the few high-wage-industry plants in the city are actually paid less than their counterparts elsewhere. Fabricated metal workers, for example, earned 22 percent *less* than the national average. Clerical, technical, and maintenance workers are well but not exorbitantly paid; they could earn as much in Detroit, Atlanta, and many other cities.[22] And industries do not behave as if labor were expensive in New York; the city specializes in labor-intensive industries. Most likely, these businesses are located in New York not because they are labor intensive but because they are information intensive. Information is the one commodity that is cheaper in New York than anywhere else—the one remaining economic advantage of the city's size and density.

The apparel and printing companies that find it worthwhile to remain in New York seem to be those that produce specialized items or lines where fashions change very rapidly and up-to-the-minute information is a vital necessity. Of course, these businesses—haute couture, for example—also require more highly skilled labor. Thus, the wage differentials in these industries frequently reflect differences in skill. Companies producing more standardized items can afford to make more capital investments and to hire less skilled workers; they usually prefer out-of-town locations. It is difficult to get hard statistics to support this explanation, but it is confirmed by everyday observation.

Between 1965 and 1975, the location quotients of most of these manufacturing specialties fell, often considerably, but they increased for hats, furs, book and periodical publishing, and jewelry (except costume jewelry) and silverware. These items are among the most labor intensive, least standardized, and highest in value-for-weight of all goods produced in the American economy. Apparel remained nearly as concentrated in New York in 1975 as it had been in 1965; the enormous loss of jobs in that sector is largely a reflection of the nationwide loss of jobs in the apparel industry due to its increasing capital-intensiveness and to foreign competition.

* * *

Manufacturing is not New York's only export sector. The city is still an exporter in many areas of wholesale trade, although from 1965 to 1975 its position slipped somewhat. Most of the slippage was, understandably, in goods distributed to local markets; the wholesale apparel business, which distributes to a national market, became *more* highly concentrated in New York. In the major categories of retail trade, only apparel and accessories are overrepresented in New York; but this concentration is not so great as it was in 1965 because the difference between sales taxes in New York and in the surrounding areas has increased, and more city residents have moved to the suburbs.

In transportation and communications, New York is underrepresented in trucking and railroads, but overrepresented in air and water transportation, telephone and telegraph communications, and radio and TV broadcasting. Data on concentration are not available for 1965 in all these categories, but the concentration of air transportation and communications in general increased between 1965 and 1975.

The financial service sector—banking, securities, insurance, and real estate—is highly concentrated in New York. Although employment in the securities industry declined sharply after peaking in

1969, this entire sector has maintained or increased its location quotient.

Nonfinancial business services, especially advertising and legal services, are another traditionally strong area for the city. Customers for these services, mainly the headquarters of major national and transnational corporations, are another large export sector. New York is losing its preeminence as a supplier of corporate services, but it still retains the most specialized services. Similarly, although corporate headquarters employment has declined both absolutely and relatively, it appears that the corporate headquarters that make the most use of specialized services stay in the city or relocate nearby within the metropolitan area.[23]

Hotels, restaurants, and personal services, all export sectors in 1965, were underrepresented by 1975; New York's value as a tourist attraction seemed, by these criteria, to have fallen. But motion pictures and theaters, a strong export sector in 1965, were even stronger by 1975, and since then, tourism seems to have recovered strongly. Between 1975 and 1977, the number of visitors to New York rose by 4 percent and their spending by 16 percent;[24] and in 1978, the numbers rose even more.

One especially bright spot in the white-collar export sector is foreign investment. The rapid growth of foreign trade and the increasing internationalization of capital markets over the last decade have brought a huge increase in the number of foreign businesses establishing offices in the United States, especially in New York City. Although no exact count is available, a 1977 survey of foreign businesses in New York identified about 2,000 such businesses and found that about 18 percent of them had arrived since 1974.[25]

About two-thirds of the foreign businesses in the city are head-quarters, representatives, or sales offices of foreign corporations. Most of the rest are banks or import/export firms; there is virtually no manufacturing and (despite the changing face of Fifth and Madison Avenues) relatively little retailing or service provision.[26]

New York has always been a center for international trade and finance; it is certainly the premier American center for world trade. A 1972 survey estimated that New York houses the American headquarters of about 60 percent of the foreign-owned corporations represented in this country.[27] Foreign businesses come to New York for more than tradition and prestige; they are attracted, like American corporations, by the variety of services available. Further-more, foreign businessmen enjoy living and working in New York. A recent survey reveals that, by a large margin, they prefer New York to any other overseas assignment, that they feel comfortable and well treated in the city, that they like New Yorkers' style of doing business, and that they appreciate the cultural events and cosmopolitan nature of the city.[28]

New York's blue-collar specialties are not directly related to one another; toy manufacturers and the diamond setters both flourish in crowded conditions, but they flourish independently. There is little or no communication between them, and one industry does not stand or fall with the success of another.

The white-collar specialties—communications, publishing, business services, finance, corporate headquarters, tourism, and culture—share with the blue-collar specialties the need for information. Corporate executives have to make decisions about a broader range of subjects than they can ever master, and they need immediate access to people with the requisite knowledge and experience. The specialists, in turn, need to keep themselves informed on the latest developments in their fields. Frequent contact and exchange of ideas seem to stimulate creative thinking by artists, executives, advertisers, or almost anyone in this group of specialties.

The white-collar export sector, though, unlike the blue-collar export sector, has closely interrelated parts. Executives depend on their consultants and financiers. The hotel, restaurant, and entertainment businesses cater to executives who are traveling or just making deals in comfortable surroundings. Everyone who wants to gather or to disseminate information depends on the publicists and the newspapers and periodical publishers. None of these industries could survive without the others.

The advantage of clustering may have been reduced in recent years with the improvement of the national communications network. Corporate headquarters that have moved to the suburbs have maintained their relationships with Park Avenue lawyers and Madison Avenue advertising agencies; the lawyers and advertisers, in turn, have reached farther afield to find clients in remote locations. Securities firms have discovered that they could function in Jersey City; New York-based banks, which once could afford to sit back and wait for business to come to them, are more aggressively seeking business outside New York. Still, there is no question that a minimum presence of all these specialties is required to make New York an attractive and desirable place. While development strategies for manufacturing could be aimed at specific industries, a white-collar development strategy would mean maintaining conditions favorable to all the white-collar specialties.[29]

An estimated 791,000 people, or 22.1 percent of those working in the city, were employed in the production of goods and services for export in 1965; 871,000 or 22.9 percent in 1969; and 818,000 or 23.1 percent in 1973.

Despite the economic fluctuations and structural changes during this period, the export sector thus has provided a fairly constant percentage of the total number of jobs in the city. But the composition of the export sector shifted radically during the 1965-73 period. The proportion of export-based jobs in manufacturing, transportation, and wholesale trade fell from 49 percent to 37 percent, and the proportion in communications (including printing and publishing), finance, and service rose from 51 percent to 63 percent.[30]

If New York had followed the national trend, the proportion of export-sector jobs in the city would have declined, especially because the average white-collar export job is generally higher paying than, for example, the average garment industry job, and thus should be able to support more local-sector jobs. But while the local sector may have grown in the metropolitan area as a whole, it has not grown in New York City because, with the growth of suburban commuting, local purchases are increasingly made outside the city limits. From 1960 to 1970, the proportion of those working in New York but living outside the city rose from 14 percent to 18 percent, an increase of 150,000 commuters. If those 150,000 commuters[31] had chosen to live in New York, they would have provided 500,000 additional jobs in the city for sales clerks, building superintendents, teachers, bakers, and shoemakers.

The export sector has been the focus of attention for those concerned with New York's economic decline, but it is not the only key to halting that decline. Another key may be reversing the exodus to the suburbs and restoring the residential and neighborhood service sector to New York. If upper-middle-income workers continue to move out, even more and better paying export jobs will be needed just to maintain the present total number of jobs in the city. Like the Red Queen in *Alice Through the Looking Glass*, New York will have to run as fast as it can to stay in the same place.

Chapter 3

Changing Demographics

Over the last generation, New York's population has changed as much as its economy. In 1950, the city was predominantly white; the largest ethnic groups were the Irish, Italians, and Jews. Today, New York is nearly half black and Hispanic. Half of the whites have left, and many of those remaining are old. Since 1970, many of the American blacks and Puerto Ricans have begun to leave; they have been replaced by immigrants from the Caribbean, Asia, and elsewhere.

These population shifts are rarely discussed dispassionately because the social and political turmoil accompanying them turned population-flow statistics into ammunition for political debates. Like the population flows of the nineteenth and early twentieth centuries, they have substantially disrupted the life of the city: fewer of the city's inhabitants are supporting themselves today (despite higher average education and income levels); families of all races have become less stable; violent crime and drug abuse have reached levels unimaginable to the prewar generation. These social dislocations have been particularly painful because the 1930s and 1940s had been, as Charles E. Silberman has pointed out, "an unusual period of domestic tranquility." The weakening of social control imposed by families and other institutions contributed to the marked rise in political tensions, which surfaced at times in bitter—and occasionally violent—confrontations. These tensions have focused on neighborhood change and on the distribution of benefits provided by the city government. Neighborhoods in the city underwent rapid change, and newcomers—whether white, black, or Hispanic—have typically faced a hostile reception from established residents. Immigrants to the city have also had to organize politically to win a share of the services and jobs provided by the city government and to protect their positions in the private sector.

MIGRATION PATTERNS

The passage of restrictive legislation in the mid-1920s brought to an end the great wave of immigration that had raised New York's population from 2 million to 7 million in fifty years. Even internal immigration- mainly southern blacks who had begun trickling into New York during World War I—came to a halt after 1929. For about fifteen years, the population remained stable, with almost no foreign immigration and only a small amount of internal migration. The ethnic composition of the city changed very little, and the population grew only by natural increase, at the same rate as the rest of the country.

After World War II, things began to move again, but in new directions. All over the country, the exodus to the suburbs accelerated as both suburban employment and commuting to city jobs grew more common. At the same time, people followed jobs out of the larger northeastern metropolitan areas—including New York. An influx of southern blacks partially offset the white exodus from the cities—again including New York. In addition, from 1945 to about 1970, New York was a magnet for Puerto Rican immigration, and since about 1968, the city has received a new wave of foreign immigration, both legal and illegal. Between 1950 and 1974, as a result of the net out-migration of whites and in-migration of blacks and Hispanics, New York's black and Hispanic population rose from about 13 percent to 42 percent.

During a period when other parts of the United States offered much better economic opportunities, the city attracted as immigrants those to whom these opportunities were largely unavailable. From 1945 to 1970, while whites were migrating in great numbers from North to South and from city to suburb, blacks were migrating from South to North and from rural area to city. After 1945, farm machinery came into wide use in the South, depriving both black and

Table 3-1.

Percentage of Nonwhites in Total Population (excluding most Hispanics)			Percentage of His-panics in New York City Population	Percentage of His-panics in U.S. Population
	NYC	Central Cities	U.S.		
1950	9.8	12.9	10.7	3.6	N.A.
1960	14.7	17.5	11.4	8.6	N.A.
1970	22.8	23.2	12.4	15.2	N.A.
1974	24.9	23.6	12.9	17.4	5.3

Source: U.S. Bureau of the Census, *Census of the Population* and *Current Population Survey.*

white of employment. The advent of manufacturing in the South provided jobs for some unemployed farmworkers. But southern rural counties had been either predominantly white (small upland farms) or predominantly black (large lowland farms that were former slave-owning plantations). And as economist Wilbur Thompson points out, manufacturing going South tended to favor white counties both because of racial prejudice and because southern whites were far less prone than southern blacks to join unions.[1] Hence, many blacks were forced to leave their homes in search of jobs, but they lacked access to the areas where manufacturing employment was growing fastest—the smaller metropolitan areas in the South and the suburbs in the North. Housing for the poor in the United States has, for the most part, been supplied by or provided by older dwellings no longer desired by the middle class. Most of the housing available to blacks in the postwar era consisted of apart-ments in older buildings in the aging central cities that whites were leaving. Another attraction of the northern cities for blacks was that they had long had small but well-established black communities, which provided information and support systems for arriving blacks.

After 1965, North-South migration began to taper off and after 1970 actually reversed, for the first time in the century. Between 1970 and 1974, there was a small net nonwhite emigration from New York.[2] But because the figures on nonwhites in New York during this period include large numbers of recent immigrations from the Caribbean, the true volume of migration to the South by blacks who were originally from the South, or whose parents were, is larger than the net figure indicates. The reversal of black migration patterns after 1970 was due to the stabilization in farm employment[3] and the rising unemployment in the northeastern cities.[4] The passage of civil rights legislation that improved, or appeared to improve, economic opportunities for blacks in the South also may have deterred some southern blacks from leaving home and encouraged some who had previously left to return.

Although the black migration affected most northern cities, Puerto Rican and foreign immigration has been concentrated in New York. In Puerto Rico, a population explosion and agricultural displacement had combined to produce high unemployment rates and grinding poverty. Before 1940, the island had been sending a trickle of emigrants to New York, but in 1945, air service between San Juan and New York was introduced, and a mass migration began. The Puerto Ricans who came to New York were more skilled and urbanized than the average Puerto Rican, but far less so than the average American.

Initially, emigrating Puerto Ricans took advantage of the low air fares to New York, and most of them settled where they landed. Since 1970, though, high unemployment in New York has led to a net emigration of Puerto Ricans from the mainland back to Puerto Rico[5] and, of those who remained, to a dispersion from New York to other cities. (It is difficult to estimate accurately the number of Puerto Ricans in New York because many people from the Caribbean, including Central America, come to New York by way of Puerto Rico or identify themselves as Puerto Ricans once they are here in order to evade immigration restrictions.)

Opponents of New York's high welfare levels have often argued that generous welfare payments attracted poor blacks and Puerto Ricans to New York. This belief motivated the attempt, in the 1960s, to impose residency requirements on welfare applicants. However, numerous studies have shown that most welfare recipients who migrated to New York originally came to the city looking for work and turned to welfare only as a last resort, usually after attempting to support themselves for several years.[6] Most observers conclude that migration (at least for persons of working age) is generally motivated by the desire for more secure or better paid employment, and until 1969, New York City appeared to have jobs available.

In the mid-1960s, population growth outstripped economic development in Central and South America, the West Indies, Asia, and poor countries elsewhere (as it had, a century earlier, in Europe), and air fares fell relative to other prices. As a result, immigration to the United States from countries of the Third World began to increase by leaps and bounds. New York, as a major international air terminal, is a convenient destination. Hence, nearly one-fifth of all legal immigrants to the United States in the past decade have settled in New York.[7] Like blacks and Puerto Ricans, foreign immigrants are generally much less mobile than most Americans. Poverty and prejudice confine many of them to central cities, and even within the cities, they tend to live in enclaves (as did the earlier European immigrants) to reduce the impact of the language and cultural barriers that separate them from the rest of American society.

An additional impediment to movement is the quota system instituted in 1968 by the Immigration and Naturalization Act. Although this system made immigration a little easier for natives of the Eastern Hemisphere, it imposed for the first time quotas on natives of the Western Hemisphere. The quotas have not been strictly enforced (whether it is possible to enforce them is still at issue), but they have kept millions of immigrants in a shadowy "undocumented" status. The illegals try to keep as low a profile as possible; the best strategy is to live surrounded by large numbers of documented fellow-countrymen so that they will not be noticeable. The need for concealment in the ghetto, of course, inhibits their search for better employment opportunities.

OVERALL TRENDS

From 1950 to 1970, the total population of New York City remained stable. During this period, other central cities lost population, while the U.S. population grew by more than 25 percent. As Table 3-2 shows, of the eighteen cities that began the period with over 500,000 inhabitants, only four—none of them in the Northeast—experienced population growth. Since the mid-1960s, the birthrate in all regions and for all races has fallen precipitously. The old central cities are now being eroded from two directions. According to population estimates made since the 1970 census, the populations of these cities have dwindled even more rapidly than in previous decades: of the eighteen cities in Table 3-2, only Houston grew from 1970 to 1975, and its growth reflects the incorporation of suburbs. Although New York's population had declined from 7.9 million in 1970 to 7.48 million in 1975, its loss was not so severe as that of most larger central cities during the same period. By 1975, seven of the eighteen cities had lost over 20 percent of their 1950 population; New York had lost only 5 percent.[8]

Within the city, Brooklyn and Manhattan have been losing population for at least twenty-five years. Queens and the Bronx grew from 1950 to 1970, but began to lose population after 1970. Staten Island is the only borough that has been growing since 1970. This pattern reflects the national trend of equalizing population density.

The suburbs around New York also felt the impact of the shift from the Northeast and the metropolitan areas. The suburbs closest

Table 3-2. Cities with over 500,000 Inhabitants in 1950 (Population in Thousands)

	1950	1970	1975
Baltimore	950	906	852
Boston[a]	801	641	637
Buffalo[a]	580	463	407
Chicago	3,621	3,367	3,099
Cincinnati	504	453	413
Cleveland[a]	918	751	639
Detroit[a]	1,850	1,511	1,335
Houston[b]	596	1,233	1,357
Los Angeles[b]	1,970	2,816	2,727
Milwaukee[b]	637	717	666
Minneapolis[a]	522	434	378
New Orleans[b]	570	593	560
New York City	7,892	7,895	7,482
Philadelphia	2,072	1,949	1,816
Pittsburgh[a]	677	520	459
St. Louis[a]	857	622	525
San Francisco	775	716	665
Washington	802	757	712

Source: U.S. Bureau of the Census, Census of the Population.

[a]Lost over 20 percent of 1950 population during a twenty-five-year period.

[b]Grew between 1950 and 1970.

to the city have actually lost population since 1970; the outer suburbs gained slightly so that the fifteen-county Standard Consolidated Statistical Area outside New York, which grew by 66 percent from 1950 to 1970, has remained stable since then, with net out-migration balancing natural increase.[9]

These demographic shifts call into question both the ability of the city as a fiscal entity to support those who cannot support themselves and the ability of the city dweller to live decently and to improve his lot.[10]

FISCAL IMPLICATIONS OF MIGRATION PATTERNS

Emigration of Labor Force Participants

The typical migrant to or from a metropolitan area is a young adult;[11] thus, most areas receiving net immigration have a disproportionate number of young adults, and most of those losing population have fewer young adults than the average. New York, which is experiencing net emigration, has an adult population considerably older than the national average. (See Table 3-3.) Detailed examination of a recent four-year period shows that

Table 3-3. Adult Population, 1974 (Percentage Distribution)

Ages	NYC	U.S.
18-24	15.9	18.5
25-44	34.3	36.4
45-64	31.7	30.0
65+	18.1	15.1
Total 18+	100.0	100.0

Source: U.S. Bureau of the Census, *Current Population Survey.*

emigration is concentrated most heavily among young adults (Table 3-4). As a result, the percentage of New York's population aged 18 to 65 has been declining steadily as that in the nation has been rising

Table 3-4. Net Migration, 1970-74, as a Percentage of 1970 Base

Age Groups	
0-13	+3.5%
14-17	−6.0
18-24	−9.5
25-34	−13.0
35-44	−12.5
45-64	−8.5
65+	−3.5
Overall rate	−6.0

Source: Twentieth Century Fund staff analysis of census data.

(Table 3-5). While New York's share of residents in this age group was higher than the national average in 1974, it is unlikely to remain so if current trends continue.

Table 3-5. Percentage of Population Ages 18-65

	NYC	U.S.
1960	61.7%	55.0%
1970	59.7	56.2
1974	58.7	57.9

Source: U.S. Bureau of the Census, *Census of the Population* and *Current Population Survey.*

Migration is selective by sex as well as by age. Throughout the 1960-74 period, the ratio of adult men to adult women in New York was far lower than the difference in their mortality rates alone would suggest. Thus, men appear to be emigrating faster than women (Table

3-6). This finding may explain the immigration of children in Table 3-4, which is initially puzzling in light of the emigration of young adults. Many children in New York (27.1 percent in 1974) live only

Table 3-6. Ratio of Males/Females Ages 15-54

	NYC		U.S.	
	Whites	Blacks	Whites	Blacks
1960	.908	.811	.974	.897
1970	.875	.805	.970	.875
1974	.932	.708	.988	.888

Source: U.S. Bureau of the Census, Census of the Population and Current Population Survey.

with their mothers; very few (0.7 percent) live only with their fathers.[12] Fathers separated from their families are much more mobile, geographically, than are mothers and children. Employers are more likely to ask a man—with or without children—than a working mother to relocate. And few working mothers with child custody voluntarily undertake the risks and difficulties of moving to a new place with children. Moreover, most public assistance goes to single-parent families with minor children. Thus, when families in New York break up, the men are more likely to leave the city, and the women and children are more likely to stay behind.

Although employment opportunities in New York have been less favorable than in the growing regions, support for the nonworking population (in the form of public assistance, Supplemental Security Income benefits, and college tuition) has been more generous than almost anywhere else.[13] As a result, labor force participants have been migrating out of New York more rapidly than nonworkers, causing the proportion of the working population to shrink during a period when the national trend has been toward labor force expansion (Table 3-7). It should come as no surprise, then, that per capita

Table 3-7. Percentage of Population Employed

	U.S.	NYC
1960	36.7	42.5
1969	38.7	40.5
1976	40.9	36.9

Source: U.S. Bureau of the Census, Census of the Population and Current Population Survey; U.S. Bureau of Labor Statistics, Employment and Earnings.

earnings[14] failed to rise as rapidly in New York as in the rest of the country (Table 3-8).

Table 3-8. Earnings per Capita[a]

	U.S.	NYC
1965	2,178	2,612
1970	3,003	3,387
1975	4,239	4,294
Increase, 1965-75	95%	64%

Source: U.S. Department of Commerce, Bureau of Economic Analysis, *Survey of Current Business*, and unpublished data; and New York State Department of Commerce, Division of Economic Research and Statistics.

[a]Labor and proprietary income net of personal contributions for social insurance.

Migration Patterns and Average Earnings Capacity

It would not be surprising if the out-migration of the white middle class and the in-migration of millions of displaced agricultural workers who arrived with few skills suitable for New York City's complex economy resulted in a lower quality resident labor force. Data directly measuring the incomes of immigrating and emigrating labor force participants are not available, but indirect evidence suggests that such a decline has in fact occurred.

Among minority group members, new arrivals to the city have the highest unemployment rates in the adult labor force,[15] in part because they must search for jobs without contacts or familiarity with the labor market. Their incomes are depressed by the lack of steady employment. In addition, once employed, they appear to work in traditionally low-paid occupations. For example, blacks and Hispanics, who are on average more recent arrivals to the city than are whites, are overrepresented as laborers, service workers, and machine operators and are underrepresented in the more highly skilled occupations. If such residents were merely replacing other low-paid residents who had left the city, the overall composition of the labor force would have remained unchanged. However, many suburban commuters to New York are former city residents and tend to be employed in occupations that pay well (in 1970, 43 percent were professionals or managers, compared to 23 percent of employed city residents[16]). Also, the predominance of men among emigrants may lower the occupational level of the remaining labor force: women are underrepresented in the higher paying professions.

The educational attainment of the city's population is quite low, as shown in Table 3-9.

Table 3-9. Educational Attainment of Population Twenty-five Years and Older

		U.S.	NYC
1960	High School 4+	41.1%	37.4%
	College 4+	7.7%	8.2%
	Median Level	10.6 years	10.1 years
1974	High school 4+	61.3%	54.2%
	College 4+	13.3%	11.1%
	Median level	12.3 years	12.1 years

Source: U.S. Bureau of the Census, Census of the Population and Current Population Survey; Bondarin, op. cit., p. 18.

Some of this discrepancy is due to the fact that younger people, who have spent more years in school than their elders, have been emigrating faster. Yet New York is below the national average for every age group. Since New York City residents enjoy unusual educational opportunities, this state of affairs is, on the face of it, puzzling. For many years, New York's public schools were regarded as among the best in the nation. Although they are less highly regarded today, nearly as many of the city's school-age children are enrolled in school as in the rest of the country. The availability of higher education in New York is still virtually unequaled elsewhere in the country. The City University of New York, which offered free college education to qualifying city high school graduates for over a century, in 1960 entered a period of rapid growth; by 1976, the city system enrolled the equivalent of 155,000 full-time students. In that year, some 79 percent of the city's high school graduates enrolled in college; only 48 percent of the nation's high school graduates in that year went to college.[17]

Thus, the only plausible explanation for the low level of education of the city's population is the pattern of migration: emigrants are, on average, better educated than immigrants. Even though the city's white residents are generally older than its black or Hispanic residents, a larger percentage of whites has been educated in New York, and whites have a higher median level of schooling (12.3 years) than blacks (11.8 years) or Hispanics (9.6 years). In the twenty-two- to twenty-nine-year age group, 2 percent of whites, 4 percent of blacks, and 15 percent of Hispanics had less than an eighth-grade education, even though the percentage of children enrolled in elementary and intermediate schools is virtually the same among whites, blacks, and Hispanics. The differences among those in their twenties can only be ascribed to migration patterns.

Finally, the earning capacity of the labor force has not increased so rapidly as it should have. In nominal terms, earnings per employed resident have increased at nearly the same rate as in the rest of the country (Table 3-10). But they should have grown faster for two

Table 3-10. Earnings per Employed Resident

	U.S.	NYC
1965	5,953	6,530
1970	8,058	8,931
1975	10,723	11,606
Increase, 1965-75	80%	78%

Source: U.S. Bureau of Economic Analysis, *National Income and Product Accounts of the United States* and unpublished data.

reasons: first, during the ten years between 1965 and 1975, inflation was much higher in New York than it was in the rest of the country; second, the labor force in New York was becoming older relative to the rest of the country (due to the selective emigration of younger adults), and older workers earn more than younger workers. Here again, a plausible interpretation of this earnings lag is that workers leaving the city were more highly paid than those arriving.[18] (It should be noted that the present lower quality of the labor force is not necessarily permanent or immutable. The prospects for reversing it are discussed in Chapter 5.)

Effects on Income and Fiscal Capacity

Because of the decreased worker/population ratio and the lowering in the quality of the resident labor force, New York, which used to be a relatively wealthy city, is now relatively poor. Median family income, which was 15 percent higher than the national average in 1950, has been below the national average since 1971. In real terms, between 1969 and 1973, median family income actually decreased (Table 3-11). According to the U.S. Bureau of the Census, which takes family size into account in its definition of poverty, the War on Poverty of the 1960s hardly touched New York (Table 3-12).

The latest income distribution figures, for 1973, reveal that 19.1 percent of New York's families, compared to only 14.6 percent of U.S. families, had annual incomes below $5,000.[19] Neither the poverty line figures nor the income distribution figures take into account the significantly higher cost of living in New York City; in real terms, then, New Yorkers are even worse off than these figures suggest.

Table 3-11. Median Family Income (Current Dollars)

	U.S.	NYC
1949	3,073	3,526
1959	5,660	6,091
1969	9,586	9,682
1970	9,867	9,905
1971	10,285	9,625
1972	11,116	10,039
1973	12,051	10,921

Source: U.S. Bureau of the Census, Census of the Population and Current Population Reports.

In summary, through migration into and out of New York, the city has been losing skilled and educated workers and gaining dependents. While the average age of New York's labor force is increasing, and age is associated with increased earnings capacity, this shift does not compensate for the other consequences of migration. Clearly, migration patterns have contributed to New York's fiscal bind. Needs have simply increased more rapidly than local sources of revenue.

Table 3-12. Families below Poverty Line

	U.S.	NYC
1960	18.4%	12.8%
1970	10.7%	11.5%

Source: U.S. Bureau of the Census, Current Population Reports.

ECONOMIC MOBILITY OF
CITY RESIDENTS

New York's migration patterns amount to more than poor blacks and Hispanics swarming to the city while the white middle class flees. Population turnover in every ethnic and age group is very high. Net out-migration results when two people move in and three people move out. The ratio of gross to net population flows among young adults is especially high.[20]

Emanuel Tobier and others have speculated that the large gross migration figures represent an "up-and-out" process.[21] According to Tobier, most black and Hispanic migrants arrived in the city with little education and few marketable skills. Most of them work their way up, and many leave the city once they have acquired sufficient skills. Those who cannot improve themselves fall back on the city's welfare system and are joined at the bottom of the social ladder by new arrivals. (A partial exception to the "up-and-out" theory should be made for the large numbers of blacks and Hispanics who have been going to college in recent years; the city seems to be keeping many of these college graduates.) The blacks and Hispanics leaving the city are probably skilled, well-established blue-collar workers. The tremendous discrepancy between the incomes of college- and high school-educated blacks in New York supports this conclusion.[22]

This "up-and-out" theory would explain why the distribution of real income among black and Hispanic families did not change between 1960 and 1968 and improved only slightly between 1969 and 1974. It is a much more cheering explanation than the alternative—namely, that most blacks and Hispanics in the city never improve their lots and are doomed to lifetimes of poverty. In addition, it is more plausible for several reasons.

First, labor market surveys in New York have demonstrated that there is considerable mobility both from lower paying to higher paying industries (from the "secondary labor market" to the "primary labor market") and from low-paying to high-paying occupations within the same industry.[23] In other words, the unappealing entry-level jobs available to young, unskilled blacks and Hispanics are not necessarily dead ends.

What is more, earnings increase with age. Mean family incomes in all ethnic groups rise steadily over most of the breadwinners' working lives; blacks reach their peak income years from 55 to 64, and whites and Hispanics from 45 to 54.[24]

Finally, education is still an important avenue of social mobility. In every ethnic group, family income rises with the education of the family head. If the adults who came to New York could not take advantage of the city's schools, many of their children have. New York's educational system may not be working well for today's minority children: public school truancy and dropout rates are very high; reading scores are very low;[25] and blacks and Hispanics do not go to college in as great numbers as do whites. Still, blacks and Hispanics receive more years of schooling in New York than elsewhere in the country.

While the "up-and-out" pattern seems to hold only for non-college-educated blacks and Hispanics, it applies to whites in general. Most young or newly arrived whites in New York are not poor—the great majority of poor whites in New York are over 65, unlike the black and Hispanic poor, who are mostly young families with children. Nor are most of the whites entering the city displaced agricultural workers; often they are recent graduates of colleges and professional schools who come from all over the country to work in Manhattan's unique white-collar complex. Many professionals and managers eventually move out to the suburbs but continue to work in New York. Others, of course, leave to live and work outside the city.

Table 3-13.

Occupations	Resident Unemployment Rate, 1977	% Job Loss, 1970-1976
Total	10.0	10.0
Professional and technical	5.8	5.0
Managerial and administrative	4.3	−32.2
Sales	9.0	21.5
Clerical	7.7	9.5
Craft Workers	11.7	15.5
Operatives, excluding transportation	13.6	} 26.1
Transportation operatives	10.3	
Laborers	17.0	8.6
Service workers	9.6	14.5

Source: U.S. Department of Labor, Bureau of Labor Statistics, Midatlantic Regional Office; New York State Department of Labor.

Table 3-13, which shows the labor conditions facing people in various occupations, offers some support for the hypotheses presented above. The general shift of the labor market toward white-collar occupations provides some opportunity for upward mobility. It also provides an incentive for college-educated workers to stay in the city (blacks and Hispanics) or near it (whites). Skilled blue-collar workers face a very poor job market and, since many of their skills are not easily transferable to new occupations, are likely to leave the New York area altogether. Unskilled laborers face a poor job market at home and are relatively immobile; they are the most likely to be unemployed.

As already mentioned, those dependent on public assistance have no incentive at all to leave New York. In 1975, AFDC and Medicaid benefits were about 50 percent above the national average, and the local contributions to Supplementary Security Income for the aged, disabled, and blind were among the highest anywhere. Most of the adults receiving public assistance who were not already working were either unable to work or illiterate and unskilled.[26]

It is easy to depict New York as a financially desperate city, daily growing smaller, poorer, older, and more dependent. But this grim picture, which may be accurate as an aggregate, is not necessarily a picture of how New York appears to the typical New Yorker. New York is still a place where many eager and ambitious young people can start at the bottom of the blue-collar ladder and either work their way up or acquire skills to find better paying jobs elsewhere; where other young and ambitious people can start at the bottom of the while-collar ladder and make it in the largest national corporations and in the professional, financial, and communications networks serving them; where a college education is available relatively easily; and where those who cannot support themselves or their families can still live decently.

To be sure, New York is not the promised land for everyone. It is shrinking now, and even if it grows again, it will not grow so fast as the natural increase of population. Hence, a certain proportion of the population, especially those who are or would like to be working in manufacturing plants, has to leave. The greatest unemployment is found among those sectors of the population who find it most difficult to migrate—teenagers, women of childbearing age, minority groups. Yet millions of people voluntarily come to New York and remain there, and it is a mistake to think that their personal prospects are as gloomy as the city's own future.

HOUSING IN NEW YORK

The changing faces of the city's neighborhoods are probably the most visible evidence of the demographic tides sweeping New York. While the "urban gentry" of young professionals carves new middle-class neighborhoods out of vacant land, obsolete commercial districts, and older but deteriorated neighborhoods, other areas are abandoned by middle-class tenants and become poverty neighborhoods; still others are abandoned by low-income tenants and become virtual wastelands. During the 1970s, the number of households in the city dropped and the average income of the remaining households failed to keep pace with inflation; as a result, the deterioration of middle-class neighborhoods and the abandonment of poor neighborhoods outpaced the "gentrification" movement.

For the last century, the primary source of housing for the poor in large cities has been the downward filtration of housing. In some times and some places, downward filtration has worked quite well. Even in New York in recent years, it has had some beneficial effects: the exodus of the white middle class provided the more recent immigrants with a greater choice of housing and substantially reduced overcrowding; it also allowed many of the oldest and worst buildings to be weeded out, diminishing greatly the number of substandard units.[27]

In some respects, however, downward filtration has worked badly in New York. First, the demographic changes have been very large and very rapid; because people judge the desirability of housing in part by the quality of housing around it, the character of entire neighborhoods has changed quite suddenly. This kind of change—whether it brings higher or lower rents—is destructive of neighborhood social stability and is painful for those tenants already in the area who would like to stay but who are forced out either by fears for their safety or by rent increases. To make matters worse, it is often the elderly who find themselves in this predicament, and people who have lived in one neighborhood for decades find it especially hard to begin anew in another.

Because the filtration process works by neighborhood, not building, its worst effects have been at the bottom end of the scale, where buildings are being abandoned. Unfortunately, the worst buildings are not the only ones that are weeded out. Once a few buildings in a neighborhood have been abandoned, they become havens for New York's large population of addicts, alcoholics, and other derelicts, who dismantle these and nearby buildings and prey on neighborhood residents. The quality of public services in the neighborhood also tends to decline. Thus, the buildings adjacent to the abandoned buildings—whatever their physical condition—become undesirable places to live, are gradually vacated, and eventually are also abandoned. The result of this sequence is the loss of potentially sound housing: nearly three quarters of the city's abandoned buildings are not considered "dilapidated."[28]

Government sponsorship of new housing has also caused instability in the housing sector. At various times over the last thirty years, New York has had available to it federal subsidies for public housing, city and state subsidies for moderate-income housing, and city tax abatements and exemptions for the construction of new housing and the conversion of nonresidential structures to housing. During the 1975-78 period, for example, when the population fell by about 300,000, about 45,000 new housing units were constructed, almost all with public aid.[29] Encouraging new building in the face of population stability or decline further accelerates the already too rapid filtration and abandonment process.

New York also has a system of rent regulation that is unusual among large cities. Because of the city's high density, about 75 percent of its households live in rental units; thus, there has always been strong political support for controls. The city's rental units have been under rent control since 1943, and most of its newer rental buildings are regulated by a rent stabilization program. Most observers agree that lifting rent controls would not stop the present abandonment of buildings: many tenants in abandoned buildings cannot even afford controlled rents, and other large cities have suffered massive abandonments without rent controls. In addition, the effect of rent controls on population shifts is unclear since below-market rents both have kept middle-class families from leaving and have encouraged poor immigrants to move to the city. However, by making rental housing a poor investment and by limiting the supply of mortgage financing available for renovation, controls have clearly contributed to the deterioration of housing.[30]

Finally, in the last decade, the filtration process has been undermined by the inflation in housing costs. Average costs have been driven up not only by the general inflation in living costs but also by unusually steep rises in fuel prices and in real estate taxes, as well as, ironically, by the elimination of many inexpensive apartments—the oldest and most dilapidated.[31] Median income of renters rose by only 25 percent from 1970 to 1978; during the same period, median rents rose by 92 percent,[32] contributing to family hardship. But even the added burden imposed on renters is not enough to offset the rising costs of housing. When the poor move into buildings once occupied by the middle class, the gap between their ability to pay and the rents needed to maintain the buildings is vastly larger than it was before the early 1970s, and the result of rents not rising to meet costs is a sudden sharp deterioration of maintenance rather than the gradual disinvestment characteristic of past decades.

As a result of these trends, about 47 percent of all households in New York occupy dwellings in need of rehabilitation (it would take an estimated $36 billion to repair those buildings[33]), about 45,000 units per year are being lost from the housing inventory, and almost 3,000 buildings per year are being seized by the city for nonpayment of taxes.[34] Even people living in apartments of acceptable quality often are affected by unpleasant and dangerous neighborhood conditions: for example, over 25 percent of all occupied rental units have boarded-up units on their streets.[35]

The effects of economic decline and population losses create a dilemma for New York. Decline feeds on itself; in the case of housing, this happens in two ways. First is the "neighborhood effect" of deterioration. When some buildings in a neighborhood deteriorate, investment in nearby buildings becomes risky; owners of and potential mortgagees of these buildings, foreseeing a decline in value, tend to disinvest rapidly. As a result, whole neighborhoods deteriorate beyond repair. Because any future revival of the city depends on the maintenance of a sound—or at least a restorable—housing stock, deterioration can lead to permanent decline.

Second, the high cost of upper-income housing makes the city unattractive to business. While the solid upper-middle-class and the newly gentrified neighborhoods do not have the problems of deterioration and disinvestment that plague much of the city, the spread of poverty neighborhoods turns these more expensive neighborhoods into enclaves or refuges. Vacancy rates in "desirable" areas are extremely low, driving rents up until many white-collar workers with families can no longer afford them. This makes it difficult for the corporate headquarters and corporate service firms, whose existence is so vital to the city's economy, to recruit executives and professionals; many such firms cite the difficulty of finding suitable housing for their employees as a major reason for leaving the city. The resulting loss of employment in turn threatens the remaining population's ability to pay for housing.

Unfortunately, policies that address these two problems often run counter to one another. Reducing the costs of upper-middle-income housing can only be achieved through such policies as regulating rents, subsidizing luxury-housing construction, and underassessing single-family housing—all of which accelerates the decline of the rest of the city's neighborhoods.

Chapter 4

City Fiscal Policies

In 1975, New York City's financial house of cards came tumbling down. Over the previous fifteen years, successive administrations had increased expenditures fivefold, making ends meet by issuing an endless variety of debt securities. To be fair, the city's officials and bankers were convinced that the city would continue to grow; its history as the center of wealth and power in America made it difficult to believe otherwise. Their optimism was confirmed by a number of beguiling developments: the boom on Wall Street, the strength of private and public construction, the rise in public employment, the increase in tax revenues. Yet all during those years, they ignored growing evidence that the city's situation was worsening. Its fiscal capacity was weakening with the decline in its competitive economic position, and its population was changing to one with less earning power. In the end, the city could not borrow in the market because it could no longer disguise the fact that it had been living dangerously beyond its means.

New York City's fiscal crisis was not caused by economic decline alone. All over the United States today, far poorer cities manage to provide an acceptable level of public services at an acceptable cost. The decline in the city's economic activity compounded its financial difficulties, but experience elsewhere makes clear that the degree of fiscal strain does not necessarily correspond to the degree of economic decline. Pittsburgh has lost more of its economic base than has New York, but its finances are relatively sound; Boston has lost less, but is hard pressed to balance its budget; and Cleveland's recent default seems to have had more to do with lack of political leadership than with economic difficulties. New York's fiscal problems, likewise, are disproportionate to its economic decline. The inescapable conclusion is that the city lived extravagantly, borrowing far too much for far too long. More prudent fiscal policies could not have avoided fiscal strain; they might, however, have averted fiscal crisis. Shortsighted policies on the local level may have exacerbated the weakening of the revenue base, and certainly were responsible for the uncontrolled growth of the local budget.

Specifically, the forces that caused the inexorable rise in expenditures to a level unsustainable by the city's resources were the increased needs of the population (which to some extent were created by local policies), the political pressures generated by rapid changes in the composition of the city's population, the illusion of reliable local and external sources of revenue, and the inflexibility of budget commitments.

THE NATIONAL CONTEXT

Before New York's sorry fiscal record is examined, it should be pointed out that, during the 1960s, other municipalities also were expanding their budgets. Nationally, per capita local government expenditures were about six times greater in 1974 than they had been in 1950. Even in constant dollars, per capita local government expenditures tripled, while real per capita personal income only doubled. Much of the increase in local government spending can be attributed to just a few sources. Payroll expenses climbed very rapidly because local government wages were rising so fast—about 40 percent faster than private nonfarm wages during the 1950-74 period. Expenditures for public welfare, health, housing, and education also skyrocketed.

Public services, like private services, are luxury items: rising incomes make resources available for more than basic necessities. In the postwar era, spending for both private and public services rose rapidly, spurred by increasing personal income. Local governments had more to spend because they received funds both directly from taxpayers and indirectly from the federal government, which in the 1960s pursued a "guns and butter" policy of waging wars in Vietnam and on domestic poverty. Lyndon Johnson's "Great Society" programs, most of which were joint federal-local efforts, were launched not because poverty was on the increase—most Americans were living better than ever before—but because poverty in the midst of plenty was held to be morally and politically intolerable. Medicaid, for example, would not have been possible during the Depression, although more people were in need of it then.[1]

NEW YORK'S BUDGET TRENDS

New York, perhaps more than any other city, embraced the war on poverty and the programs of the Great Society. The new administration of John V. Lindsay, seeking to expand its political backing at a time of racial and ethnic tension resulting from rapid demographic changes, succeeded in getting an above-average share of federal funding, which seemed a blessing at the time. But concomitant with matching requirements, the city had to increase its own spending.

Politics influenced the size and shape of New York City's budget. Winning the mayoralty is less dependent on machine politics, although New York is still heavily Democratic in its party preference, than it is dependent on coalitions that muster in support of one or another candidate. Whatever their party label and style, New York City's chief executives have tended to be liberal and generous, responsive to the demands of large blocks of voters and vocal special interests. Their common response to problems was to increase spending, rarely pausing to consider where the funding would come from. In the past, of course, a variety of sources could be tapped— the federal or state governments or the taxpayer, who, for a long time, was prepared to foot the bill.

Expenditures

As Table 4-1 shows, New York City's 1975 operating budget was more than five times the size of its 1960 budget. Both in the nation and in New York, public expenditure is sensitive to changes in income: it rises as incomes increase and falls as incomes decline, with a two- to three-year lag. Most of New York's budget explosion, especially when measured in constant dollars, was concentrated in the years 1966-71 and was a response to the boom of 1964-69. (The slower growth of the budget after 1971 reflects the slower growth of personal income after 1969.)

By almost any standard, this expansion of the budget was

Table 4-1. Expense Budget Expenditures, 1960-75 ($ Millions)

Fiscal Year	Total	Social Services & Human Resources (Welfare, etc.)[a]	Education & Libraries	Public Safety	Sanitation & Health (incl. Hospitals)	Debt Service	Pension Funds
1960	$2,245	$ 316	$ 467	$ 255	$ 263	$ 413	$221
1961	2,428	353	511	279	292	434	232
1962	2,601	385	547	304	322	447	256
1963	2,789	412	636	342	349	405	273
1964	3,098	480	687	378	400	439	293
1965	3,342	577	766	380	423	473	313
1966	3,775	710	878	435	469	553	435
1967	4,493	932	1,018	456	515	638	367
1968	5,291	1,405	1,134	489	595	655	397
1969	6,058	1,792	1,349	549	733	673	375
1970	6,701	1,888	1,569	653	828	705	424
1971	7,822	2,314	1,845	734	995	782	524
1972	8,498	2,589	2,083	751	1,045	847	488
1973	9,325	2,683	2,405	881	1,151	899	496
1974	10,247	2,923	2,314	1,015	1,218	1,141	753
1975	12,018	3,421	2,393	998	1,209	1,827	987
% increase, 1960-75	435%	982%	412%	291%	359%	342%	346%

Source: Annual Reports of the Comptroller of the City of New York.
aIncludes only welfare through 1967.

excessive. It was far greater than the national norm; local government expenditure per capita grew only about 60 percent as fast in the rest of the country as it did in New York. For each dollar added to New York City residents' personal income, about forty cents were added to the city budget. So, from 1960 to 1975, as Figure 4-1 shows, the expense budget rose steadily from 9.7 percent to an astounding 24 percent of personal income (not all of it, of course, was locally raised). By 1975, New Yorkers were paying more than twice the national average for local government services—about $1,574 per person, compared with $672 per capita for all localities,[2] or a difference of about $900 per person.

The Twentieth Century Fund staff has attempted to break down this $900 "excess" into specific components. Categorization is, necessarily, somewhat arbitrary (for example, it is difficult to allocate the high cost of medical insurance for a city social worker who, in another state, would be a state employee, if he were employed at all), and the estimates are very rough. But they add up to a figure of the same order of magnitude as the $900 per capita difference in costs for local government services between New York and all other localities.

1. Higher Cost of Living

New York's excessive expenditures are attributable to some extent to the higher cost of living in New York, as measured by the Bureau of Labor Statistics (BLS). In 1975, the BLS estimated that it cost a family of four 16 percent more to maintain an "intermediate" standard of living in New York than in the average metropolitan area.[3] This differential formed the basis for our estimate of excess costs for labor, contract services, miscellaneous costs, supplies, and equipment. Thus, compared to the national average, hospital care cost 26 percent more,[4] general medical care 10 percent more,[5] and the welfare recipient's cost of living 7 percent more.[6] Excess costs due to the high cost of living include the following:[7]

	($ Million)
Payrolls	720
Pensions (cost of living)	50
Welfare and Medicaid	180
Supplies, contracts, etc.	180
Hospitals	200
Total	1,330

Source: Twentieth Century Fund staff estimates.

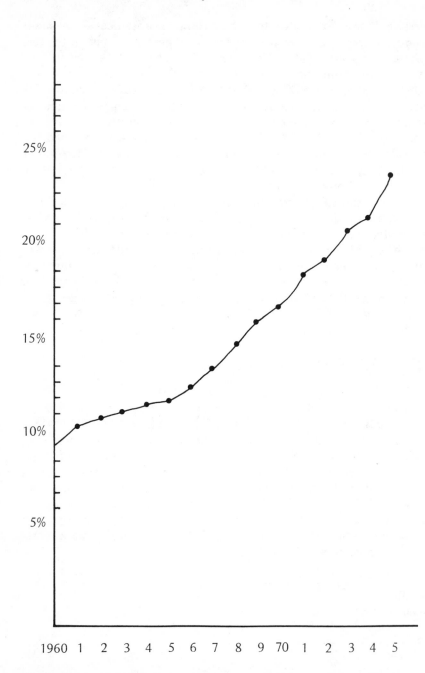

Figure 4.1. Expense budget as a percent of personal income, New York City, 1960-75. (*Sources:* Comptroller's Report; N.Y. State Dept. of Commerce.)

2. Higher Pension and Fringe Benefit Levels

Some city services were more expensive than was justified by the high cost of living. Salaries were "normal"; in October 1975, full-time employees in New York earned 16 percent more than the average municipal employee, exactly matching the cost-of-living differential. But pension costs in New York were—and are—seriously out of line with those in other cities. In fiscal 1975, city contributions to city, state, and union retirement funds totaled 19 percent of payroll, compared to about 6 percent for all localities.[8] In addition, the city contributes to the Social Security system, something done by only about a third of other local governments.

New York also grants its employees high fringe benefits. No complete and current figures on health insurance contributions of local governments are available, but a 1975 Milwaukee City Service Commission survey found that, of the largest twenty-eight cities in the United States, New York had the second highest health insurance costs and that in most cities municipal employees share costs for health insurance[9] (New York City employees do not have to contribute). Relative to the contributions made by New York State for its employees and by all employers, both public and private, for their employees,[10] New York City paid a total of $685 million in excess amounts (beyond the cost of living): $420 million in pensions, $165 million for Social Security, and $100 million for fringe benefits.

3. Higher Debt Service Costs

In 1975, New Yorkers paid $1.8 billion, or $238 per capita, for municipal debt service, while the average American paid only about $77 for local debt service. The difference reflected both a higher outstanding debt—$1,625 per person in New York compared to an average of $700 per person nationwide—and higher rates of debt retirement. (Although the interest rates on recently issued debt were high, the overall interest paid on city debt was no higher than average.[11])

New York does not have proportionally more public buildings or other infrastructures to match its enormous debt, although it does have more than average. (In conformity with its belief in permanent growth, the city until recently built too many facilities and now cannot afford the high cost of maintenance.) Only about half of the city's debt service costs were supporting real capital projects—about

Table 4-2. Expenditure Difference Between New York and the "Average Locality," Fiscal Year 1975

	$ per Capita
1. Higher cost of living	+175
2. Higher pension and fringe benefit levels	+91
3. Higher debt service costs	+161
4. Higher levels of services	+361
5. Provision of services elsewhere provided by states	+249
Total	1,037

Source: Twentieth Century Fund staff estimates.

$124 per capita compared to nearly all of the $77 per capita in other localities. The city used the rest of the debt—mainly, but not overwhelmingly, short term—to support current operations. Few other cities made a habit of borrowing to pay for operating expenses.

With the exception of about $50 per capita spent on extra infrastructure, the excess described in the above three categories yielded no tangible benefits for New York City taxpayers. Instead, it merely reflected how much more the services provided to New Yorkers cost than the same services would have if they had been purchased in the average locality. The rest of the excess, though, provided municipal services in New York exceeding those provided elsewhere.

4. Higher Levels of Services

As Lester Thurow has pointed out, New Yorkers have a taste for urban amenities; more has to be spent on them in part because they want local government services more than do most Americans.[1][2] Of course, these collective tastes may be reflecting the city's unusual political conditions, rather than the personalities of New Yorkers as individuals.

New Yorkers are no more interested in police and fire protection, education, or other "common functions" of local government than are other city dwellers; the city's expenditures, per capita, on common functions reflect national norms and living costs in New York (see Table 4-3). But New Yorkers have a strong preference for programs that redistribute income, a characteristic that stems from the city's history of absorbing successive waves of immigrants into the political process.

Table 4-3

	Direct general expenditure per capita, all local governments serving central counties, 1974-75	Employment per 10,000 all local gov'ts. serving central counties, Oct. 1974
	Common Municipal Functions Only	Common Municipal Functions Only
New York	511	243
Chicago	499	208
Houston	359	234
New Orleans	359	218
Newark	551	258
Baltimore	618	260
Denver	517	219
Boston	584	219
Detroit	496	202
Philadelphia	471	255
Los Angeles	517	206
San Francisco	523	225
New York rank	7	4
Average of other 11	499	228

Source: U.S. Bureau of the Census.

New York has a long history of providing aid to the poor. As long ago as 1847, City College was providing tuition-free higher education. The first federal public housing project in the United States was built in the city during the Depression. The New Deal itself has been interpreted as the triumph of New York liberalism.[13] Thus, in the 1960s, when spokesmen for the urban poor focused attention on urban poverty, New York responded by raising welfare benefits and by setting up a variety of new programs, many of which took advantage of federal legislation. (Although the state fixes the criteria for benefit levels and eligibility for public assistance, city voters can influence these decisions because nearly half the state's population lives in New York City.)

Even though in 1975 New York had about the same concentration of poverty as the rest of the nation, it paid more than twice as much in social services and other assistance. Admittedly, New York City had higher costs, but higher costs made up only a part of the difference. Recipients of public assistance received, in real terms, very high cash and Medicaid benefits. It is harder to estimate the excess payments for miscellaneous social services—day care, foster care, homemaker services, and so forth—but if they exceeded the national average in the same proportion as did those for public assistance and medical care, then the excess per capita for all social services was $171.

The city cannot unilaterally reduce grant levels for welfare or for Medicaid. It could, of course, lobby for such reductions at the state level, but success would mean an intolerable burden for the city's hospitals. In addition to the $976 million of Medicaid funds the city distributed directly to its residents in fiscal 1975, it also paid $326 million of Medicaid funds to voluntary hospitals and $456 million to municipal hospitals. The federal and state governments provided about 75 percent of this money. So rather than deprive the poor of medical care, a reduction in Medicaid rates would probably leave the city paying much more of this hospital bill than it does now. In other words, the city would have to curtail available health services sharply before it saved money on Medicaid.[14] Between direct provision of health services and medical payments to charitable institutions, the city spent about $210 per capita on health, compared to an average $46 for those local governments surveyed.

The educational opportunities provided by the City University (CUNY) system are much more extensive than those provided by other municipal institutions of higher learning in the United States. Few local governments finance postsecondary education programs more ambitious than small, two-year community colleges. But in 1975, New York City spent $59 per capita on CUNY, compared to an average of $7 per capita on higher education for all localities. New York State has its own system of higher education (SUNY), which was expanded under former Governor Nelson A. Rockefeller. City taxpayers help pay for these competing systems, and city residents can attend either. New York State is currently drawing up plans to take over much of CUNY.

5. Provision of Services Elsewhere Provided by States

New York City finances many services that, in most other cities, are financed by the state or federal government. For example, the city administers its own public assistance program, assuming a burden that in thirty-six states is borne by the state. Of the fourteen states that require localities to contribute to welfare and to Medicaid, only four (including New York) require localities to finance 50 percent of the nonfederal share. And the federal share is smaller in New York than in any of the three other states.[15] Thus, New York State requires its counties to pay a higher proportion of welfare costs than does any other state. The cost in 1975 of the city's social services and human resources programs totaled $3.3 billion, or $440 per capita;[16] without the city's high cost-of-living and benefit levels, its social service program would have cost much less—only about $257 per capita. But even this reduction would leave a huge gap when compared to the average of only $8 per capita for all local governments.[17]

This list of excess municipal expenditures in New York City does not include the cost of waste and inefficiency. Everyone agrees that the city government each year wastes large sums of money. Numerous studies, internal and external, agree that the city should be made to run more efficiently. The civil service system, the political patronage system, negligent accounting practices, union work rules, vacation and leave policies, the "superagency" system of organization, contracting out too many services, not contracting out enough services, and plain inertia have all been blamed, probably justifiably, for costing the city each year millions of dollars. But New York does not appear to differ from other cities in this respect; mismanagement is a nearly universal problem.

Table 4-3 compares municipal expenditures and employment for education, highways, police, fire, sanitation, parks, finance, and administration in the counties in which twelve large cities are located. Although these measures are not perfect, some degree of consensus exists about what constitutes adequate service in these categories. New York ranks seventh in expenditures and fourth in employment among the twelve cities. Its expenditures were only 2 percent above the average of the other eleven cities, although its costs were about 16 percent above the average for the urban United States. The expenditure totals for all the cities are fairly close, and Table 4-5, which provides a more detailed breakdown for the six largest cities, shows little variation on any of the lines making up "common municipal functions."[18] Although numerous studies have

Table 4-4. Summary of Higher Levels of Services ($ per Capita)

	Welfare[a]	Health	Higher Education
New York City	$307	$210	$59
"Normal" plus cost-of-living adjustment	148	59	8
Difference	$159	$151	$51

Source: Expense Budget, City of New York; *Statistical Abstract* (1977), Tables 202, 471, 476, and 544.

[a]Includes Medicaid payments to individuals.

documented the city's wastefulness and inefficiency, they have not demonstrated (or even tried to demonstrate) that New York is conspicuously more inefficient or wasteful than many other large cities. On the other hand, many of the studies reflect senior management's awareness of and concern about operating city agencies more effectively. The fact that New York has been a leader in applying advanced management techniques suggests that most other large cities harbor as much or more inefficiency.

Revenues

Between 1960 and the end of fiscal 1975 (when the fiscal crisis became headline news), New York became adept at tapping both local and intergovernmental sources of revenue. It taxed what seemed like every conceivable revenue base, and it took advantage of every applicable federal and state program.

The largest part of this financing effort was in the form of intergovernmental aid. From 1960 to 1975, local revenues increased by 306 percent, state aid by 696 percent,[19] and federal aid by 2,282 percent (see Table 4-6). Although all localities began to make more use of federal and state financing during this period, New York received close to three times as much money per capita as the average for local governments in the seventy-four Standard Metropolitan Statistical Areas (SMSAs).[20] (See Table 4-7.) Some observers have therefore viewed New York as the spoiled child of the federal government.

This interpretation is not quite fair. To begin with, about half of this aid was reimbursement for welfare and Medicaid, which are usually state responsibilities. It would be just as accurate to classify the $1.1 billion of city tax levy funds spent on public assistance, administration of public assistance, and other programs usually appearing in state budgets as city aid to the state.

If the state financed the city's welfare and Medicaid programs, it would have to raise its tax revenues, but because New York City accounts for about 44 percent of the state's personal income and 70 percent of its welfare recipients, the share paid by city residents of what are now locally borne expenses would drop from (about) 70 percent to (about) 44 percent. State financing of these programs in 1975 would have saved city residents about $400 million.

Federal revenue-sharing aid to New York also is quite high but is designed to reward local tax efforts. It could be argued that federal aid should be even higher to compensate for the city's high cost of

Table 4-5. Employment/10,000 in Oct. 1974 (all local governments in central county)

Item	NYC	Phila. County, Pa.	L.A. County	Cook County (Chicago)	Harris County (Houston)	Wayne County (Detroit)
Pop. (in thousands) 1973	7,647	1,862	6,924	5,418	1,861	2,586
(Estimated) Employees						
Total	596.4	461.7	473.5	392.1	338.63	427.2
Full-time	487.8	406.2	371.7	338.7	293.27	329.1
Part-time	108.6	55.4	101.8	53.4	45.36	98.1
Full-time equivalent						
Employment	528.2	414.5	401.1	352.5	306.99	354.3
Public welfare	36.7	5.4	19.8	0.1	0.89	0.1
Hospitals	62.5	13.3	29.2	18.1	15.73	32.9
Health	10.7	6.8	5.2	5.0	5.62	5.4
Fire protection	18.3	17.2	12.0	11.6	12.41	12.6
Housing and urban renewal	18.7	11.4	2.1	4.7	0.84	1.8
Libraries	4.8	4.4	4.6	4.3	3.04	3.8
Local utilities	61.0	44.8	29.7	29.2	7.24	21.6
Transit	57.2	39.5	7.9	22.9		11.0
Highways	10.4	6.9	8.3	9.6	9.10	10.7
Police protection	47.4	52.6	29.9	37.4	22.35	33.6
Sanitation other than sewage	15.9	16.1	3.2	7.1	5.42	8.6
Correction	8.1	5.9	9.5	2.6	3.06	3.3
All other functions	27.0	17.7	28.3	16.4	11.80	20.8
Education	176.7	166.5	180.5	170.1	186.53	164.5
Financial administration	5.6	7.5	7.7	4.1	5.37	5.4
General control	13.5	24.5	17.0	13.4	9.79	13.4
Sewerage	2.8	3.1	2.7	6.7	3.45	2.3
Other	53.1	46.3	64.0	57.2	66.86	59.9
Parks and recreation	8.2	10.2	11.6	12.3	4.34	13.3
Water supply	3.8	5.3	8.1	6.2	7.15	8.0

Table 4-6. New York City: Expense Budget Revenue, Fiscal Years 1960-75 ($ Millions)

Fiscal Year	Revenue				Intergovernmental Revenue as Percent of Total Revenue		
	Total	Local Revenue	State Funds	Federal Aid	Total Intergovt.	State Funds	Federal Aid
1960	$ 2,282	$1,796	$ 384	$ 102	21.3	16.8	4.5
1961	2,454	1,888	455	110	23.0	18.5	4.5
1962	2,579	1,951	484	144	24.3	18.8	5.6
1963	2,777	2,047	564	166	26.3	20.3	6.0
1964	3,124	2,343	599	183	25.0	19.2	5.6
1965	3,392	2,512	662	219	25.9	19.5	6.5
1966	3,894	2,576	1,010	308	33.9	25.9	7.9
1967	4,616	2,878	1,161	577	37.7	25.2	12.5
1968	5,272	3,059	1,467	746	42.0	27.8	14.2
1969	6,067	3,198	1,973	896	47.1	32.5	14.8
1970	6,705	3,638	1,993	1,074	45.6	29.7	16.0
1971	7,828	4,173	2,357	1,298	46.7	30.1	16.6
1972	8,508	4,507	2,500	1,501	47.0	29.4	17.6
1973	9,326	4,885	2,529	1,912	47.6	27.1	20.5
1974	10,248	5,475	2,752	2,021	46.6	26.9	19.7
1975	12,018	6,530	3,058	2,282	45.6	25.4	20.2
% Increase, 1960-75	426	263	696				

Source: Annual Report of the Comptroller of the City of New York.

Table 4-7. Revenues of Local Governments in 74 Major SMSA's and in New York City, 1974-75

	74 Major SMSA's		NYC	
	$ per Capita	*%*	*$ per Capita*	*%*
General revenue	809	100%	1,736	100%
State and federal aid	329	41	888	51
Property tax	285	35	349	20
Other taxes	76	9	286	16
Charges	75	9	151	9
Misc.	43	5	63	4
All taxes	361	44	635	336
Property tax/all taxes		79		55

Source: U.S. Bureau of the Census.

Note: These are cash receipts, not the accrued revenues shown in Table 4-6. A large advance payment of state aid and the inclusion of aid per capita expenditures make New York's "state and federal aid" figure seem unduly large.

living. In 1977, New York's advocates pressed for and won changes in the distribution formulas for countercyclical revenue sharing and for community development block grants on the ground that the original formulas discriminated against New York (and other high-cost localities).

In making use of intergovernmental funds, the city gave up much of its budgetary discretion. State and federal aid consists largely of categorical grants, which are restricted to the funding of specific programs; in 1975, 73 percent of federal aid and 71 percent of state aid were earmarked specifically for expenditures on health, education, and welfare (see Table 4-8). Categorical grants are designed to influence spending priorities; they appear to have been successful. For example, social service expenditures, of which the state and federal governments reimburse about 75 percent, increased by 500 percent between 1960 and 1970, although the number of families below the poverty line actually decreased (from 12.8 percent to 11.5 percent of a stable population, according to the Census Bureau).[21] Education and health expenditures, about 50 percent of which are financed by the state and federal governments, increased by 250 percent during the same period; public safety, which has been a major political issue since 1960, is financed almost entirely by the city, and increased by only 150 percent (see Table 4-1).

The original categorical grant programs were highly restrictive and, according to local officials, ill-suited to local needs. Under the Nixon administration, block grants and the revenue-sharing program were instituted, giving more discretion to local officials in the use of

Table 4-8. Intergovernmental Aid Received,a by Type, New York City ($ Millions)

Fiscal Year	Federal Aid					State Aid				
	Welfare	Medical & Health	Education	Noncategorical^b	Other Categorical^c	Welfare	Medical & Health	Education	Noncategorical^b	Other Categorical^c
1965	$124	$ 42	$ 2	$ 38	$ —	$104	$ 54	$ 294	$ 83	$ 83
1966	136	51	2	55	—	126	93	353	84	226
1967	161	73	49	111	—	126	147	410	106	328
1968	268	199	22	109	—	171	232	471	142	425
1969	377	286	51	139	—	201	317	633	253	559
1970	408	247	144	217	—	236	268	651	179	518
1971	522	326	152	175	—	252	287	687	191	657
1972	578	453	179	255	—	337	475	751	184	649
1973	705	681	161	381	130	331	412	792	163	659
1974	603	662	139	288	263	365	519	844	195	634
1975	790	632	239	349	257	527	513	1,197	221	681

Source: Reports of the Comptroller of the City of New York.

aFor Expense Budget programs.

bNot limited to specific types of expenditures. State noncategorical includes state mortgage and stock transfer taxes returned to city.

cLimited to specific types of expenditures.

funds. But as late as 1975, noncategorical state and federal grants amounted to only about one-sixth of total aid.

Taxes in New York City, like aid payments, are very high: the city, in fiscal 1975, collected $635 per capita in taxes; local governments in the seventy-four SMSAs collected only $361 per capita.[22] From 1971 to 1975, taxes became increasingly burdensome, rising after a long period of effectively stable rates from 7.7 percent to 10.2 percent of personal income. This increasing reliance on local resources relative to intergovernmental aid reflected the mounting burden of pension contributions and debt service, which are strictly local obligations. After 1969, real income was beginning to decline, and the city government was attempting to contain the budget. It managed to slow the growth of spending in many areas, but it could not cut back on pensions or debt service because they were legally mandated. In addition, the cost of debt service rose because the volume of outstanding debt, especially short term, was increasing. Thus, from 1971 to 1975, local resources were increasingly strained.

The largest local source of revenue is the real estate tax. As Table 4-9 shows, in fiscal 1975 the city levied $2.9 billion in real estate taxes, 41 percent of all locally raised revenues. But other local governments relied on property taxes, on the average, for 59 percent

Table 4-9. Locally Collected Expense Budget Revenue in New York City, Fiscal Years 1960-75 ($ Millions)

Fiscal Year	Total	Real Estate Tax	Sales and Use Tax	Business Taxes	Personal Income Tax	Other[a]
1960	$1,796	$ 979	$301	$200	$ —	$ 316
1961	1,888	1,028	306	205	—	348
1962	1,951	1,071	321	218	—	341
1963	2,047	1,135	329	262	—	321
1964	2,343	1,220	421	224	—	476
1965	2,513	1,314	446	279	—	474
1966	2,576	1,409	384	244	—	538
1967	2,878	1,573	381	252	130	541
1968	3,059	1,648	413	314	170	514
1969	3,207	1,738	445	348	201	475
1970	3,638	1,893	467	369	205	704
1971	4,173	2,080	494	301	199	1,099
1972	4,507	2,189	520	429	443	926
1973	4,885	2,468	551	431	440	995
1974	5,475	2,656	594	434	455	1,336
1975	6,530	2,896	791	444	466	1,933

Source: Annual Reports of the Comptroller of the City of New York.

[a]Mainly commercial rent—occupancy tax, charges for services, transfers from other city funds, and short-term borrowing.

of their internal funds.[23] In New York, the real estate tax was less important as a revenue source, as revenues from the personal income tax and sales tax were growing.

New York also relies on a wide variety of other taxes: sales, personal income (introduced in fiscal 1967), corporate income, and numerous business and "nuisance" taxes. These taxes made up 33 percent of the city's locally raised revenues in fiscal 1975, compared to 15 percent for all local governments in the seventy-four major SMSAs. Business taxes, the subject of considerable debate and acrimony, provided only about 8 percent of locally raised revenues and 4 percent of total revenues.

THE FISCAL CRISIS

The crude numbers explain how New York City got into such a deep financial hole. But four years after its fiscal crisis, people are still arguing about why the city had so large an expenditure budget, why its revenue base failed, and why it persisted in borrowing so much more than it could repay. While no easy answers are forthcoming, an understanding of the roots of the problem is essential to its resolution.

Why was New York City's budget so large? Three answers, by no means mutually exclusive, have been advanced: the city had unusually great needs; unusual political circumstances combined to loosen controls on spending; and sources of revenue appeared to be unusually good.

Superficially at least, the "needs" argument seems plausible. New York is the nation's largest metropolis. It is more than twice as densely populated as any other American city. During the past twenty-five years, it has undergone social disruption as waves of poor, mostly nonwhite immigrants flooded in only to find that businesses and jobs were moving out. Poverty and despair have bred drug addiction, crime, racial tension, and other forms of social pathology. The social pathology in turn has been a great burden—in addition to welfare and Medicaid expenses, the city has spent huge sums for the control of drug addiction and related crime; for the provision of compensatory education, job training, and social services; and for the renovation of blighted neighborhoods. Furthermore, city policies—or state policies strongly influenced by the city—gave dependent and social service-using individuals an incentive to stay in the city.[24]

However, the "needs" hypothesis is not strongly confirmed by empirical research. Drawing on statistical analyses of twenty-seven large-city budgets, Edward Gramlich of Cornell University has found that city spending (per capita) varies inversely with population but directly with population density.[25] City management seems to involve economies of scale. For budgetary purposes, the effects of New York's population and its density cancel each other out.

Gramlich and other researchers who consider needs and fiscal capacity as separate variables have shown that, in cities with the same per capita income, expenditures vary directly with the incidence of poverty. But in New York, the percentage of persons below the poverty line was slightly below the large-city average in 1960 and slightly above it in 1970; it has never been unusually high. Furthermore, the percentage of the population receiving public assistance in New York is normal for large cities.

Other evidence regarding New York's needs, relative to those of other cities, is conflicting. On the one hand, New York's drug-abuse problem has been severe for many years; on the other, its crime rate is about average for large cities. Again, 13 percent of New York's school population has English language difficulty, necessitating expensive compensatory programs, but public school enrollment is only 14.5 percent of the total population, compared to 21.4 percent in the rest of the country. (New Yorkers tend to have small families and to send their children to private, especially parochial, schools.) Transportation provides a third example: New York's high density makes subsidies to mass transit advisable but at the same time lowers the required expenditures for streets and highways.

In short, New York has greater needs than most localities, but its needs are not greater than those of many other large northeastern cities; they account for only part of New York's budgetary excess.

Several observers have suggested that New York has had a unique political situation that allowed the budget to expand beyond control. The most simplistic theories attribute the problem to irresponsibility on the part of the city's—and state's—political leadership.

There are many instances of the failure of political leaders to understand or to take responsibility for the consequences of their spending decisions. Mayor Robert F. Wagner declared that fiscal limitations should not curb his war on poverty and began the practice of borrowing against current expenditures. Governor Rockefeller countenanced this fiscal gimmickry and himself introduced another gimmick, the moral obligation bond, into the state's finances. John V. Lindsay, during his tenure as mayor, displayed lamentable weakness and ineptitude in dealing with the municipal unions: his administration began with a transit wage settlement that, according to one estimate, was three times greater than it should have been.[26] Lindsay later managed to get trapped into granting huge raises to the uniformed services by the pay-parity principle. He also allowed management questions to become collective-bargaining issues, making it difficult for the administration to govern effectively.

Perhaps the most glaring instance of fiscal irresponsibility was the series of expensive pension commitments made to city workers. The costs of these commitments were concealed from the public, in some cases for more than a decade, an action that can only be described as deceptive and irresponsible on the part of the city's political leaders. A series of deals among the municipal unions, the city, and the state—the increased take-home pay provision of 1960, the redefinition of the salary base and changing the city's pensions from defined-contribution to defined-benefit plans in 1963, the major benefit liberalizations and introduction of union annuity funds between 1963 and 1970, and the Heart Bill for policemen and firemen—brought about staggering increases in pension liabilities.[27] Many of these changes were only casually reported, partly because the people involved did not call attention to them or to their costs, partly because the changes were technical and complicated in nature, and partly because the costs were deferred for as long as possible. Contributions to the actuarial retirement systems were the same percentage of mean salary (15 percent) in 1973 as they had been in 1960, having been kept down by a lag in funding, a thirty-five-year amortization of unfunded liabilities, and the use of unrealistic actuarial assumptions.[28] After fiscal 1973, some of these actuarial chickens came home to roost, and pension contributions doubled in two years. (The city is still a long way from full funding of pension liabilities.) Before the fiscal crisis, however, the public had no notion of the magnitude of pension liabilities.

Many more such examples could be listed here. Yet even a full accounting of the failure of the political leadership in New York would not explain how for so many years voters came to elect and reelect such men. Although New York has a strong liberal tradition, it is highly improbable that its citizens are unusually self-destructive or that its elected leaders have been unusually weak in character and judgment. Nor would such an accounting explain why such leaders as John Lindsay began as opponents of fiscal gimmickry, lax management, and too powerful unions and went on to "give away the store." A satisfactory explanation must pinpoint the political pressures on elected officials, pressures that overcame—and continue to overcome—their attempts to contain city spending.

A more complex analysis, developed by Martin Shefter,[29] among others, identifies as the significant political development the breakdown, around 1960, of the party system in New York politics. "Machine" politics, which had functioned relatively smoothly during the demographically stable period of 1930-50, could not keep up with the rapid changes in the population, and was further weakened by reform movements. Political leaders, beginning with Mayor Wagner, found that they could do better by courting the voters directly—and without the mediating and restraining influence of the parties, they discovered that they had to promise more than they had in order to put together winning coalitions. Terry Clark provides some evidence for this theory:[30] he shows that cities tend to have more fiscal stress when power is concentrated in the office of the mayor than when power is held by strong party organizations.

According to this analysis, political instability enabled community leaders—mainly blacks and Hispanics—and the municipal labor force to improve their bargaining positions. Spokesmen for these groups could back their demands for increased pay, benefits, or services not only with their direct voting power but with their ability—amply demonstrated during the 1960s—to disrupt the city if thwarted, thereby endangering many other votes. Thus, Lindsay and Rockefeller are often charged—or credited—with "buying" labor peace and "buying" racial peace.

A variant of this theory uses, as the main political consideration, job creation rather than service delivery. Roger Starr has said: "We encourage the destruction of buildings in existence in order to put people to work using up federal subsidization for the construction of new housing elsewhere."[31] According to this theory, as the city's Democratic machine, which was a stabilizing political force for most of the first half of the century, lost its power and when political obligations became more diffused, many more jobs were promised than could be delivered without endangering the city's fiscal health. By expanding the municipal work force and by indirectly providing for thousands of other jobs, through Medicaid funds and "poverty money" and through construction contracts, Lindsay redeemed many political debts and gave the impression that the city economy was healthier than in reality it was. In the long run, these measures were harmful to the city.

These theories have some validity. Certainly, successive administrations acceded to the demands of the most vocal and powerful pressure groups; certainly, much of the city's "excess" spending not accounted for by its high cost of living was due to its largess in bestowing pension and fringe benefits and its energetic efforts to redistribute income on a large scale; and certainly, both Rockefeller and Lindsay poured public money into construction at a time when private developers were also spending money freely, generating an expensive and unsustainable boom.

But again, these political conditions were not peculiar to New

York City. Many other cities, experiencing similar population flows during the 1960s, suffered a weakening of political party structure. In New York, the political situation played an important part, but it alone does not account for the ballooning of its expenditures.

When all is said and done, what ultimately influences the level of budgetary expenditures is the level of anticipated revenues. Income changes over time are a critical determinant of local budgets; similarly, income differentials among cities seem to account for much of the variation in their spending.[32]

During the 1960s, especially the late 1960s, those responsible for drawing up the city's budget had good reason to believe that future revenues eventually would be able to pay for the commitments they were making. Both the city's tax base and the availability of state and federal funds seemed reliable, and only a few voices, such as the Citizens Budget Commission, had the temerity to warn that their great expectations might turn out to be disappointments. These warnings were dismissed by officials and ignored by virtually everyone else in New York.

In 1960, per capita income in New York was higher than in any major city except Los Angeles and San Francisco, and New York's surrounding suburban counties were far wealthier than the counties surrounding any other large city. Throughout the 1960s, per capita income for the New York metropolitan area remained about 20 percent higher than the average for all metropolitan areas. New York was the only major city in the East or Midwest where total employment remained stable during the 1960s; local unemployment was considerably below national averages. New York's retail sales increased more during the 1960s than did those in any other major city in the East or Midwest, and sales in its central business district were stronger than in any major city. Perhaps most reassuring, its assessed value was rising at a rate exceeded only by those of Houston and Los Angeles.[33]

Despite these signs of strength, which appeared so reassuring to the city's leaders, New York (and its surrounding region) was losing its place relative to the rest of the country. This trend was obscured during most of the 1960s by the national economic expansion, the city's original preeminence and wealth, the increase in public employment, and the boom on Wall Street. The office-building boom of the late 1960s was another measure of the bullish confidence in the city's future. Few believed that the city was getting in over its head financially; in fact, some did not think it was in far enough. The liberal rhetoric of the late 1960s called for diverting funds from the defense budget and spending more on schools and social services.

Apart from the city's own apparently strong revenue base, politicians were counting on state and federal aid as if it were money in the bank. The city knew it would be reimbursed for anywhere from 50 percent to 90 percent of the expenses of its various social welfare programs (the average reimbursement has fluctuated around 75 percent) and for a smaller but still significant proportion of educational and other expenses. In its dependence on outside funds, New York was, if not unique among large cities, at least in the minority. The only local governments reimbursed at higher rates for welfare and Medicaid are those serving Los Angeles, San Francisco, Newark, and Baltimore (these cities have among the highest expenditures; see Table 4-3). Most other major cities have no social programs in their city or county budgets.

The belief that programs under local control are going to be paid for by someone else is a powerful incentive for spending. Many of the econometric studies on the impact of aid show that between one and two dollars is added to the local budget for each dollar of aid.[34] In any case, even where local spending is not stimulated by federal money, the budgets of localities that manage their own welfare programs appear larger than those of localities without this responsibility.

In the late 1960s, New York was the only large American city with problems characteristic of the Northeast, with the resources characteristic of the West, and with a lack of political constraints (such as the "Democratic machine" in Chicago, the only other large city with comparable problems and resources) that might keep it from trying to use its wealth to eliminate its poverty. While no one of these factors would have been sufficient to create the swollen precrisis budgets, the three in combination made the result virtually inevitable.

The Failure of the Revenue Base. It is axiomatic that the ability to borrow depends on the capacity to repay. A city can live extravagantly on credit as long as it has sufficient money coming in. San Francisco, for example, is almost as extravagant as New York; yet its bonds have an AAA rating from Moody's and an AA rating from Standard & Poor's. San Francisco can afford to keep the commitments it has made; New York cannot because, although its revenue base began shrinking in 1969, it continued to spend, making up the difference by borrowing short term in the market. Then when its revenues fell short, it borrowed more. New York finally ended up in a position in which even the interest payments on its debt exceeded its borrowing capacity, and investors would no longer provide it with funds.

The erosion of the city's revenue base has been attributed to many different sources. Some point a finger at the slowdown in the rate of increase in state and federal aid; others blame local conditions—the tax structure (and high tax rates), the decline in population, the effects of inflation and recession, the loss of competitive position in the city's private economic sector, and the city's inability to tap revenue sources beyond its boundaries. The least persuasive of these explanations, although one favored by city officials, is that state and federal assistance failed to meet reasonable expectations.

To be sure, President Nixon, with his profound distrust of antipoverty programs, tried to dismantle the Office of Economic Opportunity, impounded funds, placed a moratorium on housing programs, and limited the amount of community development grants available to large cities. He also made no effort to introduce new programs; the momentum of the Great Society years was gone after 1969. And it is also true that the percentage of state funds declined after 1973. But the actual cutbacks in aid were minimal. In fact, intergovernmental aid never stopped growing as a percentage of the health, education, and welfare budgets. It only declined as a percentage of the total budget because the city was spending relatively less on health, education, and welfare. And this was attributable to: (1) the decline in the number of children, reducing Aid to Dependent Children grants and school enrollment; (2) a policy, initiated in the 1970s, of removing ineligibles from the welfare rolls; (3) the transfer in 1974 of 250,000 aged, disabled, and blind welfare recipients to the federal Supplemental Security Income program; and (4) the growth of debt service and pension contributions, two budget categories in which the city had never expected intergovernmental aid.

An even more popular, and superficially convincing, explanation for the post-1969 loss in the revenue base is New York's high tax rates. Over the last few years, many observers have claimed that high taxes created an "unfavorable business climate" and have called for lowering general tax rates and offering specific tax exemptions to businesses. It is an article of faith among businessmen that the city's taxes are too high. The hue and cry raised by New York business leaders in 1977 against a proposed hike in the commuter tax leaves no doubt that any attempt to increase taxes would be adamantly opposed by the business community.

It is difficult to challenge the notion that things would be different if taxes were reduced. There is no question that the combined effects of state and local taxes on businesses and individuals in New York are extraordinarily severe. Moreover, New York is virtually the only major city in the United States where the combined state and local taxes are progressive (rates rising with income levels). The rate and structure of taxation create an especially strong incentive for upper-middle-class and wealthy individuals to leave the city, and these individuals often influence business location decisions as well. A recent study showed that many corporations leaving New York have relocated nearer to the homes of their top executives.[35] Other specific instances of firms leaving the city can be traced to taxes—the brokerage firms that moved to Jersey City in response to the stock and bond transfer taxes or the printing firms that moved to avoid the sales tax on machinery. Surveys of corporate management usually cite state and city tax levels as a major consideration when thinking about relocating; they also cite city taxes as a deterrent, among others, to attracting middle management to the city.[36]

Nevertheless, empirical studies have consistently failed to document any adverse effect on business activity stemming from state and local taxes. The recent RAND report on policy impact on urban economic development cites nine studies, covering different industries, areas, and time periods, all of which conclude that state and local taxes (including personal income taxes) have no discernible impact on industry location or growth. Because taxes typically contribute only 3 percent or 4 percent of value added, and because they are largely neutralized by their deductibility from federal income taxes, high taxes do not in general drive business away, and low taxes and exemptions do not generate economic development.[37]

Moreover, the timing of the economic decline does not correspond to that of increases in the tax rate. New York's taxes have been high compared to those of other localities at least since early in this century. The slide in the city's economy did not become apparent, though, until 1969. The only major tax rate increase in recent years began in 1972, three years *after* the economic decline had begun. Before 1972, the tax burden was pretty much what it had been during the period of economic expansion.

Of course, even if the tax differentials between most localities are too small to affect locational decisionmaking, recent tax rate differences between New York and competitive locations elsewhere may have been great enough to raise costs to an unacceptable level for a significant number of businesses. There is not enough evidence to rule out high tax rates as a contributing factor in the weakening of the revenue base. But the fact remains that with so many other conditions contributing to New York's relative decline, tax rates cannot be singled out as the major cause.

Whatever its effect on business, the city's policies may have played a substantial part in driving out middle-class residents. The benefits available to middle-class residents—free college tuition, rent control, low property taxes for homeowners, and subsidized middle-income housing—may have been insufficient to compensate for progressive and very high income taxes. Because of the growth of the social service budget and municipal wages, little money was left over for improving basic services, for maintaining the infrastructure, or for amenities—such as clean parks and playgrounds—that middle-class families care about. In their view, they had to pay a great deal to live in the city, which many regarded as unsafe, unpleasant, and inconvenient. With the exception of the public transportation subsidy, only a few members of the middle class—those with college-age children or those who had stayed in one apartment for many years—enjoyed a particular benefit at any given time. The same amount of money might have been spread around to more middle-class residents in the form of tax relief or improving the city environment. Smaller benefits for a larger number might have kept more of the middle class in the city than larger benefits for a smaller number.

The city also miscalculated in its programs to improve the skills (and thereby the earning power) of the local labor force. A large amount was spent on educating and training the young. A great deal of this effort was wasted—or rather, benefited other localities—because trained young people departed for better opportunities elsewhere and less-skilled migrants arrived in their place.

Among the other causes of the erosion of the city's tax base, the tax structure is often criticized. The city can be said to have a crazy-quilt tax structure, which is the consequence of tapping as many potential revenue sources as ingenious minds could conceive. Thus, it has relied heavily on a progressive income tax since 1967, a regressive sales tax that was increased to 8 percent in 1974, as well as a property tax that is less income elastic than either.

Those who believe that the tax structure has eroded revenues point out that the lesser reliance on the real estate tax, when compared to other cities, has made the city more vulnerable whenever there is a recession in economic activity.

The real estate tax base does seem to be more recession-proof than the income and sales-tax bases. The full market value of New York City real estate increases steadily at about 5 percent a year, doing better than personal income in downswings and worse in upswings.[38] Thus, if relative tax rates remained unchanged, the real estate tax might have a stabilizing influence on revenues and the income and sales taxes a cyclically disruptive influence.

Of course, tax rates did not remain unchanged. Nominal tax rates were changed frequently, and the effective rate of the income tax

Changes in Tax Base

	Average Annual Increase in Full Valuation of Real Estate	Average Annual Increase in Personal Income
1966-69	4.8%	8.6%
1969-75	5.4%	5.1%

would have risen in any case because of the well-known effect of inflation on a progressive tax. Although the real estate tax base rose faster than personal income from 1969 to 1975, actual real estate taxes levied rose by *less* (66 percent) than sales taxes (78 percent) or personal income taxes (131 percent). To put it another way, the city avoided losing revenue on the income and sales taxes by raising income and sales tax rates.

But the tax structure may have had indirect effects on revenues. Income and sales taxes may hurt city residents more than the property tax.[39] An overreliance on income and sales taxes makes commuting relatively more desirable than living in the city, and commuters take local sector jobs with them.

The tax structure also might have adversely affected the revenue base because different industries have unequal revenue potential. This inequality was emphasized in the 1973 report of the Scott Commission on New York's economic base and fiscal capacity, which estimated the average revenue produced for the city by each job in the various sectors. Using 1970 tax rates and incomes, the report concluded that one manufacturing job produced as much revenue for the city (including taxes on business property, business income, personal income, and retail sales) as 0.71 trade jobs, 0.60 financial sector jobs, 1.11 service industry jobs, or 1.61 government jobs.[40] If these calculations are accurate, then a shift in employment from, say, the financial sector to the government sector would erode the revenue base. An actual comparison of the employment structures in 1969 and 1974 reveals that, due to its changing industrial mix, the city might have lost revenues equivalent to those produced by 40,000 manufacturing jobs even if there had been no absolute loss of employment.

Some of this change in the industrial mix was caused by city policies. Beside the increase in direct local government employment, city expenditure meant a huge rise in health-related employment and also stimulated construction employment. But the city's direct efforts to stimulate economic development had very little influence over the structure of the local economy. These efforts consisted of infrastructure projects (subway lines, for example), which benefited most segments of the economy, and relatively small individual projects (such as revitalization of commercial subcenters, the building of industrial parks, and the establishment of the new Hunts Point produce market), which shored up various ailing sectors but left the total picture virtually unchanged.

The effects of the tax structure, however, are minor compared to those of the national economic downturn. The main reason why the city's revenue base began to erode is the simple, obvious fact that forces beyond the city's control—the slowing down of the growth of the national economy and the speeding up of the dispersion of employment—caused a sudden loss of 15 percent of its jobs. There is nothing the city could conceivably have done to protect itself from the general economic recession or the relocation of industry to the South and West. But there are two traditional responses to the suburbanization of industry, which many cities have used successfully to alleviate fiscal strain. One response is to annex the suburbs. To some extent, New York is still benefiting from its 1898 annexation of Brooklyn, Queens, and Staten Island because Queens and Staten Island did not really develop until after World War II. But it has acquired no new territory since 1898. In contrast, virtually all cities in the South and West, and about half the cities in the Midwest, have expanded into formerly rural areas in recent years. This expansion has been an important fiscal safety valve. Of twenty-four midwestern cities that are fairly similar in income and structure, eleven have annexed large portions of adjacent territory since 1930; the other thirteen have remained confined within their 1930 boundaries. The per capita nonschool taxes (city and county) levied by the annexers in 1975 were only 75 percent of the taxes levied by nonannexers.[41] In other words, those cities not confined by their original boundaries are able to extend their revenue bases per resident; employment that moves away from the center can still provide revenue for the city.

The second response is to shift the provision of services to the overlying counties. Here again, New York is at a disadvantage because it already comprises five counties. According to a study of per capita nonschool tax burdens in eighteen eastern cities, the ten cities inside counties paid about 85 percent as much as the eight cities that were themselves counties.[42]

A third, and far more unusual, alternative is to institute over the entire metropolitan area a regional government that can provide services to all area residents and collect a portion of the revenues from each locality. Some planners have argued for years that metropolitan government would not only rectify fiscal imbalance but would result in more efficient delivery of government services and more rational planning for economic development, would reduce the tendency toward intrametropolitan racial segregation, and would recapture the benefits that many localities (especially large cities like New York) provide to the nontaxpaying individuals. Certainly, the 16 million residents of the New York metropolitan region have common interests that the fragmentation of local government prevents them from pursuing. A great deal of progress toward metropolitan government has been made in a few areas, notably the Minneapolis-St. Paul region, where it is generally held to have protected the large cities from fiscal strain, rationalized and improved service delivery, made development more orderly, and made the entire metropolitan area more attractive to business.

Yet insurmountable political obstacles prevent the institution of a metropolitan government in the New York region. Most importantly, the region lies within three states, raising constitutional barriers to cooperation of more than the most rudimentary kind. In addition, ethnic hostilities and long-standing bitterness between city and suburbs have discouraged cooperation, and the large cities' debt overhangs and concentrations of service-using residents (precisely the conditions that make a regional government desirable) make suburban residents unwilling to share their burdens.

In summary, much of New York's increasing difficulty in raising sufficient revenues after 1969 stemmed from the loss of jobs (especially manufacturing jobs) resulting from the nationwide recessions and the accelerated dispersion to the suburbs and the Sunbelt. The city was not able to take advantage of what little regional growth there was after 1969 because it could neither annex its suburbs, which would have enabled it to capture their revenue base, nor share its expenditure burden with them.

Why the Revenue-Expenditure Gap Persisted. The economic downturn that began in 1969 found the city locked into most of its expenditures. Legal, institutional, and political constraints prevented the city from changing programs begun or expanded in the 1960s. Municipal salaries and benefits were governed by contracts and by a provision in the state constitution protecting pension rights. Social service and public education benefit levels were mandated by state law and not easily changed. Public safety and such time-honored programs as free higher education could not be curtailed without fierce political opposition.

In addition, the city's budget included numerous fixed costs. Streets and highways, sewers, the transit system, hospitals, schools, publicly supported housing—the entire city infrastructure—had been built for a population of about 8 million. And the city had deferred to the 1970s pension liabilities incurred in the 1960s, apparently in the expectation that the population would remain stable or grow.

Finally, the matching-grant provisions of most intergovernmental aid made cutbacks in social service levels poor bargains. If cutting out four dollars' worth of service meant losing three dollars in revenue, it was hardly worth the political price.

Consequently, when Lindsay and then his successor, Beame, tried to economize, they were forced to direct most of their cost cutting to the relatively small portion of the budget that was immediately controllable. Nevertheless, after 1971 they managed to restrict real budget growth sharply.

Both tax rates and user charges were raised substantially in the 1970s. However, the political unpopularity of tax increases and the fear that high taxes were driving taxpaying individuals and businesses away kept the city from raising taxes to meet expenditures. And although it is easy to see with the benefit of hindsight what was taking place, the seriousness of the city's problems was far from clear at the time. As Dick Netzer has written, "Decisions were made on a much more ad-hoc basis, on the assumption that something would turn up to resolve the budgetary problem and that the city was not in a period of long-term continuous decline."[43] So the city turned to deficit financing apparently as a temporary expedient because the alternatives seemed more difficult or simply impossible.

This deficit financing took two forms, both questionable in nature. First, on a modest scale in the 1960s and more heavily in the 1970s, the city began to put operating expenses into the capital budget and to fund them with long-term debt. Many of the operating expenses in the capital budget, such as design, administration, maintenance, and repair of the city's capital stock, are "borderline" capital expenses. The city justified borrowing to meet these expenses on the grounds that, by prolonging the useful life of the capital stock, they would provide services to future taxpayers. Similarly, manpower training programs, also financed by capital funds, could reduce future welfare payments. This line of reasoning is not without merit, but it is not generally acceptable for accounting purposes.

Second, in the 1970s, when the city issued short-term debt, it frequently inflated the revenues it anticipated by, for example, including public housing on the property tax rolls and budgeting for state or federal aid under programs not yet enacted.[44] Then the city had to repay the debt with more debt. This strategem, in effect, put operating expenses in the capital budget: it financed current operations with revenues to be accrued for the future.

Table 4-10 shows the sum of the Citizens Budget Commission's estimate of operating expenses in the capital budget plus the city's estimates of the yearly increases in short-term debt. It is only a rough estimate (because it includes some legitimate short-term debt increases) of the city's deficit financing. As one would expect, it varies inversely with payroll employment in the city; in 1975, it reached unsustainable heights.

Table 4-10. Deficit Financing (Increase in Temporary Debt Outstanding + Issues of Funded Debt for Operating Expenses)

Fiscal Year	$ Millions
1961	12
1962	28
1963	103
1964	85
1965	236
1966	−2
1967	236
1968	126
1969	138
1970	712
1971	1,226
1972	556
1973	142
1974	1,462
1975	1,846

Source: Comptroller's Report; Citizens Budget Commission.

Ironically, the constitutional obligation to balance the budget, which was intended to force the city government to act responsibly and to live within its means, actually made matters worse: borrowing to finance operations was hidden in the budget by means of various subterfuges. The city government failed to inform the public of the city's true fiscal state and managed to postpone serious discussion about reducing expenditures until the 1975 crisis, about five years too late.

NEW YORK SINCE THE FISCAL CRISIS

Agreement will probably never be reached on who the villains of the fiscal crisis were. Some people will continue to blame the banks for backing away from city debt; others will blame the federal government for taking more money out of the city than it puts in or the local political leaders for their ostrichlike behavior; still others will insist, with former Mayor Beame, that the crisis had no villains, only victims. Yet there is general agreement that all parties must work together to restore the city's fiscal health. The federal government, the state government, the local financial institutions and other "captive" businesses, and the municipal unions all have a large stake in keeping the city from bankruptcy, and the public seems convinced that fiscal austerity on the part of the city itself is necessary for survival. The crisis has been a sobering experience, forcing some political and economic changes. To a large extent, these changes have not significantly disrupted the life of the city; however, the city's fiscal condition is not yet sound, and it remains to be seen whether or not today's policies will, in the long run, be any more sustainable than those of the past. Following is a brief summary of the changes brought about by the fiscal crisis.

Loss of Home Rule

The city no longer operates in the political environment of the past, when it was accountable for its fiscal policy only to an ill-informed and uninterested public and was assured of complicity from the state government. Today, its budgets and its fiscal plans are monitored carefully by the press, by private organizations, by the banks, and by several watchdog agencies of the federal and state governments. Furthermore, it must satisfy the federal and state governments, on which it depends for aid, that it is making fiscal progress; one of these agencies, the Financial Control Board, has been given powers over the city's budgetary, borrowing, and management decisions that before 1975 would have been unimaginable. Without doubt, this new accountability has, for the time being, brought city fiscal practices into the light of day and has made its budget figures somewhat more accurate and more meaningful. It has also provided the administration some degree of insulation from the political pressures that escalate spending.

Refinancing

The most immediate problem facing the city in 1975 was that of cash flow. With its heavy dependence on short-term debt financing, it could not, once the banks refused to underwrite its notes, pay for day-to-day operations, and as each note issue came due, it faced an endless series of crises. To allow the city some breathing space, the federal government instituted a seasonal loan program, later to be replaced by a loan guarantee program, while the state advanced some of its aid payment to the city and created a Municipal Assistance Corporation (MAC). MAC has refinanced over $5 billion of city debt with its own obligations, which are covered by sales, use, and other city taxes and are backed by the moral obligation of the state. MAC's financial relief, while desperately needed, did not improve the city's long-run position; in fact, it worsened it since its restructuring of the city's debt increased the total amount of debt service that will be needed to repay these obligations. In effect, by converting short-term to long-term debt, MAC was continuing the city's much-criticized practice of putting operating expenses into the capital budget. Thus, MAC cannot be regarded as any more than a temporary solution.

State and federal help with financing has enabled the city to continue operating, to keep paying its creditors (except during a short-lived note moratorium), to elicit investment commitments from the major banks and the municipal pension funds, and, in January 1979, to sell $125 million of notes to the general public for the first time in four years. Nevertheless, cash problems may recur. The federal loan guarantees will not be available after 1982, and MAC's existence depends upon the continued willingness of the state legislature to expand its issuing capacity and to commit city revenues to paying for its debt service. While the crisis atmosphere of 1975 no longer reigns, New York's financial situation is still precarious.

Increased State and Federal Aid

In the post-fiscal crisis period, the state and federal governments also helped New York meet the costs of service provision. From 1975 to 1979, federal aid in the expense budget increased by about one-third and state aid by about one-fifth (see Table 4-11). In addition, the state and federal governments have aided the city in several ways that do not show up in the budget. For instance, they have both begun paying some Medicaid funds directly to Medicaid providers; the federal government assumed responsibility for about 18,000 units of public housing; the state has been providing tuition assistance to students in the City University, which began charging tuition after the fiscal crisis, and has taken over the city's share of the Supplemental Security Income program. Thus, while the city has not become a "ward" of the federal government, as many expected in 1975, a large part of its progress toward solvency can be attributed to outside funding.

Table 4-11. Comparison of Federal/State Aid, Fiscal Years 1975-79 (in $ Millions) ᵃ

	Actuals			Forecast	Executive Budget
	Fiscal Year 1975	Fiscal Year 1976	Fiscal Year 1977	Fiscal Year 1978	Fiscal Year 1979
Federal Aid					
Unrestricted	$ 257	$ 263	$ 380	$ 445	$ 463
Categorical	1,911	2,327	2,421	2,705	2,429
Total federal	$2,168	$2,590	$2,801	$3,150	$2,892
% of total revenues	19.3%	20.5%	21.2%	22.8%	21.4%
State Aid					
Unrestricted	$ 492	$ 507	$ 504	$ 522	$ 724
Categorical	2,004	2,385	2,325	2,371	2,191
Total state	$2,496	$2,892	$2,829	$2,893	$2,915
% of total revenues	22.2%	22.8%	21.3%	20.9%	21.6%

Source: Executive Budget-Fiscal Year 1979, City of New York, Office of Management and Budget, p. 24.

ᵃThe federal and state aid is exclusive of the provision of disallowances.

Containing the Expense Budget

After its spectacular expansion during the 1960s and early 1970s, the expense budget has been more tightly controlled, growing by only about 10 percent from 1975 to 1979. (Even this growth is only nominal; in real terms, the budget has actually declined.) The amounts spent on all major categories in the budget have remained roughly proportional; thus, retrenchment efforts are seemingly being made across the board. However, cutbacks have in fact hurt some groups more than others.

The actual impact of the fiscal crisis on those most directly affected by it has varied. Welfare recipients, while receiving increased payments to meet the rising costs of rent and medical care, have had no increase in their basic grant since 1975. Since the city is making regular cash grants to about 900,000 persons, this involves considerable hardship. Municipal workers, however, while suffering layoffs at the beginning of the fiscal crisis, have managed, for the most part, to keep up with or even exceed the cost of living. Even the much-publicized layoffs have been partly offset by city rehirings and new hirings under the CETA program. (It should be remembered that welfare recipients have been "laid off" as well; tighter accounting procedures have eliminated about 40,000 cases in the last few years.)

The loss of power of the poor relative to the municipal workers is not surprising. The unions have not only their old weapons of votes and strikes; they have also gained a great deal of leverage by virtue of their control over the city's pension funds. Because the pension funds have been among the few institutions able and willing to invest large sums in city securities, the unions have been propelled into a "partnership" with the banks, businesses, and city administration, and their influence on issues affecting them directly and even indirectly has been greatly enhanced.

Chapter 5

New York in 1990

New York is nothing like Paris; it is nothing like London; and it is not Spokane multiplied by sixty, or Detroit multiplied by four.

E. B. White

Foretelling the future is a chancy business; all successful astrologers learn to hedge their bets. New York may be saved by a deus ex machina such as Roger Starr has hoped for—a new discovery that would do for the city what skiing has done for Vermont[1] —or it may be ruined by some equally unforeseen disaster. Even if no new developments appear out of the blue, old trends may speed up, slow down, or generate countertrends.

In the last generation, the city's economy and demography have been shaped primarily by external forces and only secondarily by local policies. It is not unreasonable to expect this pattern to hold in the future. The city government may have the power to deflect the city's development in one direction or another, but its freedom is severely limited by economic and political realities. Still, these limits do not preclude local action. If the past is any guide, public choices at the local level can significantly affect the city's future. It would be irresponsible to pretend that the future is as immutable and inescapable as the denouement of a Greek tragedy.

Because New York City's recent history has been shaped by a bewildering mix of unfavorable national—and international—developments, intertwined with excessive and sometimes deceptive local policies, there is a wide range of disagreement about its future. According to the most pessimistic view, the precipitous 1969-77 decline is the shape of things to come. Based on a continuation of 1969-77 trends, this worst-case outlook would mean another 900,000 jobs lost to the city by 1990, with the remaining population largely unemployable. No one would be left to foot the bill for city services. Proponents of this view advocate resettlement policies to remove large numbers of people in an orderly fashion and to shut down whole areas of the city.

Optimists, such as Mayor Koch, point to the revitalization of Manhattan in the last two years—packed theaters, full hotels, the success of the Citicorp Center, rising office rents, plans for new buildings, and the upturn in citywide employment. They credit the public university system with improving the work force and hope for a renaissance of "knowledge-oriented" industries during the 1980s.

This "best case," which rests largely on a sustained advance in the national economy, is excessively cheery, just as the worst case is excessively grim. Neither 1969, when the city began its slide, nor 1977, when its decline was arrested and things looked rosier in midtown Manhattan, marks a fundamental or permanent break in economic trends. A dispassionate appraisal makes it obvious that a great many forces, interacting with one another, will determine the future of New York City. Viewed realistically, the least likely course is that the city will move dramatically in one direction, up or down. Rather, New York will probably have some relatively good periods and some relatively bad ones. Its overall prospects are dependent on external influences, principally the state of the national economy and national politics, and the city's reactions to them, which in turn will be based heavily on its recent history, including its economic and demographic makeup, its physical condition, and its politics.

MACROECONOMIC TRENDS

The overall health of the national economy is probably the single most important influence on New York's economic health. The city's economy grows when nationwide unemployment is low and shrinks when it is high.[2] Figure 5-1 illustrates this relationship year to year over a twenty-five-year period; Figure 5-2 shows that the relationship holds over longer swings as well.

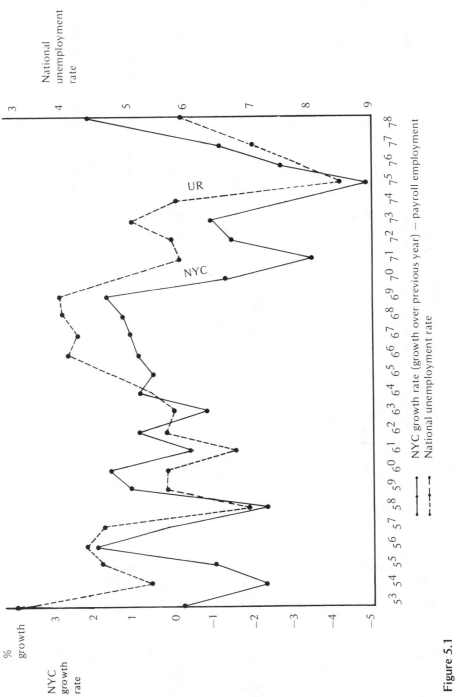

Figure 5.1

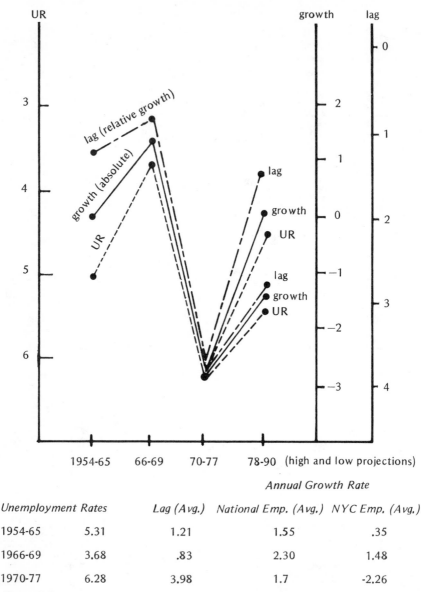

Figure 5.2.

Unemployment Rates		Lag (Avg.)	National Emp. (Avg.)	NYC Emp. (Avg.)
1954-65	5.31	1.21	1.55	.35
1966-69	3.68	.83	2.30	1.48
1970-77	6.28	3.98	1.7	-2.26

A double connection exists between national unemployment rates and jobs in the city. First, and most obvious, is the direct link: New York's economy, as an integral part of the national economy, rises and falls with national business activity. Reinforcing this direct link is another, more complex mechanism: high nationwide unemployment rates actually encourage the dispersal of industry from New York; they allay business's fear that the labor force at the projected site—usually in a less-developed area—will be insufficient. Thus, in long periods of high unemployment, both New York's absolute and relative economic positions deteriorate. Figure 5-2 also shows the relationship between unemployment and New York's relative growth.

The unemployment rates of the 1980s will be determined by a number of economic variables, some of them not well understood, and by policy decisions that will be made by politicians yet to be elected. But the unemployment rates of the 1980s may fall below those of the 1970s simply because the labor force is expected to grow much more slowly. Economist Michael Wachter has noted that the civilian labor market is relatively rigid, incapable of absorbing huge numbers of entrants at once; in particular, it was not able to "digest" the postwar baby boom very successfully after 1963.[3] However, birthrates have been falling steadily since 1962; the "baby bust" generation is now beginning to reach working age, and the Bureau of Labor Statistics predicts that labor force growth rates in the 1980s will fall to the low level of the 1950s.[4] Pressure on the labor market should diminish after 1980, and consequently, average unemployment rates should fall nationally. If this is the case, then New York will be healthier both absolutely and relatively. It will lose jobs at a less alarming rate, and its rate of job growth will not lag so far behind that of the rest of the country as it does now.

MICROECONOMIC TRENDS

Nationwide industrial trends will affect the shape of New York's economy but will have little effect on its size: the diversity of the city's economic base insulates it from most interindustry shifts. The national economy is expected to continue to shift away from goods production and toward the provision of services, and New York will most likely follow suit, becoming increasingly white collar.

Another potentially important trend is the rapid industrialization of a number of Third World countries, such as Korea, Taiwan, and Mexico. The lower production costs abroad (especially for labor) have resulted in an increase in the import of manufactured goods, with an adverse effect on manufacturing employment in New York and other major American industrial cities. The recently completed international trade agreement, which will lower tariff barriers, can be expected to accelerate this trend. The growing interdependence of the world economy also stimulates New York's white-collar sector since New York is the most favored location for the North American headquarters of multinational companies.

The city's manufacturing base may also be adversely affected by developments in the capital markets. The kind of manufacturing most suited to New York is the small, one-plant company, especially the new venture, or the specialized producer, which relies heavily on the close proximity of business services, suppliers, and, often, customers. Traditionally, New York has been a hospitable environment for small firms; the average manufacturing establishment in New York is much smaller than that in the next five largest cities.[5] However, in recent years, small firms throughout the nation have complained about being squeezed out of capital markets, partly because institutional investors prefer larger, more seasoned, and less risky investments. The increase in mergers and acquisitions in recent years and the increase between 1958 and 1972 in the number of employees per manufacturing establishment, both in New York and nationwide, tend to support this claim.[6] If small companies are, indeed, being squeezed out of capital markets, and continue to be, the erosion of manufacturing employment in New York will continue.

TRENDS IN LOCATIONAL PREFERENCES

Since World War II, large numbers of nonagricultural jobs, and the people who hold them, have migrated out of the cities and into the suburbs, out of the Northeast and into the Sunbelt. As pointed out in Chapter 2, older cities have lost favor as a location for industry and commerce for three reasons: people preferred to live elsewhere, other locations were more profitable, and the federal government encouraged the migration. There is no simple answer to the question of whether the cities will continue to lose favor or will become more competitive with the newer areas.

Political as well as economic and social prejudice against cities has been continuous for twenty-five years. But the distress in New York and in other cities has focused national attention on the "urban crisis," creating a new resolve not to let the older cities slide. Moreover, recent political developments are likely to work against continuing dispersion. The Northeast, long a highly fragmented region, has begun to coalesce politically. During the last few years, the so-called Frostbelt has been the site of the emergence of the

Coalition of Northeastern Governors, the Northeast-Midwest Economic Advancement Coalition, the Steering Committee of Northeastern Legislative Leaders, and the Council for Northeast Economic Action, which respectively unite governors, congressmen, state legislators, and community leaders. In addition, such organizations as the Conference of Mayors and the League of Cities—which sponsor research, promote self-help strategies, and work to reverse federal policies injurious to the region—have brought together big-city mayors.

Reacting to some real and serious conflicts among cities and within the region, many political leaders refuse to join such groups; others, although nominally members, do not always act in concert. Still, the coalition movement has had some success: the Northeast-Midwest Economic Advancement Coalition, for example, won favorable votes in Congress on community development and food stamp funding, targeting of countercyclical aid, and the home heating oil rebate. In other instances, these coalitions have sparked public awareness of policies that have adverse regional effects—military procurement and base siting, for example.

Another political development that seemed hopeful at one point was the formal recognition by the national administration of the concerns of declining cities and regions. Redeeming various campaign pledges, in March 1978 President Carter announced an urban policy that included revitalizing depressed economies, providing fiscal relief for cities, and ending the policies that have encouraged dispersion. Some mayors greeted some aspects of this policy package with enthusiasm; in particular, they supported the "urban impact statement," which is to accompany proposed new federal actions. Urban impact analyses by the executive branch could be an important supplement to the work of the congressional coalitions. However, many observers feel that March 1978 was the high water mark of the federal commitment to cities. The persistence of inflation in the intervening months has eroded popular, administration, and congressional support of domestic spending. Tax revolt has become increasingly widespread, and its message has not been lost on political leaders. With the related problems of inflation and energy occupying much of the public consciousness, it may be some years before cities can claim the support they seemed on the verge of receiving eighteen months ago.

These political actions, as limited as they are, seem to have generated equal and opposite reactions. The Southern Growth Policies Board, a coalition of southern states, has recently adopted an antagonistic stance and responded to the demands and assertions of the northeastern groups in a paper called "The Snowbelt and the Seven Myths."[7] Within Congress, southern and western caucuses are organizing to resist the encroachments of the Northeast-Midwest Economic Advancement Coalition. Their main concerns have been to resist the redirection of tax dollars to the distressed regions and to ensure the continued growth of the Sunbelt through the establishment of defense facilities and water projects.

A second political trend working against the cities is the loss of congressional representation and electoral college votes. The 1980 census is expected to confirm substantial population shifts that will reduce the representation of declining areas in Congress after 1982 and their importance to presidential candidates beginning in 1984. Today, congressional and executive commitment to cities and to the Northeast is tenuous; it may be more so in the 1980s.

Another conceivably important development is the resistance of the fastest growing areas to overly rapid growth. Many towns have discovered that fast development is expensive, unsettling, and unattractive. Political leaders in places as diverse as Colorado and the Connecticut suburbs adjacent to New York have found support for no-growth platforms and have sought to keep out industry and migrants by using zoning ordinances, taxation, and denial of amenities. But the United States still contains plenty of undeveloped areas; companies denied access to Boulder or Greenwich may simply move to the exurbs, and the Census Bureau found such "metropolitan spillover" increasing in the 1970s.[8] In any case, the antigrowth movement may turn out to be transitory. The slower overall growth in the 1980s may reduce the pressure on "boom towns" and defuse political opposition to development.

Technological developments undoubtedly have contributed to dispersion. Computers, air conditioners, interstate highways, and communications satellites are here to stay. New technological breakthroughs add to the impact of old breakthroughs. As time goes on, capital equipment in the older cities will become more, not less, obsolete; newer areas will be more, not less, accessible.

On the other hand, as the cities and the Northeast become less dense, and as the suburbs and the Sunbelt become more dense, some of the differences between them, and hence the relative attractiveness of the newer locations, may diminish. Weather aside, many people believe that when the South and West are sufficiently developed the nation will reach an equilibrium, after which there will be more balanced regional growth; we may even be approaching that equilibrium now.

These political and economic developments will not, generally, be felt directly by the individual or by the business executive deciding whether to stay in New York or move out. Rather, they will influence the decision indirectly, by affecting cost and noncost advantages of New York relative to other locations.

Costs

Both the increased political activism of the Northeast and the development in the Sunbelt could narrow cost differentials—especially those for taxes and energy—between New York and other locations.

Local tax differentials may be narrowed with federal help. The last recession made "fiscal relief" a national watchword. Economic stimuli—countercyclical revenue sharing, public works, and CETA employment—were applied through local governments. Especially since 1977, this relief has been targeted to the most distressed cities, reversing the "spreading" trend that began with Nixon's general revenue-sharing program. The Carter administration, in its 1980 budget, is committed to maintaining the level of fiscal relief. Although the CETA program will be cut back, countercyclical aid will be increased, thereby changing the net effect little. The administration is still committed to targeting, but the distribution of funds is uncertain. Richard Nathan of the Brookings Institution is not sure what the commitment to targeting will mean in practice, with "suburban interests, rural interests, small town interests, sunbelt interests, not to forget state governments and neighborhoods. . . reaching for the new federal cookie jar called urban policy."[9] Congress, for instance, is already pressing to dilute HUD's successful Urban Development Action Grant program by making "poverty pockets" in fiscally healthy cities eligible for these grants. Whatever targeting there is, however, will be helpful in reducing local tax differentials.

Under Carter's urban policy, federal aid should be available for renovating and maintaining infrastructure—in current usage for "soft" rather than "hard" public works. Bills are now before Congress to create a national bank to make loans (some of them subsidized) and grants for this purpose. Obviously, such a policy favors older cities over newer, growing areas. In addition, some federal funds will probably be shifted from highway projects to urban mass transit. The amounts will probably not be large—the administration asked Congress in 1978 to appropriate $1.2 billion annually for soft public works and mass transit, a sum that pales in comparison to the $11 billion that the federal government spent in 1977 on nonmass transit local projects[10]—but also may help to narrow local tax differentials.

Welfare reform also may provide fiscal relief, although the Carter program does not recognize welfare as an exclusively national responsibility. If the Carter proposal is enacted, New York State (and City) will receive relief amounting to between 20 percent and 36 percent of its current effort; most states will get only about 10 percent relief. This reform program has a long way to go to gain congressional approval. However, its implementation date has been moved up from 1981 to "immediately upon enactment of legislation." The House also is considering changes in aid formulas under the Elementary and Secondary Education Act that would give more money to inner-city schools, thus providing them with some fiscal relief; the administration supports such changes.

Congress is also considering bills for "cost equalization" of unemployment insurance taxes, which now vary from state to state. Under the proposed law, states would not be penalized for economic conditions beyond their control.

If the federal government succeeds in inducing the state governments to devote more of their resources to distressed cities, local tax differentials may be reduced. (Pessimists maintain that, because political power has shifted to the suburbs, many state governments would refuse federal aid rather than help their cities and that, in any case, the inducements to be offered by the federal government will be insufficient.)

Even without federal intervention, though, local taxes may tend to equalize themselves. The tendency toward equalization of size and density of towns should logically affect tax rates. But in practice, although an increase in population usually raises per capita expenditures, it also generates (under the current setup) more federal and state aid. Increases in population between 50,000 and 500,000 inhabitants have very little effect on per capita taxes.[11] Tax rates in large cities do not decline with population because the heaviest service users are the last to leave. The difficulties that New York City has encountered in reducing taxes argue that it will have to count more on tax increases in cities in the growth regions than on decreasing its own taxes if it is to make its own tax position more competitive.

Help may also be coming in the form of reductions in federal taxes in urban areas. The administration proposes offering a tax credit to employers who hire CETA-referred workers and a differential investment tax credit for investment in distressed areas. Together, the two programs would amount to $1.7 billion in tax expenditures annually; in 1976, the federal government provided for $7.7 billion in investment tax credits (which favor new locations).[12] Several people have suggested indexing federal personal income tax rates to regional costs of living so that people with the same real income, rather than with the same nominal income, would pay equal proportions of their income in taxes. This measure would benefit the Northeast in general and New York City in particular. However, it is not yet feasible, partly because regional cost-of-living indexes are not yet well enough developed and partly because it would not be politically popular in lower cost regions.

The effects of recent oil price increases are still unclear. On the one hand, these increases could make New York more competitive with its suburbs because the availability of mass transit and the smaller living quarters in the city cut down on individual use of energy. They also could make the goods produced in New York (e.g., apparel), which consume little energy in production, cheaper relative to goods (e.g., petroleum products) made elsewhere in the United States, raising consumer demand for them and stimulating employment in New York. On the other hand, New York depends far more heavily on oil than do most other parts of the Sunbelt, where the need for heating oil is lower and cheaper sources of energy are more readily available. Local energy prices may be reduced if the Energy Corporation of the Northeast (ENCONO) bill, proposed by the Coalition of Northeastern Governors, is passed. This proposal provides federal guarantees for loans made by an interstate energy corporation. Of course, other regions might form energy corporations of their own, and while overall energy costs might be reduced, the price differential would remain.

It is even possible that, given some reasonable changes in Interstate Commerce Commission (ICC) and Department of Agriculture regulations, the prices of food and other consumer goods could be lowered in the Northeast. These regulations, denying return trip licenses to trucks delivering food and adding unnecessary markups to dairy products, in effect make Northeasterners pay double transportation costs for many items.

Relative costs are already beginning to adjust through market mechanisms. The gap between New York's cost of living and the U.S. average has been narrowing since 1974; factory wages in New York have risen a little more slowly than the national average since 1971; other occupational earnings have also fallen behind national growth rates during the 1970s.[13]

But even if political and market mechanisms continue to reduce New York's cost disadvantages and provide some relief to New Yorkers, they probably will not significantly enhance the city's competitiveness. The range of price flexibility is small. New York, given its density and location, will always be a high-cost city. Its high-rise buildings and complex infrastructure are expensive to maintain, especially when the latter is both immense and old. It is difficult to move goods through its congested streets, and providing security, privacy, and insulation from the urban environment also adds to the cost of living. Because of these costs, the city's price levels will remain higher than the national average for the foreseeable future.

Even though prices in New York were generally becoming more favorable between 1973 and 1976, the city's employment growth rate was lagging farther and farther behind the national rate. This apparent violation of the laws of economics probably means that in recent years non-price-level considerations have been more important than price levels in determining the desirability of the New York location. While it is too soon to tell whether the narrowing of the price-level gap will eventually make the city more competitive, nonprice considerations will in the short run probably continue to be more influential.

New York's Appeal as a Place to Live and Work

Neighborhood revival movements—"brownstoning," "urban home-steading," "loft living"—and the attraction of the city's environment for contemporary living have in recent years been the subject of numerous magazine articles. Undoubtedly, many young adults earn good incomes and can enjoy the richness of city life. Middle-income families, black and white, have spurred, through a good deal of personal effort and risk, the spectacular rebuilding of neighborhoods. A recent article goes so far as to suggest a "new role for the central city" as a "home for upper and middle-class people . . . singles, couples and young families."[14] But it is unwise to assume that this rebuilding of neighborhoods, welcome as it is, represents the beginning of a trend in New York or in other cities.

It is useful to remember, however, that as early as 1958 *The New York Times* was running articles heralding the end of suburbanization and the return of the middle class to the cities. Since then, the city has become less fashionable, not more. Young, middle-class people are moving out faster than anyone else, despite the later marriages and the smaller families that might be expected to keep them in the city. In public opinion polls, the percentage of adults preferring large city life has dropped from 22 percent in 1966 to 13

percent in 1974 to 10 percent in 1977.¹ ⁵ Surely, it is more than
coincidental that those ethnic groups that have the least freedom of
choice in location have become increasingly concentrated in the large
cities.

Cities (New York in particular) may become more or less attractive to middle-income wage earners in the coming decade. The
evidence is not clear-cut or, rather, it is running in opposite
directions.

On the plus side, New York's image has improved dramatically in
the past two or three years. The fiscal crisis seems to have marked a
turning point of sorts: if New York was really in such dire straits, it
was no longer fair game for the hostile attention it had been getting
from the national media. The replacement of movies like *Death Wish*
by movies like *Manhattan* illustrates this change. In reality, as well as
in popular belief, crime may decrease as the baby boom grows up
and settles down and as the proportion of the population in the
violence-prone "criminal years" declines. Safer cities would be much
more attractive.

The expansion of international trade and of foreign business
operations, which, as already mentioned, boost New York's white-
collar economy, also bring to this country a large class of people
who find New York particularly attractive. Foreign businessmen and
their families like New York's cosmopolitan atmosphere. The city is
one of the few places where they can maintain their own communities and cultures while experiencing all the diversity New York has
to offer. Foreigners, more than many native Americans, appreciate
the city's tolerance and sophistication. What is more, with the fall of
the dollar, New York prices, although higher than elsewhere in the
United States, are low by the standards of most European and many
Asian capitals.

Another plus for New York is that the suburbs are becoming less
attractive. Many suburbs now have the violent crime, drug abuse,
high taxes, school busing, crowding, and pollution that caused their
residents to flee the cities. Suburban sprawl is no prettier than urban
blight. The "filling up" of the suburbs may eventually bring about a
return to the cities, but in the short run, it seems more likely to
accelerate development in exurbs, rural areas, small towns, and
less-developed areas of the country.

On the negative side, cities may become relatively less attractive
because of the changing age structure of the population. Typically,
many young adults who have enjoyed city life become less interested
in what the city has to offer at about thirty, when they begin to buy
homes and settle down to domestic pursuits. Because of the peculiar

age structure of the American population, the number of people reaching age thirty will be increasing rapidly during the 1980s, and the number of younger adults will be diminishing somewhat, especially toward the end of the decade.

In addition, the growth of the suburbs and of the newer regions has brought the benefits as well as the problems of the big cities: culture and prestige. Although some New Yorkers still insist that civilization is dead west of the Hudson, backwaters are no longer so dull or constricting as they once were, not only because of their growth in population, but also because of the national mass media, increasing affluence, rising education levels, and the shift to white-collar work. The federal government has encouraged the geographic decentralization of the arts through its subsidy programs. People who would once have been reluctant to leave New York City for fear of cultural isolation today feel more optimistic about what the rest of the country has to offer.

The Business Climate

The city's businesses, like its individual residents, are sensitive to crime, social unrest, and crowding; they also have an indirect stake in the quality of life because they find it difficult to recruit workers (particularly at management levels) to cities with poor images. In addition, they are influenced by the "business climate": the value of linkages to other firms and the ease of doing business.

Without government aid, the value of New York's location will probably continue to deteriorate. Firms selling to local markets will find a steady erosion of purchasing power. Firms selling to distant markets will find those distant markets growing large enough to provide for their own needs (through "import substitution"). Firms depending on New York's prestige will find other locations becoming increasingly prestigious. Also, as the concentration of American industry increases, companies can acquire prestige by sheer size; thus, the prestige of their locations becomes less important. Firms depending on the Port of New York will find that goods traded internationally are increasingly those that are more appropriately shipped through southern ports (oil, soybeans, wheat).[16]

One of the prime attractions of New York for many firms—the proximity of other firms in the same or related business—will continue to lose its force. The richer the business environment in the suburbs, the more they have to offer a relocating firm; the weaker the urban nexus, the less it has to offer. Thus, Connecticut's Fairfield County has grown dramatically in recent years as a headquarters-business service complex. In addition, the usefulness of agglomeration to some industries is likely to continue to decline. Electronic linkages can be expected to continue to improve, significantly reducing the value of face-to-face contact: the automation of the stock exchange is a case in point.

The Carter administration's urban policy includes a program designed to increase the value of older cities' locations artificially by giving inner-city firms special consideration in federal procurement decisions and, whenever possible, by locating federal offices in distressed cities. (Ironically, federal offices and contractors have even less use for urban locations—for markets, prestige, or other locational benefits—than do firms operating in the private economy, and narrow cost considerations are more relevant to them than to private firms.) But neither the procurement "set-aside" for inner-city businesses nor the number of federal offices set up is likely to be large, and these artificial measures will probably not offset the natural decline in the locational value of older cities.

Press reports of failures or relocations of New York businesses typically identify the factors triggering the decision. Usually, the businesses claim that they cannot obtain some input crucial to their success: the city delays a needed permit; the banks will not lend money; insurers will not issue policies; executives refuse to live in the area; production workers go on strike; skilled workers are in short supply; Con Ed will not install new natural gas lines; large blocks of space are not available. At some point, the firm despairs of finding what it needs in New York and closes up shop.

At least some of these availability problems may ease in the future, partly because the problem has come to public attention, partly because the city now has so many unemployed resources, and partly because resources will become increasingly scarce in locations competing with New York.

The elimination of red tape has become a priority for the city government, and a special office has been established within the Office of Economic Development to expedite the granting of needed permits for businesses. City officials are reviewing codes and regulations with a view to eliminating those that unnecessarily inhibit business. Old practices die hard, however, and sometimes more is needed than cooperation; but the improvement of the city's image has become such a political necessity that it seems reasonable to expect some progress in this area.

Political considerations may make investment capital easier to obtain in New York. Over the last few years, activist community groups have been combating redlining with modest success, and the administration has lent support to their efforts by recommending that "private sector financial institutions . . . be encouraged to provide greater resources to urban revitalization."[17] The federal government is also becoming more directly involved in supplying capital through the Economic Development Administration and the Department of Housing and Urban Development.

Office space was difficult to find in the late 1960s, was a glut on the market for most of the 1970s, and once again is becoming scarce. A number of new buildings, however, are either under construction or planned for the midtown area. If the national economy expands at a slower and steadier pace in the 1980s, serious dislocations in the office market may be avoided.

Commercial and manufacturing space may present more of a problem. The stock of buildings for commercial and manufacturing enterprises is largely old and dilapidated. As businesses move out, the buildings are demolished, neglected until they deteriorate, or converted to other (often residential) uses. Rentable space has not been allowed to accumulate. Moreover, many old buildings cannot provide space appropriate to modern manufacturing techniques and have inadequate access to transportation. But changing conditions may help solve these problems: the depopulation of the South Bronx, for example, has reached the point where it can, with relatively little disruption to the lives of residents, accommodate the wholesale demolition of existing structures and the building of a modern industrial park. Whether through the development of industrial parks or through other means, local government can help business in facilitating land assembly.

Many corporate headquarters have complained about the difficulties of recruiting middle managers to New York. To a large extent, this problem is one of cost rather than of availability. According to the Bureau of Labor Statistics, the cost-of-living differential for upper-income people is far greater than for lower-income people, and corporations are unwilling to pay the price necessary to support the New York "executive" way of life.[18] In effect, corporations rely on executives who like New York so much that they are willing to pay to live there; such executives are becoming scarce. But if prices in the New York area continue to approach the national average, executives will not have to pay a premium to live in or near the city and may become more disposed toward working there.

Energy shortages, of course, are impossible to predict. Natural gas, in short supply a few years ago, appears to be readily available once more; the State Public Service Commission has released a report citing an excess of electrical generating capacity;[19] and the Port Authority has plans to make energy from recycled garbage available for industrial use. But a concerted effort to reduce the region's dependence on oil is the only hope of avoiding energy shortages.

The most serious allegations of unavailability are businessmen's complaints of labor shortages. After a decade of high unemployment, however, these complaints are rather hard to accept. After all, more unemployed workers are in the New York labor market than anywhere else in the nation. Nor is business fleeing to avoid union truculence; the average percentage of working days lost due to work stoppages is the same for New York as for the nation—about 0.25.[20] Some observers ascribe the apparent anomaly to a labor force that does not meet business needs. According to this view, the building and transportation systems in New York increasingly favor white-collar businesses (modern offices, good public transportation; out-moded factories, poor goods delivery systems), but the pool of labor, due to migration patterns and the failure of the city's schools, is increasingly unskilled and inexperienced. Even skilled workers often have the wrong skills—an unemployed garment cutter is of little use to a bank looking for a computer programmer.[21]

If this theory is correct, and scarcity or mismatch of skills has in fact been a problem, it is likely to get worse in the coming decade. Between now and 1990, an estimated 300,000 additional foreign workers may settle in New York if the immigration laws are not more strictly enforced, and a roughly equal number of young New Yorkers will enter the labor force. These people will have few skills to offer potential employers; many of them will have language difficulties. Meanwhile, an even larger number of older, more experienced workers will have died, retired, or emigrated.

Fortunately, of all factors of production, labor is the most malleable. Most people are willing to go almost anywhere and learn almost anything that promises to improve their economic position. The foreigners arriving in New York today have made financial and personal sacrifices to emigrate; the illegals among them especially have run considerable risks. They are highly motivated people. They are also, presumably, of normal intelligence.

While the issue of structural versus demand-related unemployment is still unresolved, a strong case can be made that the low level of skills in New York—or the lack of investment in human capital—is the result, rather than the cause, of insufficient demand for labor. When training is expensive and seems unlikely to pay off in higher wages or increased job security, it becomes unattractive as an investment. To be sure, experience and education lead to higher income, but the differential may not be sufficient for many people to justify the investment. A 1975 study[22] describes the city's labor market as a "queue" in which workers are arranged in order of their desirability to employers. Training and education move up the worker in the queue, but if employers are going to select, for example, only the first ten people in the queue, the individual who, because of training, advances from position 100 to position 20 derives little benefit.

The fact that people with skills and education (at least among nonprofessionals) are more likely to move away from New York than the unskilled suggests that New York is a relatively better location for low-wage than for high-wage earners. If investment in education paid off in New York, unskilled people would be emigrating faster than skilled people or else rapidly upgrading their skills. The burgeoning supply of labor in other parts of the country tends to support the hypothesis that labor supply responds to demand. It strains credulity to argue that labor is scarce only in the largest labor market in the country. It seems most likely that a stronger effective demand for skilled labor—that is, a willingness on the part of employers to pay more of a premium for skills—might create its own supply, deterring skilled workers from emigrating and giving less skilled workers an incentive to acquire more training.

If scarcity of labor has not, in fact, been a major reason why businesses have left New York, then the other shortages—capital, space, energy, and so forth—also may have been less important than relocating companies have claimed. Such alleged shortages may have provided excuses for moving when the real reasons were not suitable for publication, or they may have accelerated decisions that would have been made in any case.

The most likely resource constraint on American business in the 1980s is a water shortage in the West. Supplying water to the West's growing population has become increasingly expensive; many proposed water projects now appear likely to cost more than they can add to the national product. The Carter administration has opposed such unprofitable projects, but although the western states have resisted its efforts with some success, they have been put on notice that they cannot take for granted a continually expanding water supply. Government unwillingness to endlessly finance water projects may curtail western growth and in the process, almost inevitably, may improve New York's competitive position.

* * *

These developments can be summarized as follows: between now and 1990, there will probably be stabler, more moderate growth in the national economy; increasing difficulty and cost in finding new suburban and Sunbelt locations for business but fewer compelling reasons to stay in the older cities; and some commitment to change and also some resistance at the state and national levels.

In short, real and strong forces are pulling in opposite directions. As a result, in the foreseeable future, New York may experience some easing in the cost and difficulty of doing business, and it may be able to line up enough political support to obtain some fiscal breathing room. But the city is most unlikely to regain its leading edge of national growth. New York will not capture its lost glory; it will not be "revitalized." At least for the next decade, it will continue to be a disfavored location and to lag behind national growth rates, although less so than in the recent past.

An extension of Figure 5-2, using national projections furnished by the Bureau of Labor Statistics (BLS) and the Bureau of Economic Analysis, yields the conclusion that stability in the total number of jobs is compatible with a slight lag behind national growth rates when unemployment rates are moderately low, as they are expected to be in the 1980s. These projections are based on rather optimistic assessments of future unemployment rates. If the national unemployment rate does not fall so rapidly as the Bureau of Economic Analysis expects, but averages 5.5 percent in the 1980s (the Congressional Budget Office projection for the next five years), the job total in New York in 1990 may be as much as 10 percent or 15 percent below today's. This economic forecast is not inconsistent with the predictions for 1985 made by the New York State Department of Labor and the Temporary Commission for City Finances.[2 3]

Even if the number of jobs does not change much over the next decade, the composition of the job market will certainly change. Nationwide, the BLS predicts that the basic trends of recent years will continue: manufacturing employment will become less important and service industry employment (especially business and health services) more important. The trend away from blue-collar jobs to service and white-collar jobs also will continue.[2 4] These trends may be mirrored, or even magnified, in New York. Some of New York's manufacturing specialties—apparel, printing and publishing, leather— are expected to do particularly poorly; some of its service specialties — business services, health and hospitals, entertainment—are expected to do particularly well.

The BLS predicts that finance will be a national growth industry. New York's financial community is unlikely to share in these gains because most of the growth will be in retailing financial services to individuals and will follow the markets. Moreover, even "high finance" is increasingly being provided at the regional level. The centralization of the stock market may offset whatever gains accrue from the development of New York as an international financial center.

While the BLS forecasts no dramatic changes in the proportion of jobs in construction, trade, or transportation and public utilities, construction jobs in New York may increase slightly. The Westway, if built, the office buildings now planned, and the long-deferred rehabilitation of existing buildings and infrastructure should be sufficient to lift the construction industry out of its current depressed condition. Trade should decline slightly, with the shrinking of the local market, and the transportation, communications, and utility sectors, which depend partly on local markets and partly on New York's nodal role, also may decline somewhat.

The BLS predicts that in the future the federal government will employ a smaller percentage of the national work force, although if the government does carry out a deliberate policy of retaining federal employment in the inner city the absolute number of federal employees in New York City may not decline. State and local government employees are expected to increase very rapidly nationwide, but without massive federal help, it will for a long time be politically impossible for New York to hire many more municipal workers.

Job openings, according to State Department of Labor projections (see Table 5-1), will favor city residents over commuters and women over men. Relatively fewer jobs (24 percent of existing jobs) will open up in occupations favored by commuters—professional, managerial, and sales. More jobs (30 percent of existing jobs) will become available in clerical, blue-collar, and service positions, which are largely filled by city residents. Fewer jobs (19 percent of existing jobs) will be available in managerial, professional, sales, and blue-collar occupations, all traditionally male; more jobs (42 percent of existing jobs) will open up in clerical and service occupations, largely female. A relatively strong demand for women residents may help absorb into the labor market the thousands of welfare mothers whose children will be growing up.

As in the recent past, low-level job openings will be more numerous than those for skilled jobs. In such a situation, workers will have little incentive to improve their skills, and educated and skilled workers, especially men, will continue to emigrate at higher than average rates. Earnings per person will stagnate, or at least lag behind national growth, both because of the changing job mix and

Table 5-1. Occupational Distribution of Jobs to Be Filled in New York City, 1976-85

Occupation	Employment 1976	Jobs to Be Filled, 1976-85
All Occupations	3,436,100	956,800
White-collar occupations	2,148,900	730,100
Professional and technical workers	583,800	166,500
Managers and administrators	439,400	88,900
Sales workers	235,400	56,400
Clerical workers	890,300	418,300
Blue-collar occupations	840,200	77,400
Craft and kindred workers	337,600	33,100
Operatives	395,800	39,100
Nonfarm laborers	106,800	5,200
Service workers	448,900	149,300

Source: New York State Department of Labor.

because clerical and service occupations have little potential for productivity increases. The decline in manufacturing employment and the predominance of low-level job openings should continue to hamper the city's efforts to increase its tax revenues.

If foreign immigration is not sharply restricted, the working-age population in New York will increase much faster than the available jobs. Even if the employment level remains stable, out-migration will probably remain at the level of the 1970s, a level that was not rapid enough to keep pace with the alarming rate at which jobs vanished. The 1978 unemployment rate of 9.8 percent, 40 percent above the national rate, indicates a backlog of potential emigrants. A number of individuals, kept in the city by unemployment benefits, working spouses, sentimental attachments, or poor prospects for employment elsewhere, will probably move out in the 1980s. The emigrants will probably be disproportionately white, although perhaps less so than in the past. Whites still have a far better chance of finding acceptable housing and employment in their new locations than do blacks, but it is not unreasonable to expect a decline in discrimination.

The low emigration of the elderly and the immigration of young children (because of the family composition of foreign immigrants) are likely to continue, and if they do, they will offset the decline in the working-age population, as shown in Table 5-2.

We also expect a continuation of the increase in black, Hispanic, and foreign-born population. The white population is old (median age 41.2) and more likely to emigrate; the black and Hispanic

Table 5-2. Age Structure of the Population of New York City (in Millions)[a]

	1974	1990 (Projected)
0-17	2.13	2.25
18-65	4.42	4.00
65+	0.95	1.25
Totals	7.50	7.50

Source: Twentieth Century Fund staff estimates for 1990, Census Bureau for 1974.

[a]This estimate assumes 3.2 million jobs, 2.85 million employed residents, a slight increase in labor force participation rates for 18-65-year-olds (BEA), a 4 percent unemployment rate (BLS), Census Bureau projections of the national age structure in 1990, and the continuance of the age-specific migration rates derived in Chapter 3. Because of the very large number of assumptions, nearly all of them rough, the estimate should be used with caution. But BEA's projections for New York State also involve a stable population and lagging per capita income for the city.

populations are young (25 and 22.9 years, respectively) and more likely to immigrate. Geographically, the only source of net immigration will be from overseas.

Some of the needs of the 1990 population will be quite different from those of today's population. The number of recipients of Aid to Dependent Children will probably continue to fall: it declined by 7 percent from 1972 to 1976, despite high unemployment, in part because of the declining birthrate. The birthrate will probably continue to fall; by all accounts, welfare is used very little by foreign immigrants in New York; and we expect much higher rates of employment of the working-age population. However, the expected increases in the non-working-age population and in low-level jobs point to a rise in the number of medically indigent residents (a broader category than indigent) and increased demand for publicly subsidized medical services. The current surplus of hospital beds may vanish as the city's population ages.

Public school enrollment, which has been falling since 1971, will probably fall for a few more years and then rise slightly as the number of children increases and as more of those children are nonwhite (nonwhites in New York make heavier use of the public schools than do whites, a large percentage of whom attend private schools).

The increase in the percentage of persons over 65 will be a source of fiscal strain. Senior citizens—at least those choosing to remain in New York—have below-average incomes; much of their income comes from nontaxable sources; and they are heavy users of other city services.

Other demands on the city's budget during the 1980s will be

determined not by the changing composition of the population but by prior commitments or by basic "housekeeping" needs. In the first category are pension contributions and debt service costs on debt already incurred.

Payments for pension funds are mandated by commitments made when the city's economy was stronger. Revisions, which require the approval of the state legislature and find strong opposition from the powerful union lobby, have been too little and too late. Eventually, pension costs will fall because the city has fewer employees than it did a few years ago. It also has undertaken to provide less generous benefits to those hired after June 30, 1973, than to those hired prior to that date. In the meantime, however, the actuarial funds must reduce as quickly as possible their billions of dollars of unfunded accrued liability, which they accumulated by delaying contributions. Retirement costs, therefore, will not soon fall.

Debt service on debt already incurred also is virtually inescapable. Unlike retirement costs, funded debt repayments have not been delayed. The debt service on the funded debt outstanding as of June 30, 1976, was $1.478 billion in fiscal 1977, but it will be only $275 million by fiscal 1987.[25] The city has rolled over short-term debt in the past, and is stretching some of it out through the Municipal Assistance Corporation, but if the city reduces its deficit in accordance with the federal plan, debt service for short-term debt should after a few years decrease correspondingly.

In the second category are expenses for general government, uniformed services, and maintenance and rebuilding of the city's housing stock and infrastructure. Some of the investment in housing and infrastructure will be capital spending, calling for the issuance of new debt. General government expenses are, within a large range, insensitive to changes in city size or composition. The demand for police, fire, and sanitation services is relatively fixed. Violence, robbery, and arson may decline if the city has a stabler, more fully employed population with fewer teenagers and young adults, but even then, it will be difficult to justify cutting back police and fire protection by very much. A certain number of people are needed just to patrol a given area, and today's force is widely regarded as a "bare-bones" operation.

A strong demand will continue for housing subsidies and renovation. Abandonment and burnings should become less commonplace as the population stabilizes over the next decade, but the prospects for maintaining housing in the future do not look bright. If real average earnings and the proportion of workers in the population do not rise very much, and if housing costs continue to rise relative to the consumer price index, the population in 1990 will be no more able to afford the housing stock than it is today. To prevent irreversible deterioration, the city government will be under pressure to increase its investment in housing rehabilitation. At present, the city is using Community Development funds to operate the thousands of buildings that have been seized for nonpayment of taxes, but it is not clear that they will be able to continue using such funds for this purpose. If housing becomes less profitable to provide, more buildings are seized, and Community Development funds are cut off, the operation of these units will be an enormous burden to the city.

The city's infrastructure faces similar problems. Much of the city's infrastructure is old and in serious disrepair, and in recent years, it has been replaced or repaired much too slowly.* The city will have to maintain minimal standards of public safety and to allow business to function. Much more money is required to meet federal pollution standards and to make New York's "quality of life" competitive with that of other cities (quality of life is not simply a luxury; it attracts and keeps businesses).

In summary, we expect much more stability in the next decade than we have had in the last. The economy will stabilize, with more white-collar and service employment and less manufacturing; we expect productivity and earnings to lag. The population will also remain about the same size, and there will be more children, old people, nonwhites, Hispanics, and recent immigrants. The needs of the population will be different from those of today, but equally hard to meet. Unless federal and state assistance reaches a level not previously imagined, it will be impossible to provide the public services that city residents have come to expect. However, expectations seem to be catching up with circumstances; perhaps the city in the 1980s, despite shortages of funds, will avoid the crisis atmosphere of the 1970s because it will no longer be trying to live in the style thought possible in the 1960s.

New York faces an unenviable and uncertain future. There will always be a New York. But although it is not Spokane or Newark or Detroit multiplied, its position is more vulnerable now than it ever was in the past. Manhattan may thrive even under the worst of circumstances, but if it is surrounded by declining and decaying activity, social and political tensions may well increase. Although the city may avoid a tailspin like the one it experienced from 1969 to 1976, the chances are that real growth is no longer possible. The problem, then, is how best to manage stability and decline.

*See Appendix.

Chapter 6

Policy Options

Like its predecessors, the Koch administration faces a seemingly constant flow of critical decisions—how to reduce the excess of hospital beds; whether the police should patrol singly or in pairs; where to deploy the sanitation department's scarce equipment in a snowstorm; what attitude to take when the leader of a municipal union threatens to strike. Those decisions have to be made under pressure and frequently in dramatic circumstances, with television cameras and newspaper reporters on the scene. But unlike its predecessors, this administration has to take account of a new perspective—the necessity of making pressing short-term decisions without worsening the city's still precarious long-term situation.

Previously, City Hall left the future to take care of itself. Today, it no longer has that luxury. What the municipal administration now does in the short run can affect the city's ability to recover from the brink of bankruptcy and to set a sustainable course for the future. Yet some of the decisions that appear so important and get so much news coverage are not so critical as others that receive little if any publicity.

There is wide agreement concerning some of the measures that the city has to take to improve its long-run position. For example, the city must continually carry out management reforms. (One observer compares these to certain domestic chores that go unnoticed as long as they are done but are missed when they are left undone.[1]) The city must communicate to business convincingly that it is not hostile; it must eliminate unneeded red tape and listen seriously to the complaints of the business community. It must manage its finances so as to inspire investor confidence. It also has to take a tough stance in bargaining with its own unions over wages and work rules; it must gain the confidence and cooperation of the unions in improving management and personnel procedures. In addition, in the private sector, it must foster cooperation between labor and management. Greater flexibility in budgeting is also vital. The implementation of these policies will not be easy; any proposed specific changes generate controversy. But these problems are, by and large, technical.

The fundamental policy decisions facing the city will be even harder to make because the liberal coalition of the 1960s and early 1970s– which itself was a long way from unanimity—collapsed when the market for city bonds did. Today, despite what seems like a more cooperative working relationship among government, business, and unions, there are serious disagreements about the proper role of the municipal government that make it difficult to implement any consistent or effective policy for governing the city.

There are disagreements about the scope of the city government, especially about the extensive social services provided to the residents of New York. The tax revolt movement of the last few years—which has not passed by New York—calls into question whether government in general should be as large a component of the economy as it is today. Similarly, there is doubt about the effectiveness of social services; few New Yorkers today are confident that social problems can be solved by "throwing money at them." Others, however, would prefer to see the city heavily involved in social service delivery.

Nor is there a consensus about the way in which the burdens of taxation and the benefits of public services should be divided. Here the argument is between those who would attempt to attract middle-class residents to New York by providing them with better services (education, parks, clean streets) and lowering their tax burden while spending less on the poor, and those who deplore the subsidies to the middle class already in effect and call for a fairer allocation of burdens and benefits.

The relationship between the city and the state and federal governments is also at issue. There is a trade-off between autonomy and increased funding; money often comes with strings attached, either in the form of taking over or regulating the particular program being funded or in the form of increased monitoring of city operations and budgeting in general. It is by no means clear whether or not increases in funding are worth their political price. Even if there is agreement that increased state and federal roles are justified, the questions of which programs are most useful to the city and merit an increased lobbying effort remain unanswered.

Perhaps the most serious disputes are those concerning the relationship between the public and private sectors. While public encouragement of private enterprise has become increasingly popular, and increasingly sophisticated, many citizens still have strong feelings about "giveaways" to businesses and resent the hypocrisy of corporations that preach free enterprise and then blackmail local governments into subsidizing them. If the city is to have an economic development policy, it must face the issue of what kinds of industries should be encouraged—those likely to thrive in New York, those likely to provide jobs for the city's unemployed residents, or those that are faring the worst and are most in need of shoring up. Another alternative is a neutral development policy that stimulates private business in general without favoring any particular industry. Similarly, there is disagreement about whether incentives to business should help them no matter where they want to locate or whether the incentives should be formulated to encourage industries to return to the city's most devastated areas.

THE BASIS FOR MAKING CHOICES

Some, but not all, of these issues involve competing values. Different segments of the city's population have different preferences and needs. There is no one correct answer to the question of how far the rich should be taxed to pay for services to the poor; or whether a neighborhood of young, childless professionals is more valuable to the city than a working-class family neighborhood; or whether it is better to adjust the city's labor force (through migration) to fit the job structure or to encourage job development that will make the economy fit the labor force. There are essentially only three ways to resolve conflicts of values politically. The first method is building a consensus by convincing a majority of voters to adopt a common set of values. For example, John Lindsay attempted to build a coalition of liberals and the poor in New York in the 1960s; the fiscal crisis created something of a consensus for retrenchment in 1975. But New York is a difficult place in which to achieve a consensus. The population is so heterogeneous, and political divisions are so bitter and so deeply felt, that large numbers of New Yorkers can agree on anything only rarely. The uncertain atmosphere of 1979, with the fiscal crisis temporarily lifted but still threatening to reappear, is an environment more conducive to jockeying for position and protecting earlier gains than to consensus-building.

A second method is imposing a minority view on an unwilling population. This is a risky procedure for a politician, but less risky if the minority has political strength out of proportion to its numbers. In this way, the municipal unions have been able to exercise a great deal of power since the early 1960s. The policy favored by the business community, which calls for reducing taxes, social services, and regulation and for granting special incentives for business expansion, is the most likely to be imposed on the city if a minority view should indeed prevail. The business community, which must be encouraged to stay if the city is to avoid bankruptcy, has been able to substantially increase its influence over policy since the fiscal crisis. However, even this group is not free of conflicts, and no one faction may be strong enough to impose its policies on the rest.

Finally, disputes are most often resolved by logrolling—offering enough concessions to enough groups to win an electoral majority. Given the slim chances of creating a lasting consensus or of one group being able to maintain its leverage over the rest, this seems like the most practical means of reconciling the diversity of interests in New York today. There are many opportunities for balancing claims. Cutbacks in services are easier to accept if they affect all groups; a reduction in business taxes can be balanced by a reduction in the unemployment rate; Times Square can be renewed at the same time that small industrial parks are built in the Bronx. In fact, it is likely that little can be done in the city over the long term if most constituencies are not kept at least minimally satisfied.

Logrolling—accommodation of interests—has other benefits as well. It produces results that are at least roughly in accord with most people's sense of justice or fair play; it does not impose a minority's, or even a majority's, interest on the rest of the city, where unrepresented interests may bear a disproportionate burden. Finally, logrolling avoids basing the city's future on a single eventuality (such as the chance of being able to stem the exodus of manufacturing jobs) when the future appears so uncertain. It is likely to produce a more neutral and more conservative policy than that likely to be produced by imposing the interests of a single group on the rest of the city.

However, there are two problems with a policy based on the satisfaction of numerous diverse constituencies. First, it creates—or at least does nothing to resist—pressures for greater expenditures than the city can afford. When any slack at all appears in the city's budget—as it has this year—so many claims are made on it that it cannot be used to reduce the city debt overhang. With all the city constituencies clamoring for various types of tax reduction and service increases, with the long-term fiscal outlook remaining bleak, and with no restraining mechanisms such as a powerful political party, one could argue that the Financial Control Board should be made a permanent institution if another fiscal crisis is to be avoided.

Second, such a policy is incoherent and ineffective. An equal division of benefits may result in all groups becoming equally disaffected with the administration. There appears to be a threshold below which the effects of the city's efforts are not perceived; a substantial incentive is necessary to stimulate any action. Thus, if the administration tries to use its limited resources to do something for everyone, it may not be able to do enough for any group to win political support or to induce marginal residents or businesses to remain in the city. It may make more sense—in terms of providing the most service or the most economic development per dollar invested or making the best use of the city's influence in Albany and Washington (which is as scarce as its financial resources)—to focus the city's resources on a single goal, or a consistent set of goals.

Not all policy questions turn entirely on competing values. When decisions are being made about economic development, we must ask not only who a proposed policy is intended to benefit and what activities it is intended to encourage, but also how likely it is to achieve its goal, and how much the city will receive for each dollar expended. For example, we might want to choose a new convention center over an equal investment in industrial parks if we determined that such a center would bring more and better paying jobs into the city. (Unfortunately, assessing the results of an economic development program, even in retrospect, is a highly inexact science. Economists disagree wildly on the direct effects of development—how many of the new jobs would have been added without the development program—and even more wildly on the "multiplier," or spin-off, effects of development.) A judgment made on grounds of effectiveness might countervene a judgment made on other grounds. For example, the industrial park might be chosen over the convention center, even if it were a net loss to the city, because it might do more to reduce local unemployment by hiring more neighborhood residents.

Thus, a direction for policy must be chosen that takes into account not only the competing claims and values of the city's various constituencies but also makes effective use of the limited funds available—in other words, choosing a policy of balancing competing claims by implementing the most cost-effective projects for each competing group.

THE CHOICES AVAILABLE

Although New York has numerous distinct constituencies, many of which have coalesced around only one or two issues, they can be grouped into several broad categories: the poor (welfare recipients, the aged poor, and others more or less permanently outside the labor force); resident taxpayers (the "middle class") and neighborhood businesses; the "elite" New York businesses; the businesses that manufacture and distribute goods in the national and international markets; and the municipal unions. These five interest groups correspond to the five major sources of personal income in the city: transfer payments; public employment; and three types of private employment— the local sector, the white-collar export sector, and the blue-collar export sector. There may be somewhat uneasy alliances within some of these categories (for example, the first category includes both many criminals and their victims; the second category includes both landlords and tenants); but we will show that a fairly coherent and internally consistent policy program can be drawn up for four of these groups. The fifth, the municipal unions, has a more limited range of interests than the others. Although they are concerned in the short run with their members' welfare and in the long run with the city's solvency, and although they often take positions on subjects not directly affecting them, they are essentially neutral on many of the development issues we are concerned with here. The next section will present a detailed strategy for each of the other four interest groups (the first is a "shrinkage" strategy, the second, third, and fourth are economic development strategies), and finally, we will consider how the four programs might best be integrated.

"Shrinkage" Strategy

1. A strategy designed to help the city's poor would concentrate on delivering assistance and social services, while providing relatively fewer benefits to middle-class residents or to businesses. To some extent, this policy was for a long time the unofficial choice in New York and elsewhere, as George Sterblieb and Norton Long lamented

as early as 1971,[2] but it has never been pursued to its logical conclusion.

Such a policy has several things to recommend it. First, it is humane, and New York has a long tradition of initiating humane policies. New Yorkers have a deep sense of responsibility to those in need. When levels of support have to be reduced, many taxpayers as well as recipients are distressed.

It also is something New York can do well. As a result of past policies, New York has a vast support system. The municipal health and hospital system, the welfare bureaucracy, the city's charitable institutions, and the community antipoverty agencies have acquired an enormous expertise and organizational capacity for managing and relieving the effects of poverty.

It also is apparent that the clientele for income support and health and social services is growing, if only because the city's elderly population is increasing.

The growing awareness that poverty and health are national responsibilities may make such a policy easier to finance in the future than it has been in the past. If welfare reform and a national health program are enacted in the next few years, New York may be able to combine a high level of service with fiscal stability. In effect, the city would be contracting with the federal government to deliver services to its own needy residents.

Finally, by declaring that New York has irretrievably lost its locational advantages for most forms of public and private enterprises (except social service delivery), the city would eliminate the necessity of carrying out expensive and risky economic development programs. Few such programs have been notably successful in New York or elsewhere.

Additions to the infrastructure, even in forms that would benefit growing industries (for example, the World Trade Center), have not been fully utilized. In a declining city, building new housing speeds the deterioration of old housing. Tax abatements for industry have been criticized on several grounds: they subsidize the federal government (local taxes being deductible from federal taxes); they tend to be used for projects that, according to many surveys,[3] would have been carried out in any case; and they are very expensive. Large-scale projects like industrial parks can be administrative nightmares—the Flatlands Industrial Park in Brooklyn took a decade to build. In general, development efforts do not seem to have generated many jobs in the private economy. The major effect has been to increase the proportion of workers dependent, directly or indirectly, on government payrolls and contracts. Whether no economic development policy could have made the city more attractive to business, whether the city's inability to provide sufficient incentives for development is due to resistance from "captive" taxpayers and other would-be recipients of city expenditures, or whether the development projects undertaken were poor choices is unclear. Whatever the reason for this failure, many people have lost faith in development and regard it as throwing good money after bad.

Concentrating on social services, though, has its drawbacks. Offering first-rate social services means diverting funds and attention from maintenance of the city's physical environment; the city's primary function would be caring for those left behind by the modern world. Many people—including the poor themselves—find the notion of living in such a reservation distasteful and insulting. The idea that New York may become a place where nothing important happens, where those with ambition plan their escapes, is frightening and depressing. It is incompatible with the images of New York as the "Big Apple," as a trend-setter, as the transformer of immigrants into citizens—images as powerful as that of the generous and protective city. Even if these other images are no longer realistic, it will not be easy to give them up: the adverse public reactions to Roger Starr's call for "planned shrinkage"[4] give some indication of the political obstacles to the lowering of sights. And the economic revival of the last year and a half indicates that the city's economy is not demonstrably beyond redemption. In these circumstances, a policy of abandonment is much harder to defend.

Yet it is worth exploring what policies are suited to our city-as-charitable institution. If the city devoted its resources to transfer payments rather than to productive activities, it could not only avoid development projects but also minimize other public expenditures currently undertaken to enhance the "business climate." If its energies were devoted to taking care of the poor, the city would not need to offer much postsecondary education, vocational training, or other educational "frills." It could keep basic services to the minimum necessary to maintain social order and to meet federal regulations. It would not have to construct new transit lines, or housing, or sewage lines.

The city could further reduce costs by relocating some of its excess residents—those unemployed workers who are likely to find jobs elsewhere. Relocation policies have been used both in Europe and in this country with some success; our American experience includes Depression-era programs as well as some pilot programs in 1963. The more successful policies include interregional job banks (where workers laid off in one area are automatically hired in another); travel and moving assistance; visiting allowances for people working far from home and living allowances to train for and to become established near a new job. Perhaps, since so many of the unemployed are youths who are not as mobile or independent as older workers, the city—or the state—might undertake a program of supervised relocation and training for youth, similar to the CCC of the 1930s but for private sector jobs. Although many of the city's unemployed will emigrate even without assistance, the city could take the initiative in order to speed up the process and make it less painful for both individuals and the city.

With the depopulation that has already occurred and that could be induced by relocation policies, the city could shrink to a smaller and more manageable size through large-scale demolition of housing and of obsolete industrial structures. Some authorities favor a "thinning" approach; others argue that a "clustering and clearing" strategy is more appropriate for a shrinking population.[5]

Clustering and clearing through a coordinated policy of public and private red-lining have been advocated on the ground that this strategy would preserve communities and would save energy, transportation, and public service delivery costs. These arguments are debatable. Neighborhood preservation programs are more likely to succeed in neighborhoods whose residents have some hope for upward mobility; a neighborhood with a high proportion of poor and desperate residents may not be able to generate a sense of community.[6] A neighborhood "triage" plan proposed to the city of St. Louis provoked considerable interracial and interneighborhood tension.[7] No one wants *his* neighborhood to be cleared. In fact, the announcement that an area was to be cleared would completely devalue its real estate. The city would have to operate some sort of land bank to reimburse property owners and to make sure that disinvestment and depopulation were carried out in an orderly manner.

As for savings on public service delivery, Thomas Muller, one of the leading authorities on local finances, says that they are "probably minor and would be insufficient by themselves to justify such a decrease."[8] In addition, large cleared areas would require some public investment to be made useful and safe as malls or parks.

Two things can be said, nonetheless for clustering and clearing. One is that much of the depopulation has already taken place, and whether by accident or by design of financial institutions, it has taken place in clusters. Some neighborhoods have decayed; others have not. It would make sense to make this de facto policy de jure as well. Second, clustering and clearing would facilitate the assembly of large tracts of land for future population growth.

Thinning, on the other hand, would provide more privacy and

would make sections of the city more attractive for its residents as they approached suburban densities. There would be numerous small vacant lots, which could be turned over to private or neighborhood use and could become amenities without much city investment.

If the city is not pursuing business, it does not have to worry about business reaction to its tax policies and can therefore continue to levy high and progressive taxes. It might also raise some revenue by selling to the suburbs at least some of its excess infrastructure capacity—water, sewage treatment buses, or whatever becomes unnecessary if the population declines.

Under a welfare strategy, the federal and state governments would become even more important as revenue sources. In fact, the city would have to develop a "foreign policy" design to maximize flows of transfer funds, lobbying the state and federal governments for formulas favorable to New York in the dispensation of welfare, health, housing assistance, Social Security, and other transferred funds. It would be equally important to identify and draw on all existing sources of funds and to spend them.

In summary, a strategy that focused on the needs of the service-consuming population could be undertaken only by leaving the middle class and the city's businesses to fend for themselves, by making the city smaller and more manageable, and by devoting the city's lobbying efforts to securing welfare reform and other increases in poverty funds.

Economic Development Strategies

Despite its unimpressive record to date, economic development in the last few years has become extremely popular. States and localities have pledged to hoist themselves up by their own boot-straps, and the federal government is committed to helping them do so. Today's domestic programs are more place- than people-oriented. The urban programs of the 1960s called for relief of distress and for services to individuals; those of the 1970s attempt to improve the business climate in order to create jobs. The urban crisis is no longer defined as a public sector problem but as a private sector problem. In essence, urban policy is increasingly macroeconomic policy applied at the local level.

Much of this interest in economic development seems to be an exercise of moral will, a reluctance to admit failure or to give up the cities as lost causes. It is an American tradition to struggle against the odds, to look for new frontiers to conquer, to meet challenges head-on. The case for economic development, however, does not have to rest on this base alone; several more solid arguments can be advanced in its defense.

First, national unemployment rates have been high since 1970. They are especially, and unacceptably, high in New York and in some of the nation's other large, aging cities. This differential is likely to be a fact of life in the foreseeable future. Only a few options are available for public policy in dealing with these unemployment differentials. One is to provide relief—unemployment insurance and welfare—directly to the victims. Of course, providing income support for hundreds of thousands of potentially productive workers is extremely expensive. In addition, because few new jobs are opening up, the ratio of long-term unemployed to total unemployed is very large in New York—50 percent higher than the national average.[9] In other words, New York does not have a constant flow of workers in and out of jobs, as the rest of the country does; workers laid off in New York tend to have a hard time getting back to work. Long-term unemployment leaves personal and social scars; its effects cannot be made up merely by replacing income.

Drawback

Another approach is the large-scale use of relocation policies to move workers to the available jobs, which was mentioned as part of the "planned shrinkage" strategy. This policy also has its drawbacks. Many people do not like to pull up roots, and would prefer to stay in the places they know, among the people they know. Moreover, some of those who would be relocated might have only recently migrated from depressed rural areas in the American South or Puerto Rico. The arguments advanced for their leaving the countryside fifteen and twenty years ago are essentially those made for their leaving the city today. Where will they be asked to leave tomorrow? The prospects of creating a permanent migrant class that is never absorbed into the economic mainstream is not pleasant.

The last option is to put people to work where they live—in other words, economic development. Given the difficulties of other approaches to unemployment, the failures of economic development programs look less serious.

A similar argument can be made for putting New York's capital assets back to work. New York has an excellent harbor and port facilities, the most extensive public transportation system in the nation, a multitude of schools and hospitals: a good, though run-down, municipal infrastructure. It also has a large private capital stock, including much basically sound housing and office space, and externalities generated by clusters of firms in various industries

assets

where geographical proximity is still important, most notably the advanced business service sector. The city still has attractions as a place to live and work, and sentimental attachments for many of its residents. But in the past twenty-five years, changes in technology, market conditions, individual preferences, and national policies have reduced the ability of many of New York's assets to generate real income. As a consequence, investment is being directed away from New York and toward more profitable locations, and many of the city's capital assets are unused or underused.

Some observers argue that regional decline is an efficient response to changed circumstances and that any attempt to reverse it will reduce the total national product. But although regional decline is well understood as a response to changing circumstances, the efficiency of the process is not self-evident. If the adjustment mechanisms are not working well, the decline may have been greater than was warranted by real social costs.

Examples of such market failure are not hard to find. Privately owned real estate cannot be easily moved around or reorganized; it has a notoriously "sticky" market, and when its value dips below the outstanding value of the mortgage on it, owners are often tempted to settle for getting the building's value as scrap or through insurance claims. Other types of market failure from which New York may have suffered include the prejudices of banks against small companies and self-fulfilling expectations of neighborhood decline.

Worst of all, there is no market at all for publicly owned assets. If, like some of the new planned communities, New York City were owned by a single developer, and it diminished in value, the developer could sell it at a loss and the life of the city could continue uninterrupted. Old capital assets would not be replaced, but sound stock would not be abandoned. But the "owners" of New York are its taxpayers, both individuals and businesses, and they are not forced to take responsibility for their capital losses. For the price of hiring a moving van, they can rid themselves of their share of New York and trade it for a piece of another community whose assets have been increasing in value. This exchange, when it takes place, worsens the position of those left behind. It increases not only their share of the original capital loss but also the loss itself because, with a smaller population, the infrastructure cannot be used efficiently. As these losses grow, they prompt still more people to leave. Thus, although a change in the value of corporate assets is followed by rapid equilibration in an orderly market, a decline in the value of a city's assets can set in motion a vicious downward spiral, causing the city to shrink much faster than it ought to.

If this explanation of New York's decline is correct, then those remaining in the foundering city have every right and obligation to try to reverse a process that is impoverishing them. By offering temporary incentives to newcomers, they can encourage utilization of the existing capital assets, and by adding new, more appropriate assets to the city's stock, they can raise the overall rate of return and reduce the temptation to leave.

Those remaining in the city, of course, are the so-called captive businesses and individuals. Economic development policy requires these taxpayers to pay the costs of luring others back; the captives, by definition, have a stake in the city's welfare, and may reap substantial benefits, monetary or otherwise, from their New York location.

Thus, economic development is justifiable both psychologically and practically. But it can take any of several forms.

2. One strategy with a great deal of political appeal is encouragement of the local sector (sometimes called import substitution). The key to a local sector strategy is to induce more people to live in the city independent of the growth of the export sector. Because people tend to shop, bank, and get haircuts in the neighborhoods in which they live and to buy locally printed newspapers and locally baked bread, an increase in the number of city residents would lead to an increase in local sector jobs in the city.

This strategy, with its emphasis on local self-reliance, would be a source of civic pride. Rather than plead with outsiders to invest in New York, New Yorkers would support one another. The strengthening of the local market would attract investment. According to one school of thought, "Almost anything that a government can do to reduce the uncertainty about sales is more likely to successfully induce business people to go ahead and invest than any other kind of public action."[10]

The local sector may be the only possible source of growth for New York. Local or regional markets in many parts of the country are now large enough to establish their own sources of supply. (Small markets do not permit efficient production of many goods and services.) For example, the volume of manufacturing in the South today supports large headquarters-business service-finance complexes in Atlanta and Houston. If other cities are practicing import substitution, New York may have no one left to export to. (This view is disputed, however, by Stanback and Drennan, who argue that functions are "passed down" from larger to smaller centers as the whole economy grows and that the largest centers—such as New York—must keep looking for broader markets and higher levels of specialization.[11])

Another advantage of this strategy arises from the composition of the local sector of the economy. Small businesses—typical of retail, personal services, or light manufacturing—are especially able to absorb the immigrants arriving in New York and to give them opportunities for upward mobility.

The most serious objection to local sector strategy is that it depends for its success on the city becoming an attractive place to live. It is still too early to tell whether the young professionals transforming such areas of the city as lower Manhattan will prove to be the vanguard of a significant "back-to-the-city" movement. If this promise turns out to be illusory, a neighborhood strategy will be futile.

If it is to succeed, a local sector strategy must be designed to appeal to those metropolitan area residents who have the choice of living in the city or the suburbs and who, for some reason, incline toward the suburbs. This minority of metropolitan area residents is the "swing vote" that could make a great difference to the city's future.

This group can itself be divided into two distinct subgroups: one is made up of people working in New York and either living in the suburbs or likely to move there (the latter are usually young families with children and at least one white-collar worker). The second, and smaller, subgroup consists of people working in the suburbs but living, or likely to live, in the city.

The commuters (or potential commuters) from the suburbs are, for the most part, people who require and are in a position to demand a safe and pleasant living environment. They can only be persuaded to choose city living if they can be assured of good basic services, an educational policy that focuses on the needs of the more academically oriented students, and a renewal of the city's infrastructure, especially its mass transportation system. They also need more affordable and more easily available housing. They would appreciate relaxation of the regulations governing housing cooperatives so that they could buy apartments more easily and take advantage of the federal income tax deductions for homeownership. But they would require a varied choice of locations, types of neighborhoods, and types of housing because the freedom (real or perceived) of city dwellers to pursue an unconventional pattern of life is often what makes people choose the city over the suburbs as a place to live. Policies to facilitate conversion of loft space to residences (which would be incompatible with a blue-collar strategy) or "gentrification" of formerly lower income neighborhoods (which would be unacceptable under a welfare strategy) would attract this group.

The second target group, the reverse commuters, are mainly low-income, blue-collar workers, who, for reasons of cost, discrimination, or family ties, can more easily find satisfactory housing in the city. They are not usually so demanding as the suburbanites because they have fewer choices. But they need easy transportation to their suburban jobs. Improved public transportation for those going in the "wrong direction" might be a profitable investment.

For the most part, though, residents (or potential residents) do not have to be stratified. Many policies that will appeal to all or most of them do exist.

The local sector strategy is a neighborhood strategy. It requires support and coordination of all the successful community self-help devices that have been introduced over the last decade or so— community development corporations, neighborhood housing services, tenant management, "sweat" equity, urban homesteading, anti-red-lining, block associations—enabling residents to take an active part in maintaining and rebuilding their neighborhoods. Past experience has shown that opportunities for self-reliance create a sense of commitment and result in better physical preservation of the neighborhood.[1][2]

The city could take an active role in neighborhood preservation. It is already working in this direction with historic preservation districts, tax abatements and federal block grants for housing renovation, and a well thought out policy of providing support to neighborhood commercial strips. (The city's economic recovery plan calls for storefront renovations, beautification projects, pedestrian malls, street improvements, self-help security projects, urban renewal, zoning, tax incentives, and allocation of block grant funds to joint public/private efforts.) In addition, the city could grant automatic property tax relief for small improvements or, even better, could convert the property tax to a site-value tax to maintain a permanent incentive for improvements. (A site-value tax system assesses the lot but not the buildings on it; unlike the system now in use, it does not penalize improvements of property by increased taxation.) It could charge a stiff fee for abandonment. Finally, it could train the long-term unemployed to maintain and repair housing and supply them with technical support and low-cost materials. Such training programs have been successful in several instances, perhaps the best known being the Morrisania Project in the Bronx and the Portland Youth Project.

With the population dwindling, building new housing seems unnecessary, but the city should stand ready to build—or subsidize the building of—low- and moderate-income housing.

The goal of attracting people to live in the city calls for a pro-individual rather than a pro-business policy and an emphasis on "livability" rather than on more narrowly construed economic development projects. ("Pro-individual" in this context means catering to the individual who has some choice about where to live. Tax cuts and service improvements would leave little money in the budget for social services.) For example, a pro-individual policy calls for lowering taxes on personal income, retail sales, and residential property, rather than reducing business taxes. However, the local sector strategy can include measures to stimulate economic development. Development funds could be channeled (and in fact, are now being channeled) to the larger subcenters—downtown Brooklyn, Jamaica, and Fordham Road—to enhance their attractiveness as locations for nonheadquarters offices and large retail complexes. These areas could benefit from integrated transportation access, better parking, and such amenities as malls.

If the city pursues a local strategy, it will need to direct its Washington lobbying efforts toward such programs as the Comprehensive Education and Training Act (which trains the unemployed to work in city and nonprofit agencies), federal funding of infrastructure maintenance, community development grants, and aid to education. In addition, as part of its effort to provide basic services efficiently and cheaply, it should consider passing some of these functions to higher levels of government—water and sewage to regional authorities, for example. Some such steps have already been taken with the state's assumption of parts of the higher education and court systems.

3. Another strategy involves supporting the blue-collar export sector of the economy— attempting to reinstate New York as an important location for the manufacture and distribution of goods to national markets. The blue-collar export sector consists of the port and other transportation facilities and the manufacturing and wholesaling of several specialized types of consumer goods—apparel, jewelry, toys, cosmetics, and others. It has been declining faster than any other sector in recent years.

The strategy has won support on two grounds. One is known as the "worst-first" argument: since this sector (particularly manufacturing) is doing so poorly, it is most in need of attention. To put it another way, the losses in the manufacturing sector are responsible for New York's economic decline; if they can be halted, the city as a whole will recover. The Temporary Commission on City Finance subscribed to this point of view: "The major weakness in the city's economy has been in manufacturing. . . . An attempt must be made to retain and possibly even expand, the city's manufacturing base. . . . This is necessary to halt job losses."[13]

But the worst-first approach is not by any means universally accepted. Stanback and Drennan, for example, call it "a logical fallacy and a dangerous misuse of resources."[14] New York declined in the first place as a center for manufacture and distribution of goods because of such trends as the shift of population away from the Northeast and the consequent loss of access to markets, the obsolescence of industrial plants and industrial neighborhoods in New York, the loss of manufacturing jobs in the United States as a whole, and the increased capital-intensiveness and routinization of manufacturing. These changes cannot be wished away, and the city's chances of reversing them or their effects are slim.

The other possible justification for the blue-collar strategy is that it would preserve what is most valuable about New York: the richness of its economic and social fabric, which generates innovations and institutions that benefit society as a whole.

The social argument is tinged with nostalgia for New York as a "melting pot" and for small-business industries, such as the garment industry, as sources of upward mobility. In New York and in other cities, these industries allowed generations of immigrants, despite their lack of formal education or training, to support themselves, to raise families, and, in some cases, to buy their own businesses. In addition, the steady employment and the ease of entry into the work force they provided strengthened the ethnic neighborhood as a mediating structure; that is, hiring was done through neighborhood channels, rather than through school placement offices or governmental or private employment exchanges. The strong ethnic neighborhoods, in turn, provided moral and financial support for later generations to rise out of the ghettos.

But manufacturing is not necessarily the only avenue, or even the best avenue, of upward mobility. The social transformation process of the nineteenth and early twentieth centuries was very slow and painful. Labor-intensive manufacturing has always offered low wages and poor working conditions; in fact, pessimism about opportunities for upward mobility helped to motivate New York's turn-of-the-century manufacturing workers to embrace the emerging union movement. In any case, the manufacturing export sector is becoming more and more specialized and is calling for higher and higher levels of skills. These industries may no longer be the best place for most of the new immigrants to start. A local sector strategy might offer better opportunities for transformation of immigrants; the last few years have seen a proliferation of small groceries, fruit stands, and restaurants run by recent immigrants.

The economic innovation part of the argument rests on the fact that, in New York, small companies can easily rent space, hire workers, and purchase all sorts of materials and expertise to try out new processes and products. Consequently, a large number of patents have originated in New York. When the new process becomes routinized, or a reliable market has been established for the new product, the operation is moved to an out-of-town location, and the cycle begins all over again. A continuing erosion of New York's manufacturing base might thus interfere with technological development in the country as a whole.

However, this argument overstates the role of small companies in innovation. Market research and product development today are planned at corporate headquarters, financed with the aid of the companies' credit ratings, and executed at any convenient location. Product development is, in short, as routinized as mass production. Although some legitimate questions have been raised about the adequacy of corporate and government funding for basic research in recent years, technical innovation will not come to a halt if New York and other large manufacturing cities continue to decline.

A blue-collar strategy would depend on development projects favoring light industry, wholesaling, and transportation of goods. Improved access, changed traffic patterns, and the elimination of nonconforming uses would make profitable manufacturing neighborhoods more profitable. The city could protect marginal areas from the encroachments of residential developers, abandon obsolete and unsalvageable areas, and move clusters of closely linked industries to new, specially prepared locations (as it already has done with what is now the Hunts Point Produce Market). Moving industries would have the additional advantage of spreading more evenly around the city manufacturing and wholesaling, once heavily concentrated in Manhattan and the city's waterfront.

The city could direct its tax abatement program to manufacturing companies setting up business in the city, expanding their plants, or hiring new workers. Tax abatement and other measures for recruiting industry are most likely to succeed if they are geared to the needs of those industries for which New York is a reasonable location. New York's comparative advantage in manufacturing is in small, high value-per-weight, nonstandardized items; diamond jewelry is the archetypical example. This field is rather narrow, but not every item of this sort is currently being manufactured in New York. New products should be carefully analyzed for their potential suitability to New York.

One of the most important components of this strategy is the improvement of goods transportation systems. Improved access is needed for plants, warehouses, and industrial neighborhoods; in addition, goods must be able to get in and out of the city itself more efficiently. Container facilities must be installed in those parts of the Port of New York still lacking them. Physical restrictions on rail lines serving the city must be removed so that large conventional cars and "piggyback" cars can enter the city. A freight facility in the Bronx, Queens, or Brooklyn, and a rail ferry for the shipment of container freight between New Jersey and the Brooklyn waterfront are also necessary if transportation costs are to be made competitive with those in other regions. Westway, or some scaled-down version of the lower West Side Highway, must be built for goods that enter the city by truck. Bridges must be repaired and maintained.

Another aspect of this strategy is building up the supply of skilled labor for specialized industries. The city must shift educational funds from academic programming to specific vocational and technical training, and give a high priority to achieving minimum levels of competence for all students. It could establish or expand work-study programs for youngsters entering manufacturing and port-related industries.

Industry also needs better police and fire protection than it is currently getting. Some industrial neighborhoods are alleged to be emptying out because theft, vandalism, and arson by local youth gangs make it impossible to operate at a profit.

In addition, the city could expand and improve its program of aid to small businesses, offering management advice and identifying business policies that make better use of local resources. New York business could learn from any of several programs that have been successful elsewhere: the Selby bindery plant in St. Paul, which has an entirely part-time work force; a learning-on-layoff program in Chicago; several government-organized consortia of small businesses for training programs; and regional job banks.

It would not be necessary (or possible) under this strategy to provide more than the minimum of services to city residents. Mass transit, parks and recreation, welfare and social services, and housing development programs could be slighted; taxes on manufacturing and wholesaling would be lowered relative to other taxes.

"Foreign policy" efforts under the goods-export strategy would concentrate on making changes in federal programs, such as the investment tax and employment tax credits, transportation industry regulation, and highway building, that would lower industrial costs in New York, and on inducing the state to lower its business taxes.

④ Perhaps the most popular strategy for New York (as least among those whose views reach print) is to support the white-collar export sector—that section of the economy consisting of corporate headquarters and the legal, advertising, and other services supporting them, finance, communications, publishing and printing, the arts, and the tourist industry.

The white-collar export sector is the strongest part of New York's economy. Despite the much publicized loss of corporate headquarters, securities industry employment, and printing and publishing, the sector as a whole grew slightly between 1969 and 1973, which were disastrous years for the New York economy. Foreign business, especially foreign banking, has been the most vital industry in New York. Furthermore, the American economy as a whole is becoming increasingly white collar. Measures to benefit this sector, therefore, might have a large payoff.

The sector also offers (for the most part) good working conditions and relatively high wages. It is relatively clean and does not add to New York's air pollution problems. It attracts talented and ambitious young people to New York. It is modern, sophisticated, and often exciting. Above all, it is a tremendous source of civic pride: it is the justification for New Yorkers' feeling that they live in the capital of the world.

But it also has its drawbacks First, it is a Manhattan strategy. Most of the businesses involved in this sector are located in the Central Business District (59th Street to the Battery); measures to benefit these enterprises would help the outer boroughs only to the extent that outer-borough residents are employed in corporate service jobs. The strategy also is elitist. Although the white-collar sector employs a good many clerical and service workers and other lower- to mid-level employees, it also employs many of the most powerful and highly paid people in America. A policy that provides services to the wealthy at the expense of the poor runs contrary to the inclinations of many New Yorkers. Moreover, many white-collar workers live outside the city. Although these people are assets to the city, a policy of providing jobs mainly for commuters and new arrivals would do little to put unemployed residents back to work—one of the primary goals of economic development.

A headquarters strategy calls for economic development projects that benefit the midtown and downtown office districts. A Convention Center, such as the one now being planned, is an obvious centerpiece to the strategy; a real cleanup and renovation of Times Square is another; significant mass transit improvements are also important. The city would need to continue providing tax incentives for new office buildings and amenities in the Central Business District—pedestrian malls, waterfront and "vestpocket" parks, seating in the numerous office plazas that are theoretically open to the public. It would have to keep midtown much cleaner and safer and repair its streets. It would provide stronger support for cultural institutions and continue to advertise New York's attractions as a tourist and convention location.

Because white-collar employment is growing nationally and because many white-collar workers are highly skilled, they are much more mobile than, for example, garment industry workers, and their preferences are much more important in determining the location of firms, especially corporate headquarters. Thus, a headquarters strategy would have to make the city as attractive as possible to professional and managerial workers, both those who prefer to live in the city and those who prefer to commute. The city would have to improve suburban transit and its links with subway transit and make it easier to drive cars into the city, to the extent that such measures are consistent with EPA regulations. The city should encourage construction of upper-income housing, make it easier to buy co-ops and to convert lofts to residences, and continue its low assessments on single-family housing.

Certain businesses should be the targets of vigorous recruitment efforts. Foreign companies, for example, would be encouraged by the facilitation of international air travel and the deregulation of foreign banks. Everything possible must be done to keep New York the world's foremost money market. Stock transfer taxes must be eliminated; banking regulations altered so that New York can capture the "offshore" banking business now going to the Bahamas; and plans for the centralized stock market must be drawn up so as to keep as much business as possible in New York. Finally, the city must selectively recruit the headquarters of companies entering an active growth phase; according to a recent study, such companies make the most use of advertising, marketing, and financing services.[15]

For the most part, however, economic development strategies, rather than being selective, should be aimed at the whole white-collar export sector since the various industries have many of the same needs.

The city must improve its educational system if it is to attract high-level employees from outside New York. It must offer both schools to which such employees would want to send their children—more "magnet" schools, a more selective CUNY—and other schools that emphasize basic skills and produce competent clerical workers to staff the offices.

The headquarters policy requires less progressive income taxes and lower taxes on retail sales and residential property. Perhaps the city should imitate Ireland by exempting resident artists from local taxation. Except for nuisance taxes, such as the stock transfer tax, business taxes would not have to be lowered since the white-collar sector depends more on amenities than on tax advantages.

If this strategy were successful, it would increase the local tax base somewhat. The city would still have to make some cutbacks, however, probably in income support, social services, and amenities for poor neighborhoods.

Foreign policy for the city would be very difficult. Since the strategy means keeping New York America's premier city, the city would have to direct its lobbying efforts at limiting direct air flights between other cities in the United States and overseas, centralizing federal aid to the arts once again, limiting the implementation of the national stock market system, and trying to obtain special treatment for companies headquartered in New York. Since these programs are largely unjustifiable in national or equity terms, and are likely to arouse hostility elsewhere, they would have to be conducted with great caution.

* * *

If the city administration were to publicly adopt one of these four strategies, it would serve as a guide to policymakers. For example, one of the divisive issues in New York in the last two years has been the South Bronx, large parts of which have been gutted and abandoned. Despite a general agreement that "something should be done," and despite a federal and city commitment to do something, it has been difficult to devise a plan for the area that is satisfactory to everyone.

If the city were following a welfare strategy—giving up economic development as a lost cause and concentrating on the needs of the service-using populations—there would be little question about the future of the South Bronx. Large areas of it would be razed, and the inhabitants would be relocated to still vital areas of the city. Existing hospitals, schools, and other public facilities would be closed and construction of new facilities would stop.

A local-sector strategy, on the other hand, would call for rehabilitating the still-salvageable buildings in the South Bronx, constructing as much new housing as can be built with available federal funds, launching a concerted effort to make the neighborhood safe and livable once again, offering strong support to tenant and community organizations interested in rebuilding the neighborhood, and making funds available for renovation of commercial strips in the area. If this strategy were successful, it would draw people—perhaps former residents—into the South Bronx, thus relieving pressure in other housing markets in New York, lowering apartment rents generally (or slowing their rise), and ultimately, encouraging people to live in New York who might otherwise stay in or move to the suburbs.

In a blue-collar strategy, the unused acres in the South Bronx would be used to create large, modern, self-contained industrial parks, which could be new homes for existing industries, such as the garment industry, or made available to companies wishing to set up new plants in New York. Construction of such plants, of roadways providing access to them, and of other necessary infrastructure, possibly including electrical generating plants, would proceed simultaneously with the training of neighborhood residents (and, possibly, unemployed residents of other parts of the city) to work in the factories that were going to open in the industrial parks. Once the area was stabilized by sources of steady employment, revitalization of the residential areas adjacent to the industrial parks would follow.

Finally, a white-collar strategy would find little immediate use for the devastated areas of the South Bronx. In the short run, the South Bronx might be subject to a "clearing and cutting" operation similar to what it might receive under a welfare strategy. Proponents of a white-collar strategy would argue, however, that, in the long run, directing economic development aid to a Manhattan corporate-service complex and using manpower training programs to provide the work force needed by these businesses are the most effective ways to produce the economic growth necessary to stimulate a demand for real estate. With a strong city economy, the South Bronx, which is close to Manhattan, served by subway and bus routes, and equipped with water, sewers, and other infrastructure, may appear an attractive location and thus may be redeveloped by private interests.

However, for reasons discussed earlier, it is neither politically practical nor even desirable for the city to adopt and pursue any one of these strategies. The policy problem, then, is to integrate the most promising features of each strategy without having programs that cancel out one another's effects. To some extent, the various strategies are irreconcilable; for example, they have entirely different implications for tax policy. The neighborhood strategy calls for the tax burden to be shifted toward businesses and away from individuals; the blue-collar strategy calls for the opposite. But a balanced overall policy, making key concessions to all major interests, is possible.

While the purpose of this background paper is to clarify the options facing the city administration rather than to choose among them, we can at least suggest how the various strategies might be combined. The first step in combining the three economic develop-ment strategies is to evaluate policy proposals in terms of their effectiveness in keeping residents and businesses in New York, and the next step is to select those that are most effective in retaining taxpayers and reject those which are most discouraging to them. For example, loft conversion to unconventional living space may be highly desirable under a local-sector or white-collar policy, but under a mixed policy, it might be wiser to limit legal conversions and enforce the law against unauthorized conversions if the loss of manufacturing jobs exceeds the gain in middle-class taxpayers and the local-sector jobs generated by them. Encouragement of co-oping might be an alternative, non-job-destroying means of rebuilding the middle class.

The most difficult task is to balance economic development against the needs of welfare recipients and other social service users and municipal workers. Economic solutions can be found that will meet the needs of these groups in the manner least destructive to the city's private economy. But ultimately, choices must be made in which one interest must benefit at the expense of another. And these choices are, finally, political and depend on the relative influence and willingness of the various interest groups to accept them. There is no one best solution.

* * *

A failure to make hard choices now means that the city will continue to fritter away what options it has left, making it even more vulnerable to outside forces. The merit in examining the potential courses of action, which are not entirely mutually exclusive, is that it underlines the danger in pursuing a policy of drift, of being hostage to the host of short-term considerations, in particular, the pressing need to stave off fiscal disaster, which has unintended—and probably unfortunate—consequences for the long run.

With its limited resources and dwindling leverage, the city can least afford a policy of drift. A refusal to face realities and instead to hope for the best will not only prove injurious to the economic well being of many New Yorkers but also might incite political troubles. Certainly, Mayor Koch's proclaimed desire to remain as the city's chief executive for twelve years would be dashed as soon as it becomes clear to New York voters that his roseate vision of the future cannot be realized.

In the past, the time horizon of the city's political leaders was short. It did not have to be otherwise. Even in the dark days of the

Great Depression, there was faith in the future of the city and the nation. But the nation's growth cannot be counted on to bail out New York over the long run. Even though there is no assurance that the city can really shape its future, it must make the attempt to formulate policies that point in the direction that makes the most of what the city has to offer.

There is no need to be unduly pessimistic and to despair about the notion of managing—or guiding—decline. On the contrary, it presents a fresh opportunity for New York to act as a pacesetter for those sections of the nation afflicted with similar problems. Facing up to decline does not have to result in heartless or ruthless policies that, in any case, would be politically impossible. Instead, the objective should be a searching out for ways and means to make the city more livable and more productive for a somewhat smaller number of New Yorkers. Indeed, the city may well respond more positively and cooperatively to the challenge of adversity than to business—and politics—as usual. But what is needed most is a realistic strategy and the political will to work toward it.

Notes

CHAPTER 1

1. *Partisan Review*, Summer 1977.

CHAPTER 2

1. *Statistical Abstract of the United States, 1977*, Table 1373.
2. *Employment and Earnings*, Bureau of Labor Statistics.
3. Wilbur Thompson, "Economic Process and Employment Problems in Declining Metropolitan Areas," *Post-Industrial America*, ed. George Sternlieb and James W. Hughes (New Brunswick, N.J.: Center for Urban Policy Research, 1975), p. 189. Thompson gives as an example the shift from metal working to electrical machinery.
4. U.S. Federal Highway Administration, *Highway Statistics*, annual.
5. *Statistical Abstract, 1977*, Table 749.
6. Ibid., Table 708.
7. Ibid., Table 1353.
8. *Statistical Abstract, 1977*, Table 1050.
9. Ibid., Table 1097.
10. Ibid., Table 1365.
11. Here and elsewhere in this paper, "export" and "import" refer to interregional rather than international trade.
12. This fourth category is officially considered to be in the service sector but is really more closely related to the goods sector.

13. *Employment and Earnings*, Bureau of Labor Statistics.
14. This chapter uses employment rather than, for example, value-added or income as the basic economic indicator. There are fairly accurate data on employment, and the concept is a readily understandable one. Value-added data are not readily available, and income statistics can be misleading because of inflation and because income cannot always be measured where earned.
15. Bureau of Labor Statistics, Middle Atlantic Regional Office.
16. *Statistical Abstract, 1977*, Tables 1363, 1325, and 625.
17. *Employment and Earnings*, Bureau of Labor Statistics.
18. Ibid.
19. Shift-share analysis conducted by the Twentieth Century Fund staff for the years 1965-75. A shift-share analysis distinguishes growth or decline caused by an area's specific industrial mix from that caused by the competitiveness of its location. Shift-share analysis is not a very reliable tool because it is hard to break industrial categories down precisely enough to make the local industry really correspond to the national industry. Still, the analysis confirms the intuitive guess that New York has declined because it is an uncompetitive location rather than because its mix of industries was unfavorable.
20. Michael Greenberg and Nicholas Valente, "Recent Economic Trends in the Major North-Eastern Metropolises," *Post-Industrial America*, ed. George Sternlieb and James W. Hughes (New Brunswick, N.J.: Center for Urban Policy Research, 1975), p. 86.
21. The location quotient is the proportion of New York employment in a given industry divided by the proportion of national employment in the same industry. We have had to ignore apparent specializations that seem merely to reflect unusual consumption patterns in New York—for example, taxicabs. All the location quotients are calculated by the Twentieth Century Fund staff from the Bureau of Labor Statistics, *Employment and Earnings*, 1965 and 1975.
22. All wage comparisons from *Employment and Earnings*, Bureau of Labor Statistics.
23. See Conservation of Human Resources Project, Columbia University, *The Corporate Headquarters Complex*, December 1977, p. 44.
24. New York Convention and Visitors Bureau, unpublished data.
25. David Heaps and Patricia Hopkins, *1977 Census of Foreign-Owned Business in New York City* (New York University—GBA Working Paper #78-45, April 1978), pp. 1, 20.
26. Ibid., p. 11.
27. H. Georgiadis, "The Requirements of Foreign Multinational Enterprises Operating in the United States" (New York City Economic Development Administration, September 1972).
28. "The Touche Ross Survey of Foreign Businessmen in New York," conducted for Touche Ross & Company by McBain & Small, Inc. (New York, June 1978).
29. For a fuller discussion of these issues, see Edgar M. Hoover and Raymond Vernon, *Anatomy of a Metropolis* (New York: Doubleday/Anchor, 1962), pp. 74-109; and Conservation of Human Resources Project, *The Corporate Headquarters Complex*.
30. *Economic and Demographic Trends in New York City: The Outlook for the Future*, Temporary Commission on City Finances, 13th Interim Report, May 1977, pp. 32, 34.
31. New York State Department of Labor from the Decennial Census.

CHAPTER 3

1. Wilbur Thompson, "Economic Processes and Employment Problems in Declining Metropolitan Areas," *Post-Industrial America*, ed. George Sternlieb and James W. Hughes (New Brunswick, N.J.: Center for Urban Policy Research, 1975), p. 190.
2. U.S. Bureau of the Census, *Current Population Survey*.
3. *Statistical Abstract of the United States, 1977*, Table 661.
4. Bureau of Labor Statistics, Middle Atlantic Regional Office.
5. *Statistical Abstract*, Table 1485.
6. See, for example, David M. DeFerranti, et al., *The Welfare and Non-welfare Poor in New York City*, R-1381-NYC (The Rand Corporation, 1974); Miriam Ostow and Anne B. Dutka, *Work and Welfare in New York City* (Baltimore: Johns Hopkins University Press, 1975), p. 76; and Rita M. Maldonado, "Why Puerto Ricans Migrated to the United States in 1947-73," *Monthly Labor Review*, Vol. 99 No. 9, pp. 7-14.
7. Immigration and Naturalization Service, Annual Reports.
8. All the population figures cited in the discussion come from the Census Bureau decennial counts and intercensal estimates. Many observers, including some officials of the Census Bureau, believe that recent figures are unreliable because they miss most of the estimated 8 million undocumented (illegal) aliens in the United States. The Census Bureau is now attempting to estimate its undercount.

   The immigration and Naturalization Services and the New York City Department of City Planning estimate that there are about 750,000 undocumented aliens in New York City, most of whom have arrived since 1968. If all or most of these are uncounted by the census, then the city's population has not declined at all since 1970; it may even have grown.

   However, independent counts of subpopulations tend to confirm the census figures. For example, census estimates of school-age children are highly consistent with actual school enrollment. Undocumented immigrants are believed to make heavy use of the public schools; if their children had not been counted in the census, school enrollment figures would exceed the census count of children. In addition, declining employment and welfare rolls, as well as the abandonment of several hundred thousand housing units, point to a decline in population. We believe, therefore, that most of the undocumented aliens are in fact counted and that the census estimate of total population, at least in New York, is reasonably accurate.
9. U.S. Bureau of the Census.
10. For these purposes, aggregate figures hide more than they disclose; a more detailed analysis is necessary. Unfortunately, the detailed demographic data available on New York are not very good. Many of the answers given to the questions asked by the Census Bureau and other agencies are untruthful; even the truthful answers are not always correct (for example, Arley Bondarin, *New York City's Population—1974*, New School for Social Research, Center for New York City Affairs, 1976, points out that people tend to underestimate their own incomes because they forget about minor or irregular sources of income). To make matters worse, the intercensal estimates are based on small samples, not on complete counts. In general, the finer the breakdown, the smaller the sample and the less reliable the estimate. For example, it is possible to make fairly good estimates of the city's total Hispanic population but not of the average income of young Hispanic women working in white-collar jobs. Finally, it is hard to get

up-to-date figures. Most of the available census data on New York are for 1973 or 1974; anything may have happened since then. In the pages that follow, therefore, the reader must keep in mind that the conclusions in this chapter represent the piecing together of a puzzle from the data collected by the Census Bureau, the Bureau of Labor Statistics, the Bureau of Economic Analysis, and other agencies, rather than universally accepted facts.

11. Thomas Muller, "The Declining & Growing Metropolis—A Fiscal Comparison," in *Post-Industrial America*, ed. George Sternlieb and James W. Hughes (New Brunswick, N.J.: Center for Urban Policy Research, 1975), p. 199; Julie Da Vanzo, "Who Moves and Why," *Challenge*, Vol. 21, No. 4, pp. 55-57.

12. Arley Bondarin, op. cit., p. 34. It is often suggested that the estimates of female-headed families are exaggerated because many reported family break-ups are only nominal, having been engineered to obtain more public assistance money. However, a study by Blanche Bernstein and William Meezan ("The Impact of Welfare on Family Stability," New York, New School for Social Research, Center for New York City Affairs, June 1975) indicates that only about 7 percent of all aid-to-dependent-children cases fit into this category. There are enough genuinely broken families to support the theory that men are more likely to emigrate than women.

13. See Chapter 4.

14. Earnings, here and elsewhere in this paper, are defined as labor and proprietary income net of personal contributions for social insurance.

15. Emanuel Tobier, "Economic Development Strategy for the City," *Agenda for a City*, ed. Lyle C. Fitch and Annmarie Hauck Walsh (Beverly Hills: Sage Publications, 1970), p. 44.

16. New York State Department of Labor, from 1970 Census of Population. Of course, suburban commuters are not identical to emigrants from the city. Many commuters never lived in New York; many emigrants no longer work in the city. Still, the two categories overlap enough to suggest that those leaving the city have not been primarily low-paid workers.

17. Bureau of Labor Statistics.

18. It is equally true, of course, that the earnings lag is caused by a decline in the demand for labor in New York, but this explanation does not conflict with that given above. Such a decline in demand can be expected to lead to the emigration of those with the best prospects for employment elsewhere.

19. U.S. Bureau of the Census, *Current Population Reports.*

20. Ibid.

21. Tobier, op. cit. A considerable body of research confirms that, for the nation as a whole, black rural-urban migrants have been "among the most successful of the city's residents at overcoming personal disadvantages." (Peter A. Morrison, "New York State's Transition to Stability," in *The Decline of New York in the 1970's*, Center for Social Analysis, State University of New York at Binghamton, May 1977, p. 11.) The black migration to the cities did not merely transport poverty from one location to another; in many instances, it improved the lot of the migrants.

22. Arley Bondarin, op. cit., p. 64.

23. Ruth Fabricant Lowell, *The Labor Market in New York City* (City of New York, Human Resources Administration, Division of Policy Research, May 1975).

24. Very few Hispanics in New York are over 55; estimates of their incomes are probably highly unreliable.

25. According to the Board of Education, only 42.6 percent of students in grades 2 through 9 were reading at or above grade level in 1976 (compared

to 50 percent nationally). Much of this discrepancy can be attributed to the extraordinarily high percentage of pupils in private schools (23.8 percent, compared to 9.4 percent nationally), who presumably have high average reading levels, and to the high percentage of non-English-speaking pupils in the public schools (13.1 percent with at least some English language difficulty). Still, it cannot be claimed that city schools are doing a good job of educating their students.

26. See Chapter 4.
27. Peter Marcuse, *Rental Housing in the City of New York, Supply and Condition 1975-1978,* January 1979, pp. 138, 141.
28. Ibid., p. 6.
29. Ibid.
30. For a fuller exposition of these arguments, see the *Fifteenth Interim Report of the Temporary Commission on City Finances,* June 1977.
31. See George Sternlieb and James W. Hughes with Carl Horowitz, *Enhancing the Supply of Land & Buildings in Central Cities: The Local & State Government Role,* prepared for the HUD National Conference on Housing Costs, February 1979.
32. U.S. Bureau of the Census, *NYC Housing and Vacancy Surveys.*
33. New York City Planning Commission, *Report on the Fifth Year Community Development Plan & Program,* p. 11.
34. Ibid., p. 13.
35. Marcuse, op. cit., p. 7.

CHAPTER 4

1. The connection between income and local government expenditures is often obscured because it takes several years for a change in income levels to produce a corresponding adjustment in expenditures; public recognition of changes in income takes time, and still more time is required to translate this recognition into expenditures. Budgets are drawn up in the year before the expenditures are made, and many commitments are mandated by law or made years in advance; as a result, they are fairly inflexible. Statistical studies by the Twentieth Century Fund staff confirm a significant relationship between income and local government expenditures; expenditure changes correspond fairly closely to income changes of two or three years earlier. In general, an extra dollar of income will lead to an extra thirty cents of local government spending. See Stephen Barro, *Fiscal Conditions, The Urban Impacts of Federal Policies Vol. 3* (Santa Monica: Rand Institute, 1978), pp. 148-150. Other studies have shown that municipal unions tend to win greater concessions in times of prosperity because they and the public know that "the money can be found somehow."
2. U.S. Department of Commerce, Bureau of the Census, *Government Finances, 1975* (Washington, D.C.: U.S. Government Printing Office, 1976).
3. U.S. Department of Labor, Bureau of Labor Statistics, Middle Atlantic Regional Office.
4. U.S. Department of Commerce, Bureau of the Census, *Statistical Abstract of the United States, 1976* (Washington, D.C.: U.S. Government Printing Office, 1977).
5. U.S. Department of Labor, Bureau of Labor Statistics, Middle Atlantic Regional Office.
6. Ibid.
7. Breakdown of expenditure by object from Annual Reports of the Comptrol-

ler, as reprinted in the *Eighth Interim Report to the Mayor by the Temporary Commission on City Finances*, October 1976, p. 23.

8. *Sixth Interim Report to the Mayor by the Temporary Commission on City Finances*, May 1976, p. 11; *Statistical Abstract, 1977*, Tables 331 and 489.

9. Milwaukee Civil Service Commission, *Municipal Fringe Benefits and Related Pay Practices* (Milwaukee: City Service Commission Classification Division, October 1975).

10. *Seventh Interim Report to the Mayor by the Temporary Commission on City Finances*, June 1976, p. 21; *Statistical Abstract, 1977*, Table 523.

11. Expense Budget, City of New York, *Statistical Abstract, 1977*, Tables 463 and 472.

12. Lester C. Thurow, "New York: A Declining Activity," *New York Affairs*, Vol. 4, No. 3 (Summer/Fall 1977), pp. 14-23.

13. Bernard Gifford, "New York City: The Political Economy of Cosmopolitan Liberalism," *The Future and the Past: Essays on Programs, and the Annual Report 1976-77* (New York: Russell Sage Foundation, 1978), pp. 169-200.

14. The city could save money by cutting back on marginal services, such as eyeglasses, that the city hospital system would not have to cover.

15. John P. Keith and David Geyer, "In New York Welfare *is* Different," *The Journal of the Institute for Socioeconomic Studies*, Vol. 1, No. 1 (Summer 1976), pp. 68-86.

16. New York City Expense Budget, 1974-75.

17. *Government Finances, 1975*. This figure represents an average in which the majority of local governments have zero expenditures.

18. This chapter has used the same set of figures to argue that New York is not (relatively) inefficient and that it does not provide an unusual level of basic services. Obviously, they could be interpreted to mean that New York is extremely inefficient and provides very poor basic services, or that it is extremely efficient and provides a very high level of basic services. This is a matter of judgment. We find the first explanation most plausible.

19. These "state aid" figures include state mortgage and stock transfer taxes returned to the city. The city prefers to classify this aid (which amounted to $221 million in 1975) as locally raised revenue since it did, after all, originate in the city.

20. *Government Finances, 1975*.

21. Social services spending may have increased, at least in part, because it is more sensitive to changes in local income than is spending in other categories.

22. *Government Finances, 1975*.

23. Ibid.

24. There is no hard evidence on how many welfare recipients were discouraged from leaving New York City by the size and array of their benefits. Logic, however, suggests that, once received, the city's benefits were large enough to satisfy some people, particularly when it could be combined with untaxed income from one or another source.

25. Edward Gramlich, "The New York City Fiscal Crisis: What Happened and What is to be Done," *American Economic Review*, Vol. 66, No. 2 (May 1976), pp. 415-429.

26. Ken Auletta, *The Streets Were Paved With Gold* (New York: Random House, 1979), p. 60. The estimate was made by labor mediator Theodore Kheel.

27. Defined-benefit plans guarantee workers a certain retirement income. Thus, if the investments in the pension fund appreciate more slowly than was

anticipated, the city has to contribute more than it had planned. The increased take-home-pay provision was an assumption by the city government of most of the employees' contributions to the plans. Prior to 1963, the base for computing retirement income was the average of the retiree's three or five highest paid years; after 1963, the base was the final year's salary or the salary in effect at the time of retirement; on this basis, pensions can increase drastically if the employee receives a last-minute promotion or works overtime during his last year. The Heart Bill states that all policemen's and firemen's heart conditions are presumed service-related and therefore that policemen and firemen with heart disease can receive an extra disability pension.

28. *Seventh Interim Report to the Mayor*, passim.
29. Martin Shefter, "New York City's Fiscal Crisis, The Politics of Inflation and Retrenchment," *The Public Interest*, No. 48 (Summer 1977), pp. 98-127.
30. Terry N. Clark, "How Many More New Yorks?" *New York Affairs*, Vol. 3, No. 4, pp. 18-27.
31. Roger Starr, "The Dilemmas of Governmental Responses," *Post-Industrial America: Metropolitan Decline and Inter-Regional Job Shifts*, ed., George Steinlieb and James Hughes (New Brunswick, N.J.: Center for Urban Policy Research, 1975), p. 250.
32. See note 1.
33. Advisory Commission on Intergovernmental Relations, *Trends in Metropolitan America* (Washington, D.C.: U.S. Government Printing Office, February 1977).
34. Barro, op. cit., p. 141.
35. William H. Whyte, "End of the Exodus: The Logic of Headquarters City," *New York*, September 20, 1976, pp. 88-89.
36. See, for example, *Central City Business—Plans and Problems*, prepared for the use of the Subcommittee on Fiscal and Intergovernmental Policy of the Joint Economic Committee, 95th Congress, 2nd Session (Washington, D.C.: U.S. Governmet Printing Office, 1979).
37. Roger C. Vaughan, *The Urban Impacts of Federal Policies, Vol. II: Economic Development* (Santa Monica: Rand Institute, 1977), pp. 72-73. An exception is the recent study by Ronald E. Grieson, William Hanovitch, Albert M. Levenson, and Richard D. Morgenstern, "The Effect of Business Taxation on the Location of Industry," *Journal of Urban Economics*, 4, 170-185, which finds that the 1966 increase in taxes on manufacturing accounts for about two-thirds of the 1966-71 loss in manufacturing employment.
38. The 1977 increase of 2 percent, which seems alarmingly low, is actually due to the removal of public housing and city property from the tax rolls, where they never belonged.
39. Commuters account for only a small part of the income and sales taxes collected, but probably a larger proportion of property tax collections.
40. State Study Commission for New York City, *New York City: Economic Base and Fiscal Capacity—Summary*, 1973, p. 36.
41. Advisory Commission on Intergovernmental Relations Trends in Metropolitan America.
42. Ibid.
43. Dick Netzer, "The New York City Fiscal Crisis," *The Decline of New York in the 1970s*, Benjamin Chinitz, ed. (Binghamton: Center for Social Analysis, 1977), p. 162.

44. Short-term debt can be used legitimately to finance construction if long-term interest rates are temporarily high, or to smooth out fluctuations in revenues. Hence, it can be expected to rise as tax and intergovernmental revenues increase and as long-term debt issues rise.

CHAPTER 5

1. Roger Starr, "The Dilemmas of Governmental Responses," ed., George Sternlieb and James W. Hughes, *Post-Industrial America* (New Brunswick, N.J.: Center for Urban Policy Research, 1975), p. 253.
2. Twentieth Century Fund staff analysis shows that city employment growth appears to be more closely related to unemployment rates than to other indicators of economic health, such as the growth rates of the Gross National Product or nationwide employment levels.
3. Michael L. Wachter, "The Changing Cyclical Responsiveness of Wage Inflation," *Brookings Papers on Economic Activity (1:1976)* (Washington, D.C.: The Brookings Institution, 1976), pp. 115-167.
4. *Statistical Abstract, 1977*, Table 626.
5. U.S. Department of Commerce, Bureau of the Census, *Census of Manufactures, 1972* (Washington, D.C.: U.S. Government Printing Office, 1973).
6. Ibid., and *Census of Manufactures, 1958*.
7. E. Blaine Liner, "The Snowbelt and the Seven Myths," paper prepared for Southern Growth Policies Board, January 1978.
8. See Peter A. Morrison, "Overview of Demographic Trends Shaping the Nation's Future." Testimony before the Joint Economic Committee, May 31, 1978.
9. Richard P. Nathan, "The Outlook for Federal Grants to Cities," ed., Roy Bahl, *The Fiscal Outlook for Cities* (Syracuse: Syracuse University Press, 1978), p. 88.
10. *Statistical Abstract, 1977*, Table 464.
11. U.S. Department of Commerce, Bureau of the Census, *City Government Finances*, 1974-75 (Washington, D.C.: U.S. Government Printing Office, 1976).
12. *Statistical Abstract, 1977*, Table 419.
13. U.S. Department of Labor, Bureau of Labor Statistics, Middle Atlantic Regional Office.
14. Kevin Balfe, "The Economic Role of the City," *Commentary*, Vol. 2, No. 1 (January 1978), p. 12; based on presentations at the National Council for Urban Economic Development 10th Annual Conference.
15. The first two polls were Gallup polls and the third was conducted by Louis Harris and Associates. They are quoted in the President's Urban and Regional Group report, "A New Partnership to Conserve America's Communities: A National Urban Policy," March 1978, p. I-17.
16. See Judy Rubin and Phil Baum, *Analysis of Arab Trade in Major U.S. Ports* (mimeo), prepared for Commission on International Affairs, American Jewish Congress, New York, 1976.
17. President's Urban and Regional Group report, "A New Partnership to Conserve America's Communities," p. 11.
18. The U.S. Department of Labor, Bureau of Labor Statistics, Middle Atlantic Regional Office reports that "higher level" budget in the New York area in the autumn of 1974 was 23% above the national average, while the "intermediate" level was only 16% above average.

19. Charles A. Zielinski, "Report on Summer 1978 Electric Demand/Supply and Consolidated Edison's System," Public Service Commission, June 1978.
20. Bureau of Labor Statistics, Middle Atlantic Regional Office.
21. Conservation of Human Resources Project, *An Economic Development Agenda for New York City*, December 1975, pp. 9-12.
22. Ruth Fabricant Lowell, *The Labor Market in New York City*, Human Resources Administration, City of New York, 1975.
23. *Thirteenth Interim Report to the Mayor of the Temporary Commission on City Finances*, May 1977, p. 61.
24. Bureau of Labor Statistics, *Monthly Labor Review*, November 1976.
25. The City of New York, Official Statement, "General Obligation Serial Bonds," November 1976, p. 59.

CHAPTER 6

1. Blanche D. Blank, "The Myth of Management Magic," *New York Affairs*, Vol. 4, No. 2, pp. 24-32.
2. George Sternlieb, "The City as Sandbox," and Norton Long, "The City as Reservation," *The Public Interest*, 25 (Fall 1971), pp. 14-21 and 22-38 (respectively).
3. See Bennett Harrison and Sandra Kanter, "The Political Economy of State 'Job-Creation' Business Incentives," ed., George Sternlieb and James W. Hughes, *Revitalizing the Northeast: Prelude to an Agenda* (New Brunswick, N.J.: Center for Urban Policy Research, 1978), pp. 264-266.
4. For a description of the "planned shrinkage" idea and the public reaction to it, see Roger Starr, "Making New York Smaller," ed., Sternlieb and Hughes, op. cit.
5. For a fuller discussion, see Wilbur R. Thompson, "Land Management Strategies for Central City Depopulation," in Committee Print of the Subcommittee on the City, *How Cities Can Grow Old Gracefully*, Committee on Banking, Finance and Urban Affairs, U.S. House of Representatives, 95th Congress, 1st Session (Washington, D.C.: U.S. Government Printing Office, 1977), pp. 67-78.
6. Alan Kravitz, "The Other Neighborhoods—Building Community Institutions," in *How Cities Can Grow Old Gracefully*, pp. 91-96.
7. S. Jerome Pratter, "Strategies for City Investment," in *How Cities Can Grow Old Gracefully*, pp. 79-90.
8. Thomas Muller, "Service Costs in the Declining City," in *How Cities Can Grow Old Gracefully*, p. 129.
9. U.S. Bureau of Labor Statistics, *Handbook of Labor Statistics*; and Middle Atlantic Regional Office.
10. Harrison and Kanter, op. cit., p. 256.
11. Thomas M. Stanback, Jr., and Matthew Drennan, *The Transformation of the Urban Economic Base: Information Paper*, Conservation of Human Resources Project, Columbia University, 1977.
12. Kravitz, op. cit., pp. 91-96.
13. The Temporary Commission on City Finances, "Taxation and Manufacturing in the Northeast," in Sternlieb and Hughes, ed., op. cit., p. 279.
14. Stanback and Drennan, op. cit.
15. Conservation of Human Resources Project, Columbia University, *The Corporate Headquarters Complex in New York City*, 1977, p. 16.

Capital Construction Needs of New York City in the 1977-86 Period

David A. Grossman
President, The Nova Institute

Preface: Events since the Study Was Completed

This examination of New York City's capital needs in the 1977-86 decade was completed in February 1977. At that time, the city had little hope of meeting even its most basic capital needs. Fiscal crisis had foreclosed the city's access to the municipal bond market. Even access to the resources of the municipal employee pension funds and to federal and state aid permitted only "bare-bones" capital budgets in fiscal years 1976 to 1978.

The purpose of the study was to assess the amount of capital funding needed to forestall decay and deterioration of the city's physical plant. Conducted at a time when no adequate source of financing was in sight, the study found a sharp contrast between municipal needs and the capacity to address them. The report was circulated in draft form to the municipal agencies and others who contributed data to the city's central budgeting and planning agencies: the Office of Management and Budget and the Department of City Planning.

In January 1978, the new administration of Mayor Edward I. Koch issued its Financial Plan for the next four fiscal years (1979 to 1982). The plan, substantially developed during the last months of

An earlier draft of this paper on Capital Construction Needs, by David A. Grossman, was released in January 1978.

the administration of Mayor Abraham D. Beame, focused on actions essential to close the expense budget gap, to fund out the remaining short-term deficit, and to provide long-term financing for a capital program. The central features of the Financial Plan were a ten-year forecast of city capital needs and a proposal for federal guarantees to enable the city to borrow the capital funds needed for the first four years of the ten-year construction program. The city's analysis of capital needs included many pages of the text of this study. (See *The New York Times*, January 29 and 30, 1978.)

After nine months of major effort by public and private organizations, both houses of Congress approved legislation to provide federal guarantees for long-term borrowing by New York City. In August 1978, President Jimmy Carter signed the bills into law in a ceremony at City Hall.

Meanwhile, the federal government had begun to examine the infrastructure needs of older cities throughout the nation. In July 1977, the Joint Economic Committee of the Congress stated that "[m]aintenance and upgrading of the public infrastructure, and particularly reversing the downward trend in capital expenditures, appears to be the single greatest problem facing our nation's cities."

Federal agencies have responded to this recognition of need by undertaking major analyses of national public works needs. In October 1977, the U.S. Department of Housing and Urban Development directed the Urban Institute to undertake a study of urban infrastructure needs. In September 1978, the U.S. Department of Commerce awarded a contract for a national study of public works investment to provide the basis for a report by the Public Works Committees of the Congress.

In the nearly two years since this study was completed, the city has acquired the means to engage in a major effort at infrastructure improvement. And the growing recognition that infrastructure is a critical national urban problem seems likely to result in increased and refocused federal aid programs. New York as well as other cities should benefit from this policy shift. New York has only begun to address its capital needs, but the prospects now appear far more promising than in 1977, and the financing for at least the next four-year period now appears to be in place.

David A. Grossman
December 1978

Chapter A1

Introduction

In a high density urban environment, a sound physical infrastructure—streets, subways, water and sewer lines, and other public facilities—is essential to overall economic and social health. New York City's public infrastructure has long been one of the city's major assets. It has fostered the growth and development of what may well be the world's most complex urban environment. And the city's public agencies have a long tradition of pioneering in the application of innovative and imaginative solutions to the problems of high population density. If New York City is to overcome its present difficulties and construct a solid economy for the next decade, investment in the maintenance and development of its physical infrastructure will have to be among its priority concerns.

CAPITAL CONSTRUCTION IN THE PAST DECADE

The New York City fiscal crisis of 1975 brought publicly financed construction in the city to a near standstill. From 1969 to 1975, public investment in capital construction had been heavy (except in 1971, when the city postponed building awards in order to induce contractors and unions to accept minority workers on the job), peaking in 1973, when over $1.1 billion in city construction contracts were awarded. (See Table A1-1.) Part of this increase reflected inflation, but most of it represented a sharp increase in actual new construction.

Table A1-1. New York City Construction Awards by Years, 1966-76[a]

Fiscal Year	Construction Awards ($ Millions)
1966	$204.3
1967	248.4
1968	216.2
1969	464.4
1970	722.8
1971	406.7[b]
1972	920.0
1973	1,111.6
1974	698.4
1975	761.6
1976	316.2

Source: Annual Reports of the Director of Construction, City of New York.

[a]Includes only amount of construction award, not architectural or engineering costs, land, furniture and equipment, etc.

[b]A moratorium on many construction awards was imposed during this year to help implement a minority employment program.

In 1976, city construction contract awards amounted to only $316 million, the lowest level since 1968, and 70 percent of these were for transit projects largely funded by federal grants. Because of the fiscal crisis, only small amounts of city funds were available for new construction or even maintenance.

Table A1-2 shows the distribution of city contract awards over the past decade. Education projects accounted for the largest amount of new construction (29 percent), and water pollution control ran a close second (22 percent). The table accurately indicates the percentage distribution of total city infrastructure investment by category, but it does not include all such funds; city agencies spent additional hundreds of millions of dollars in maintenance and minor rehabilitation efforts to maintain the quality of the municipal plant. Moreover, major parts of the infrastructure are financed and constructed by state agencies, regional authorities, and private utilities. Comparable data are not available on these activities.

Table A1-2. Construction Awards by New York City Agencies by Major Categories, 1966-76

Agency or Function	Total Construction Awards (in $ Millions)	Percent of Total
Education[a]	$1,775.5	29.2%
Water pollution control	1,342.5	22.1
Transit	990.9	16.3
Public buildings[b]	529.8	8.7
Health and hospitals[c]	494.1	8.1
Water supply	328.2	5.4
Highways and traffic	266.2	4.3
Parks and museums	208.3	3.4
Ports and terminals	113.2	1.8
Sanitation	22.0	0.4
Total	$6,070.6	100.0

Source: Annual Reports of the Director of Construction.

[a]Includes Board of Education, Educational Construction Fund and CUNY.

[b]Includes facilities for courts, correction, police, fire, branch libraries and other facilities under jurisdiction of the Department of Public Works.

[c]Includes State HFA projects.

PROBLEMS FACING THE INFRASTRUCTURE

New York must make a continuing investment in the many aspects of its complex physical infrastructure if it is to maintain its vitality as a place to live and work. Planning to meet these capital needs, financing the necessary improvements, and completing construction projects on schedule to meet changing public requirements are challenging tasks.

The challenge looms especially great in the coming decade. New York City must confront and resolve the serious fiscal problems that have closed off its access to the security markets and brought its construction programs to a virtual halt. The long-term erosion of the city's economy, characterized at first by continuing losses in factory jobs and more recently by declines in total employment, will strain the city's capacity to finance infrastructure improvements while placing new and costly demands on some physical systems.

Investment in the physical infrastructure must meet:

1. *Maintenance requirements.* Some minimum level of annual investment is needed simply to combat the effects of decay and deterioration. For example, the city's 6,000 miles of streets and water mains are currently being renewed at rates that approximate a 200-year replacement cycle. Whatever the optimal replacement cycle may be, it seems unreasonable to expect street paving or water pipes to hold up for two centuries. The maintenance requirement has two aspects: First, the city must invest enough each year to keep system quality from deteriorating; second, because the city has failed to make such investments consistently, many municipal facilities now need major repairs. Inadequate maintenance is largely responsible for the collapse of portions of the West Side Highway. The equally exposed elevated rapid transit structures have been relatively well maintained, and are in substantially sound condition, although they are older than the West Side Highway.
2. *New capacity requirements.* A substantial part of New York City's $6 billion in construction awards between 1966 and 1976 went to meet new capacity requirements or to replace wholly obsolete facilities. The city built, among other things, new schools and colleges to provide for substantially increased enrollment; water pollution control plants to treat raw wastes and extension of sewers to unserved areas; and additions to the stock of prisons, police stations, and courts.
3. *Changing standards.* Another factor that generates demand for construction—one that is not always clearly distinguishable from new capacity considerations—is changes in the standards for public services. Air and water quality standards have risen markedly in recent years; in response, New York City has installed costly control systems on municipal incinerators and upgraded water pollution control facilities from primary to secondary treatment capacity. Environmental concerns, requirements that facilities such as buses and subways be adapted to the needs of the handicapped, and hearings to allow community comment and participation in facility design are all changes in standards that, however desirable, have both increased construction costs and created new demands.

RISING CONSTRUCTION COSTS

Apart from these abiding problems, infrastructure investment in the 1970s has encountered rising costs for construction relative to the general price structure. In recent years, the United States has experienced the most rapid inflation in its history, and in most years of the past decade, construction costs in New York City have risen as much as twice as fast as the general cost-of-living index. The recession of 1974-76 slowed this inflation temporarily, but most construction agencies in the city are anticipating cost increases of 5 percent to 7 percent annually—and are hoping that they will not be higher. In the past decade, the costs of many construction projects have doubled or even tripled over the three to five years from start of design to ground breaking.

Infrastructure Priorities and Needs

In view of New York City's difficult fiscal plight, future planning for the maintenance and upgrading of the city's physical infrastructure must be influenced by careful attention to priorities. Ultimately, priorities for the spending of public funds are decided by the political process, subject to the constraints of the marketplace that determine the amount of current revenue and borrowing that is available to finance construction. Within this context, however, it is important to consider what ought to be the construction priorities for New York. It is suggested that these can best be divided into three categories:

First priority would be assigned to maintenance of those physical elements that are absolutely critical to continued operation of a high-density urban center. The major urban systems in this category are water supply and distribution, electricity, mass transit, and the arterial highway system. Significant failures or shortfalls in service availability in these four systems would strike at the heart of urban life.

Second priority would be assigned to systems of less critical importance but whose operation is nonetheless essential to a viable city: air transportation, solid waste collection and disposal, and the components of the sewer and sewage treatment system essential to prevent flooding and to avoid serious health problems.

Third priority items include the complex of public buildings that contain important public services, such as schools and colleges, hospitals, and police and fire stations. Fortunately, New York City has already invested heavily in these elements in recent years so that there are few urgent problems to be addressed. Also included in these third priority items are capital facilities to assist in expansion of the city's economy (such as industrial parks) and important elements of urban amenity, such as parks and museums.

These three categories roughly correspond to the four priorities set forth by the City Planning Commission in its 1966-67 Capital Improvement Plan:[1] maintenance of vital services, maintenance of public facilities, reinforcement of revenue-producing and job-generating projects, and protection of the urban environment.

Within each urban system, some elements have higher priority than others. For example, maintaining the existing subway system is clearly of more immediate importance than constructing a new Second Avenue subway. But it is often difficult to judge whether a major capital investment is of critical importance or only desirable; the Third City Water Tunnel presents the city with one of its most difficult decisions in this regard. It also is difficult to determine the level of investment necessary to maintain a system in operating condition; at current replacement rates, some ancient water and sewer lines will have to last for more than a century.

MASS TRANSIT

New York City's mass transit system is operated by the Transit Authority (TA), a major subdivision of the state-chartered Metropolitan Transportation Authority (MTA). The mass transit system has two major components: rail rapid transit and surface operations.

The rail rapid transit system consists of 6,700 subway cars operating on 232 miles of track (137 miles underground, 72 miles of elevated structure, and 23 miles of open cut). At present, the system carries about 1 billion passengers per year, down from an average of about 1.3 billion per year in the 1960s. Another MTA subsidiary, Staten Island Rapid Transit Operating Authority, operates an additional 52 cars on a single rail line on Staten Island.

The surface transit system is primarily composed of 4,400 buses operated by the TA and its subsidiary Manhattan and Bronx Surface Transit Operating Authority. The public bus system carries about 700 million passengers per year.

In the past decade, transit construction, involving major investments both in the existing rail system and equipment and in construction of new subway routes, has been a major capital investment priority for the city. From 1966 to 1976, 16 percent of all city construction funds were allocated to transit. In 1976, when total city construction starts fell sharply due to the fiscal crisis, transit accounted for $224 million of the $316 million in new construction, but much of the money for transit was supplied by the federal government.

The New Route Program

In 1968, New York City committed itself to a major expansion of its rapid transit system. As approved by the Board of Estimate, the expansion program was to include a new Second Avenue subway running the length of Manhattan and into the Bronx; major additions to the main trunk line from Jamaica, Queens, into Manhattan; an additional line reaching farther out into Queens along the Long Island Expressway; and some short additional sections in Brooklyn. In the years since then, as the anticipated cost of subway construction has increased sharply, federal assistance has been less than was hoped for, and the availability of city capital funds has diminished, forcing a major cutback in these construction plans. At present, the "new route" construction program to which the city and the MTA are committed calls only for completion of the Queens "trunk" route from Sixth and Seventh avenues in Manhattan through the new 63rd Street tunnel to the Jamaica area in Queens by the mid-1980s.

Some construction has been completed on the Second Avenue line, but all work on this $2 billion facility is now suspended. It seems unlikely that any additional construction on the Second Avenue line will be undertaken prior to the 1980s.

The low-priority lines in Brooklyn have been postponed indefinitely, and none of the subway construction planned in connection with an expanded Long Island Expressway has even been scheduled.

Table A2-1 presents data on present commitments and potential additions that were part of the 1968 plan for subway expansion. The financing expected to be available for the committed construction (essentially the Queens trunk line) consists of about $100 million per year—one-half of anticipated federal grants of about $200 million per year—together with about another $40 million per year in city funds and state grants (from the $600 million made available through a 1967 bond issue).

Table A2-1. Major Mass Transit Capital Projects Under Way or Planned in New
York City (in Millions of 1974/75 Dollars)

Item	Committed by End of 1975	Remaining Cost
Transit Authority facilities		
1. 63rd Street Subway	$170.9	$ 470.3
2. Archer Avenue-S.E. Queens line	82.4	354.6
3. Queens high-speed bypass	0.4	349.2
Subtotal, priority routes*a*	253.7	1,174.1
4. Second Avenue subway north of 42nd Street	79.5	1,042.2
5. Second Avenue subway south of 42nd Street	44.1*b*	1,065.0
6. Bronx high-speed bypass	3.2	282.1
Subtotal, Transit Authority	380.5	3,563.4
MTA facilities		
7. East Side LIRR access via 63rd Street tunnel	83.2	500
8. JFK Airport rail access	—	400
Subtotal, MTA	83.2	900
Total, New York City	$463.7	$4,463.4

Source: From Table 6, Regional Plan Association, *Financing Public Transportation*
(1976, reprinted by permission of the RPA). Table 6 cites as sources the MTA and Tri-State
Regional Planning Commission.

*a*Includes portion attributable to Second Avenue Subway.

*b*More than $25.8 million of this amount has been uncommitted since the date of the
RPA study.

The Existing System Program

New York City's six-year transportation program policy statement of
1975[2] allocated nearly equal construction funding to the existing
system ($1.35 billion) and to the new routes program ($1.47 billion
for completion of the Queens trunk line). This policy has been
substantially followed since 1975.

Table A2-2 shows the major elements of the existing system
program. Major allocations are assigned to track and tunnel rehabilitation, signal system replacement and modernization, upgrading of
the power system, noise abatement and station modernization, air
conditioning for existing IRT cars, and maintaining the bus replacement cycle. The city's estimate of needs for subway system improvement averages about $177 million per year over the six-year period.

In its five-year (1977-82) program,[3] the Tri-State Regional Plan-

Table A2-2. New York City Program for Improvements to Existing Transit System, Fiscal 1975-80

Program Area	Proposal Allocation (in $ Millions)
Subway lines	
Rehabilitation of track, tunnels and structures	$ 93.6
Signal modernization	150.1
Noise abatement program	151.9
Station improvements	182.8
Rehabilitate power system	185.2
Other (communication facilities, repair	
water conditions, maintenance equipment, etc.)	68.5
Subtotal	$ 832.1
Subway Car Fleet[a]	
Air-condition older cars	96.1
Rehabilitate maintenance facility	100.2
Other (debt service on car purchase)	32.6
Subtotal	$ 228.9
Bus System	
New buses (15-year cycle)	110.9
Other (depot improvements, etc.)	43.6
Subtotal	$ 154.5
Staten Island Rapid Transit	5.0
Engineering staff costs	134.0
Total	$1,354.5

Source: New York City Transportation Policy and Programs (March 1975), p. 14.
[a]Does not include funds for new car purchases in connection with new lines.

ning Commission estimated the capital needs of the existing rapid transit system (excluding the bus system) as $1.1 billion, or an average of $210 million per year. (See Table A2-3.)

The Tri-State estimates differ from those of the city in both itemization and relative costs.

Current city appropriations for the existing rail rapid transit system amount to about $110 million per year. This figure does not include new equipment purchase, retrofit, or engineering costs; the inclusion of such costs would raise appropriations to about the level called for in the city's six-year program.

The TA considers this figure the minimum needed to maintain the system's present operating condition. Although TA engineers have apparently not made detailed analyses of the trade-off between capital investment in the existing system and the costs of increased maintenance, slower operating speeds, and more breakdowns, they

Table A2-3. Tri-State Program for New York City Subway System Maintenance and Rehabilitation, 1977-82

Category of Need	Estimated Needs (in $ Millions)
Track and structure	$ 119
Signal modernization	194
Station improvements	165
Electrification modernization	227
Yard and shop improvements	163
Line equipment rehabilitation	50
Equipment retrofit and purchase	156
Subtotal	$1,050
Staten Island Rapid Transit (overhaul of power, signals, shops and track)	22
Total	$1,072

Source: Maintaining Mobility, Tri-State Regional Planning Commission.

are convinced that the two figures are about the same. They estimate that an additional annual investment of as much as $100 million per year is required to achieve a faster, quieter running system (with welded track and major improvements in station amenities).

Major Unmet Needs

The city has made heavy investments in new operating equipment in the past ten years. Over 2,000 new subway cars, equivalent to one-third of the entire fleet, have been delivered in the past decade or are currently on order. As a result, the subway system will not need to make major new equipment purchases prior to the mid-1980s. The single major equipment item called for in the next eight years is about $60 to $75 million for retrofit air conditioning of the IRT cars. By the mid-1980s, though, the city will need to replace subway cars that by then will be about thirty-five years old. New cars now cost close to $600,000 each (compared to the $300,000 paid for each of the R-46 cars now being delivered); by the mid-1980s, with continuing inflation, they could cost nearly $1 million each. Thus, from 1985 to 1995, the city may need $1 to $2 billion for 1,000 new subway cars.

The city has spent very little money in recent years on the modernization of subway stations. Data on the cost of such modernization are scarce and unreliable, but significantly, upgrading the appearance and design of major existing stations is likely to cost $10 to $25 million per station. A modernization program would have to function within major constraints on time and space because the stations would have to stay open while the work went on.

Sometime during the next decade, the seventy miles of antiquated elevated structures still operated by the Transit Authority will require renovation or replacement;[4] this project involves potential expenditures of major proportions but can probably be postponed until the mid-1980s, if the TA continues to invest sufficient operating funds to maintain and paint these structures. Several elevated structures have been or are being removed: the Third Avenue El in the Bronx has been replaced by a bus line, and much of the Jamaica El will be replaced by work being done on the Queens trunk system.

Surface Transit System

The most expensive item in the TA's surface operations budget is bus replacement. The present replacement cycle is fifteen years; TA personnel point out that good private systems use their buses for only ten to twelve years. At current costs of about $65,000 per vehicle, replacement of one-tenth of the TA's 4,400 buses each decade would cost about $30 million per year—about $10 million per year more than replacement on a fifteen-year cycle. This amount is obviously substantial, but it is a minor item relative to the enormous cost of rapid transit facilities and equipment.

STREETS AND HIGHWAYS

The city and state transportation agencies share responsibility for the street and highway system of New York City, financing the operation of the system from city capital funds, state grants and direct expenditures, and federal grants. The major arterial system, including the interstate system of limited access highways, is financed almost wholly with federal and state funds; federal grants cover up to 90 percent of the total cost of the interstate expressways. The city has sole responsibility for most of the 5,300 miles of paved streets within the five boroughs, although some federal and state funds are available for safety and traffic improvements.

The Arterial System

The arterial highway system has been the focus of recent planning and programming efforts by the New York State Department of Transportation and the Tri-State Regional Planning Commission, a

Table A2-4. Tri-State Regional Planning Commission Estimate of Arterial Highway Needs, New York City, 1977-82

Tri-State Identification No.	Item	Estimated Five-Year Requirement (in $ Millions)
1-3	Highways on Staten Island (West Shore extension, Richmond Avenue improvement, Richmond Parkway extension, Shore Front drive)	$ 2+
7	Highways in Brooklyn (Ocean Parkway Reconstruction)	15
12	Highways in Manhattan (West Side Highway)	1,000
16	Highways in the Bronx (Sheridan Expressway improvements)	No estimate
21	Highways in Queens —Long Island Expressway corridor improvements —Nassau Expressway	45 11
—	Other Regional Highway improvements in New York City (rehabilitation, safety, drainage, landscaping)	343
—	Subregional Highway improvements in NYC (street widening, intersection improvements, bikeways, etc.)	262
	Subtotal, NYC highways	$1,678+

Source: Tri-State Estimates (from *Maintaining Mobility*).

federally required body that reviews transportation projects (and other major regional projects) scheduled to receive federal funds.

Tables A2-4, A2-5, and A2-6 depict five-year projections of major highway construction projects. The projections differ in detail and cover slightly different time periods but present substantially similar views of the major priorities for arterial highway construction in the

Table A2-5. State Department of Transportation Highway Improvement Program, 1976-81 Region 10 (New York City and Nassau)

	Planned Expenditures (in $ Millions)	Percentage of Statewide Total
Interstate expressways	$ 650	41.4%
Other highway funds	737	38.8
Five-year total	$1,387	39.9

Source: Five-Year Transportation Program for New York State.

city. The Tri-State five-year program (Table A2-4) projects $1,678 million in expenditures for the 1977-82 period, or about $336 million per year. The state program (Table A2-5) includes about $1,387 million in expenditures, or about $277 million per year.

The single most significant arterial project planned for the city is the billion-dollar Westway underground roadway to replace the obsolete West Side Highway from 42nd Street to the Battery. This project will take over five years to complete. Tri-State estimates that Westway will cost $1 billion; the state projection of its ultimate cost,

Table A2-6. New York City Highway Projects in State's Five-Year Transportation Program, 1976-81

Category and/or Project	Planned Expenditures
Interstate Highways	
Westway, Manhattan	$1,600[a]
Major Deegan Expwy, Bronx	5
Brooklyn Queens Expwy	16
Van Wyck-Nassau Interchange	25
Long Island Expwy, Queens	251
I-278, Brooklyn	23
Miscellaneous projects	8
Subtotal, interstate systems	$1,928
Urban Highways	
FDR Drive, Manhattan	6
Harlem River Drive, Manhattan	8
Henry Hudson Parkway, Manhattan	16
Bronx River Parkway, Bronx	6
Van Wyck Expressway, Queens	8
Interborough Parkway, Queens	23
Various post-1981 projects	166[b]
Subtotal, urban highways	$ 233
Miscellaneous Smaller Projects[c]	
Reconditioning and preservation	51
Safety	120
Traffic operations	122
Other	102
Subtotal, smaller projects	$ 395
Total, all items above[d]	$2,556

Source: Five-Year Transportation Program for New York State.

[a]Westway project is estimated to cost $1 billion in 1975 prices; project not expected to be complete by 1981.

[b]Part of this expenditure may be committed prior to 1981.

[c]Data includes Nassau County as well as New York City.

[d]State plan over-programs by about 25% to take into account unanticipated delays. Costs escalated at 9% per year.

at 9 percent escalation per year, is $1.6 billion (but not all of this amount is included in the state five-year plan).

Table A2-6 presents a somewhat more detailed program of major highway improvements drawn from the state's five-year program. It includes, in addition to Westway, a $251 million project that would expand the capacity of the Long Island Expressway in Queens from Maurice Avenue (where a two-level roadway from the Brooklyn Queens Expressway interchange now ends) to the vicinity of Flushing Meadow Park. This is one of the most heavily utilized commuter and commercial routes in the entire city. Both sides of the expressway are heavily developed, and it will not be easy to design an expansion plan that the community will accept.

The Tri-State study of regional transportation includes a very generalized statement of major highway needs by "corridors" within the city. The four major projects it suggests for the post-1982 period are:

1. An east west expressway crossing Manhattan in the Canal-Delancey Street area. (This highly controversial proposal has been suspended for a number of years because of fierce community opposition.)
2. A replacement for the still unfinished portion of the Clearview Expressway in Queens.
3. Improvement of congested Hylan Boulevard in Staten Island.
4. Improvements in the Pennsylvania Avenue corridor in southern Queens.

For the foreseeable future, except for "targets of opportunity," such as the short but very costly Westway, the period of major highway building in New York City appears to be over. Growing antagonism to the displacement of housing and jobs by new highways, environmental problems, and the growing belief that the city must place its future reliance on mass transit have all contributed to this outcome.

The Existing Street System

New York City's 5,300 miles of paved streets range in scale from eight-lane divided roadways equipped with computer-controlled traffic signals (such as Queens Boulevard) to fifty-foot pavements serving single-family residences on Staten Island. Most of these streets show the results of too little maintenance and too much wear and weather. Since about 1973, the city's Highways Department has filled over 1 million potholes per year.

Pothole filling and other continuing maintenance, such as resurfacing, are necessary components of a street improvement program. In recent years, New York City has spent on the order of $40 million per year for salaries and materials in its street maintenance program. But all too many streets in New York City still need major reconstruction of roadway, underpavement, sidewalk, and drainage systems.

In the past decade, contract awards for street construction averaged $20 million per year; this amount is sufficient to rebuild (or, in some cases, to construct) only about forty miles of roadway per year at an average cost of about $500,000 per mile. At this rate, the average city street would be rebuilt every century and a half.

It is difficult to determine precisely how long street construction should last under conditions of normal maintenance. According to the city's former highways commissioner, Anthony Ameruso, the optimal replacement cycle is twenty-five years; street reconstruction at this rate would cost New York City about $100 million per year, without taking into account either cost escalation or the present backlog of streets in substandard condition. A forty-year-replacement cycle would cost $60 million per year, several times as much as was expended on average during each of the past ten years.

Barring a major change in the availability of capital funds or an unforeseen technological breakthrough in the technique and cost of street construction, the city's streets face continued deterioration.

Bridges and Structures

The street system of New York City includes 1,200 bridges or other elevated structures over twenty feet in length, including highway overpasses, railroad crossing bridges, and waterway bridges. The latter group includes the giant Brooklyn, Manhattan, Williamsburg, and Queensboro bridges over the East River.

In recent years, the city's bridge construction and rehabilitation program has spent $10 to $15 million per year. The city's bridge engineers calculate that $60 million per year would be needed for a "crash" program to reconstruct about half of the estimated 24 million square feet of bridge deck in a ten-year period (at an estimated cost of $50 per square foot). The same amount of reconstruction over a twenty-year period would still cost $30 million per year, or $300 million in the next decade.

The major waterway bridges are in sound condition but require periodic rehabilitation as well as painting. Painting, which should be done every ten years, costs over $1 million per bridge. Of the large bridges, the Queensboro Bridge is the most in need of major repairs. These are estimated to cost about $16 million.

The city has built few bridges in recent years. For some time, the city has been planning to replace an operating bridge over the Flushing River in Queens with a high-level fixed bridge at a cost of about $13 million (about half of which would be for utility relocation). The city could recoup at least part of this amount because the new bridge would have lower operating costs and would offer greater potential for barge shipment to industries located on the river beyond the bridge.

WATER SUPPLY AND DISTRIBUTION

A dependable supply of pure water, in sufficient quantities and at adequate pressures, is absolutely essential to the operation of an urban center. New York City has been fortunate in the past in its water supply. As the city grew, city agencies secured rights to extensive watershed areas and constructed a system of distribution that reached into virtually every corner of the five boroughs. Today, the city must continue expanding its sources and maintaining the system in order to maintain its access to this vital resource.

The Supply System

New York City's water supply system brings fresh water to the city from locations as distant as 125 miles away. The city's supply system is based on two extensive watershed areas in the Catskill Mountains and a smaller area (the Croton watershed) in Westchester County.

Two great underground pipes, the Delaware and Catskill aqueducts, carry water from the upstate reservoir system to Kensico Reservoir, located north of White Plains at the southern end of the Croton watershed area. From Kensico, another aqueduct carries the water about a dozen miles south to Hillview Reservoir in the Bronx. Smaller aqueducts extend directly from the Croton system into the city, bypassing Kensico and Hillview.

The reservoir system provides an average of about 1,400 million gallons per day (MGD) to New York City and about another 100 MGD to other communities in the metropolitan region. The system constitutes virtually all of the city's fresh water supply. In 1974, private water companies in Queens supplied a total of about 60 MGD to city residents, this private supply is drawn largely from underground sources within the city. The city is acquiring these private companies, and within a few years will be responsible for the entire supply system.

The upstate watershed, reservoir, and aqueduct system contributes one of New York City's most valuable and irreplaceable assets. Protection of the city's supply system, as well as its expansion to increase the dependable yield in drought years, presents difficult problems. Urban development pressures on the Croton watershed (which accounts for about 15 percent of the total supply) have been increasing and may force the city to install treatment facilities—at an estimated cost of $200 million—sometime in the next decade. The growing demand for water for recreational uses in the Catskill watershed area is imposing similar but less intense pressures on the remainder of the city supply.

At the same time, the water supply demands of other counties in the metropolitan region, especially Nassau and Suffolk, are growing. The ground water supplies of these counties may well not be sufficient or adequately protected against infiltration of salt water or pollution. These needs may threaten the city's undisturbed use of its water supplies.

To date, New York City has opposed proposals for regional or state systems that would control the city's resources. Although willing to cooperate in regional action to increase supply, the city will not give up control over its own resources.

Under state law, the Board of Water Supply (an independent authority that has since been disbanded) planned and supervised construction of the city's upstate reservoir and aqueduct facilities. The city Department of Water Resources operates and maintains the system. The department does not at present see the need for major capital investment in the reservoir or aqueduct system in the next decade (beyond the possible installation of treatment facilities at Croton). The department is no longer actively seeking funds for a bypass aqueduct at the Rondout Reservoir. But the system will require continuing maintenance investment, including some costly repairs. For example, a five-foot crack at the forty-foot level in the Croton Dam is currently being investigated and may need major repair.

Hudson River "Flood-Skimming"

From 1962 to 1966, the Northeast experienced the most severe drought on record (although rainfall records suggest that New York City's situation was actually worse in the 1830-60 period). As a result of the drought, the U.S. Army Corps of Engineers began a study of water supply needs in the entire Northeast. Good engineering practice and Corps policy call for basing safe yield estimates for water supply systems on the worst-recorded situation. On this basis, a safe yield for New York City's water supply system would be about 1,290 MGD.

The Corps estimates that regional need by the year 2000 will be 390 MGD higher than this figure. The Corps based this estimate on a forecast that the population of the metropolitan region would be about 15 million in 2000; this figure is higher by 2 million people than that of the Tri-State Regional Planning Commission.

The State of New York, according to the Corps report,[5] arrived at about the same supply deficit as the Corps, despite the difference in population forecasts, because it assumed lower safe yields from Nassau County underground supplies, future unavailability of ground water in Brooklyn and Queens, higher per capita consumption, and lower potential savings from conservation programs. Thus, the Corps took as its target the addition of about 400 MGD of safe yield to the regional supply system.

The Corps considered as many as sixty different possible projects to meet the 400 MGD need. It finally narrowed the possibilities to three essentially similar variations on a single concept. The proposed project would take water from the Hudson River at a point near Rhinebeck (about eighty-five miles north of the Battery), treat it, and convey it to New York City's Kensico Reservoir via underground aqueducts. From Kensico the water would be distributed via the Third City Water Tunnel and an extension into Nassau County.

The design is based on the assumption that during at least part of the year the Hudson retains more water than is needed to prevent the saltwater front from moving too far to the north. The city can store this excess water in its Kensico and Hillview Reservoirs and Catskill water in upstate reservoirs. Thus, the city could take full advantage of reservoir capacity in anticipation of a drought.

The three variant designs studied by the Corps differ in the site of the treatment plant and the route to be taken by tunnels to Kensico. They do not appear to differ significantly in cost or feasibility.

The Corps estimates the cost of the proposed project in 1975 dollars as follows:

	($ in Millions)
Intake, pumping station, and treatment plant	$ 400
Tunnels to Kensico Reservoir	900
Third City Water Tunnel plus Nassau extension	2,300
Total construction cost	$3,600
Interest during construction	900
Total estimated cost	$4,500

The Corps proposed that the federal government finance the facility initially (over a fifty-year period at 6.75 percent interest) but that the state or affected communities pay the annual cost of debt service, which is estimated at about $300 million for the fifty-year period. (At present, New York City's total annual debt service is about $1,800 million.)

The project is expected to take five years to design and an additional eight years to construct. If design were to begin at once, it would not be complete before 1990. But given the time that is likely to be consumed in arguments over environmental and financing issues, a target completion date of 2000 seems more reasonable.

The Distribution System

The city's water distribution system comprises the two major water tunnels that deliver water from Hillview Reservoir to the city and the mains that connect these tunnels to individual consumers. City Water Tunnel No. 1 delivers water to the Bronx and Manhattan; City Water Tunnel No. 2 carries water to Queens, to Brooklyn, and—via a recently constructed Richmond Tunnel—to the Silver Lake storage area on Staten Island.

Tunnels 1 and 2 are now about fifty-five and forty years old, respectively. In 1970, concerned with their age and the serious problems that a breakdown in either tunnel would cause, the city began construction of a third water tunnel. This facility, twenty to twenty-five feet in diameter and as much as 300 feet beneath the earth's surface, was initially planned to run from Hillview to mid-Manhattan and then cross into Queens, where it would connect to Tunnel No. 2 and loop back through Queens and to Hillview and Kensico reservoirs. The first stage, from Hillview to mid-Manhattan, was bid at $200 million; the city estimated that the entire loop would cost about $1 billion.

Unfortunately, the digging of Tunnel No. 3 ran into a series of delays and unforeseen physical problems in its passage through deep rock beneath the city. The contractors demanded extra payments in multimillion dollar amounts and, when the city refused, stopped work and sued the city for $200 million in damages. Because of the fiscal crisis, the city was unable to pay for additional work—even if the lawsuit had been resolved—and work on the tunnel came to a halt.

According to current city estimates, completing the first stage of Tunnel No. 3 will cost up to $600 million. Extending the tunnel to lower Manhattan to relieve water supply problems in that congested business district would cost another $600 million. The city has nowhere to turn for these funds. Meanwhile, the possibility of an outage in one of the two existing tunnels continues to loom as a serious threat to the city.

The system of smaller distribution mains ranges from pipes six feet in diameter down to some older lines in Manhattan only six inches in diameter. The Department of Water Resources has set ten inches as the minimum diameter for new work, and wants to replace the antiquated six-inch lines as soon as feasible. These smaller diameter lines, laid as long ago as 1870, are a source of major trouble in the distribution system; they serve 11 percent of Manhattan and account for about 40 percent of the breaks that occur each year in that borough.

Another major repair problem in the distribution system centers on the 20,000 trunk valves. Six percent of these valves are in such poor condition that they cannot be closed when a line break occurs.

The entire distribution system encompasses 6,100 miles of water mains of various sizes. In recent years, construction of new mains has proceeded slowly; in 1974—even before the fiscal crisis—the Department of Water Resources constructed only forty-two miles of new main. Of these, twenty miles were net additions to the system (mostly in Staten Island growth areas); only twenty-two miles replaced obsolete mains. At twenty-two miles per year, replacing the entire system would take 277 years.

The department's objective is to increase the replacement rate to seventy-five miles per year, or a replacement cycle of about eighty years. At an estimated $250,000 per mile of main, the target eighty-year cycle would cost about $20 million per year, about twice as much as the Department of Water Resources has spent in recent years. Over the 1977-86 decade, replacement at this rate would cost about $240 million (assuming a 5 percent rate of cost escalation).

The eighty-year replacement cycle is still too slow to maintain the distribution system in good condition. Current installations of ductile iron are expected to be good for sixty to seventy-five years. However, the existing distribution system was mostly constructed of cast iron, good for only about fifty years of trouble-free service.

Universal Metering

Most of New York's residential structures pay for water on a front foot basis rather than on a metered basis. There have been vigorous arguments about the desirability of requiring universal metering in the city as a method of conserving water use. The Department of Water Resources has consistently argued that universal metering would not save significantly on consumption; in Philadelphia, for example, a switch to metering has had negligible effects on water use.

Proponents of metering, among them a recent Temporary State Commission on the Water Supply Needs of Southeastern New York, argue that it could save over 240 MGD. This amount, together with the proposed Hudson River flood-skimming project, could be sufficient to meet regional water needs through the year 2020.

Metering the 800,000 residential structures in New York City would cost more than $100 million. Under present regulations, this cost would have to be borne by the private owners of metered buildings.

The Troubled Water Supply Situation

Until a few years ago, the city financed the capital investment needs of its water supply system by issuing bonds outside the constitutional debt limit, meeting long-range water needs through an end run around the competitive budgetary arena. But since the onset of the fiscal crisis, the city has been unable to sell bonds at all, within or outside the debt limit.

Since the difficult drought years of 1964 and 1965, New York City's water supply and distribution system has been adequate. The state of the supply system largely justifies a sense of security, but the potential for breakdown at key points in the distribution system is a matter for serious concern.

ELECTRICITY

An adequate supply of electrical energy is critically important for New York City's economy in the 1980s and 1990s. Planning, obtaining necessary approvals, and constructing electrical generating and transmission facilities typically take seven to thirteen years; the planning for the next two decades is already well under way.

In response to the requirements of the Public Service law of New York State, the New York Power Pool—an agency composed of the seven private utility companies and the Power Authority of the State of New York (PASNY)—has developed a detailed planning process that results each year in the submission of a twenty-year plan (termed the Section 149-b Plan after the law that requires it[6]) to the State Public Service Commission. The most recent plan, the 1976 version, contains year-by-year forecasts of electrical energy needs by utility company areas through 1996.

The key demand requirement that generating and transmission facilities serving New York City must meet is summer peak demand, largely a result of the growth in use of air conditioning. New York is expected to remain a summer peak demand area throughout the next twenty years.

Table A2-7 shows forecasts of peak summer electrical demand for the Consolidated Edison (Con Ed) service area (which includes all of New York City except the Rockaway peninsula plus most of Westchester County) for 1976, 1986, and 1996. It also shows increases in PASNY peak demands above the 1975 level; prior to 1975, virtually all PASNY's service went to industrial users, utilities, and municipal systems outside New York City; with the recent acquisition of two Con Ed plants, the authority has begun to provide electrical energy to the New York City Transit Authority and to other public consumers in and near the city. A significant proportion of PASNY's future expansion plans are designed to help meet public agency energy needs in the city and adjacent areas.

Table A2-7. Peak Summer Electricity Demands, New York City Area[a] (in Megawatts)

	1966	1976	1986	1996	% Increase 1976-86
Consolidated Edison	6,154	7,845	9,350	12,275	19
PASNY[b]	—	1,270	2,330	3,930	84
Total	6,154	9,115	11,680	16,205	28

Source: Con Ed data from Section 149-b Report; PASNY data from PASNY officials.
[a]Con Ed service area (includes most of Westchester).
[b]PASNY data is for 1975, 1985 and 1995.

Table A2-8 indicates that the forecast peak demands for Con Ed are expected to grow more slowly than is demand in the state as a whole. Even when PASNY demand forecasts are added to Con Ed's forecasts, the total growth forecast for the New York City area can be seen to be slower than for the state as a whole. The overall state demand peak is expected to increase by 4 percent a year during the late 1970s, declining to 3.5 percent per year by 1990.

The New York Power Pool bases its peak electrical demand forecasts on detailed utility-by-utility analyses checked against an econometric mode forecast for the entire state. The 1976 forecasts resemble those made in 1974 and 1975 but represent a major downward adjustment from earlier forecasts. For example, the Power Pool now forecasts a 1990 peak load of 35,700 megawatts (MW), some 14,000 MW or 39 percent lower than was forecast for the same date in 1973. The downward adjustment may reflect the severe

Table A2-8. Peak Summer Electricity Demands, New York City Area Compared to State of New York Total (in Megawatts)

Year	New York City Area[a]	New York State Total	New York City Area as a Percentage of New York State Total
1966	6,154	13,609	45.2%
1976	9,115	21,000	43.4%
1986	11,680	30,890	37.8%
1996	16,205	43,550	37.2%

Source: New York City area from Table A2-1; New York State data from Section 149-b report.

[a]Area and data as defined in Table A2-1 (includes PASNY).

effects of the OPEC oil price increases (most oil used in New York State is imported) and the recent economic difficulties of the state in general and New York City in particular.

The Section 149-b report shows that planning for electrical energy production and transmission capacity in the state is now based on sharply reduced demand levels. To some degree, these forecasts may be self-fulfilling: if the capacity is not built, businesses and industries that require electrical energy may locate elsewhere in the nation where the supply is less constrained; moreover, heavy demands on existing capacity require reliance on older, less efficient, and more expensive generating plants. Because constructing electrical facilities involves long lead times, once plans are made, they cannot be easily revised.

Responsibility for the Electrical System

Until 1972, Con Ed had virtually complete responsibility for production and distribution of electricity to New York City. In that year, the legislature authorized PASNY to construct two plants to meet needs of the MTA, which serves New York City and the surrounding counties but which has its heaviest electrical needs concentrated in the city subway system. Then, with the economic downturn of 1973 and the concurrent sharp rises in fuel oil prices, Con Ed ran into fiscal difficulties that were resolved, in significant part, by its sale of two large partially complete generating facilities—the Astoria No. 6 plant and the Indian Point No. 3 nuclear facility—to PASNY.

Plans for New Generating Capacity

Over the next two decades, additional generating capacity is essential to meet New York City's forecast peak electrical demand, even if demand does not exceed the present forecasts. Table A2-9 lists the generating facilities planned by Con Ed and PASNY. In addition to these facilities, one other plan will add significantly to available supply. Hydro Quebec, a Canadian public utility that operates hydroelectric facilities on the St. Lawrence River, has entered into an agreement with PASNY to exchange up to 800,000 kilowatts of electrical energy. During the seven warmer months of the year (when New York City loads peak), PASNY plans to provide most of this supply to Con Ed, and is building a new transmission line (at an estimated cost of $233 million) to carry this power from Massena on the St. Lawrence River to a point near Utica where it can be transferred to existing transmission lines.

Table A2-9. New Generating Facilities Planned to Serve New York City Area, 1978-91

Facility[a]	Target Service Date	Owner	Maximum Capability (MW)	Estimated Cost ($ Millions)
Prattsville (Schoharie Reservoir)	1982	RASNY	1,000	$ 330
Staten Island Fossil/Refuse	1982	RASNY	700	500
Greene County Nuclear	1984	PASNY	1,200	1,600
Cornwall No. 1-4	1987	Con Ed	1,000	} 1,017
Cornwall No. 5-8	1988	Con Ed	1,000	
Mid-Hudson Nuclear No. 1	1989	ESPRI[b]	1,300	N/A
Mid-Hudson Nuclear No. 2	1991	ESPRI[b]	1,300	N/A
Total			7,500	

Sources: NYPP Section 149-b Report (Vol. 2, pp. 8-9) and interviews with Con Ed and PASNY officials.

[a]Not included in table are three planned upgrading-projects: PASNY Indian Point No. 3 of 92 MW in 1978 and 68 MW in 1980 and Con Ed Indian Point No. 2 of 160 MW in 1979.

[b]Con Ed plans to finance these facilities until ESPRI is approved.

As can be seen from Table A2-9, only PASNY has construction plans for generating plants to serve the city before 1985. Con Ed's major new facilities are scheduled to come into operation well after that date.

In constructing many of the planned new generating facilities, PASNY will confront the difficult tasks of obtaining the necessary governmental approvals, especially from environmental protection agencies, and overcoming lawsuits against plant siting and design. The planning schedules for these future PASNY and Con Ed facilities include some provisions for delay in the performance of these tasks, but it is not at all certain that the planned target dates can be met. Con Ed's Cornwall facility is a particular problem in this regard; it has long been opposed by well-organized environmental groups.

Another open issue is the safety of nuclear facilities. At least one of the near-term major city-serving facilities is planned as a nuclear power plant (the PASNY plant in Greene County). In addition, Con Ed plans to build two nuclear facilities in the mid-Hudson area in the 1990s.

Plans for New Transmission Capacity

Transmission facilities also are needed to carry power from the planned new generating facilities to locations within New York City from which it can enter Con Ed's distribution system. Table A2-10 presents a summary of Con Ed's planned expenditures for trans-mission facilities by major categories for the 1976-86 period. In the mid-to-late-1980s, Con Ed also may have to spend up to $1 billion to construct a major direct current (DC) transmission facility from northern Westchester to the city. This corridor along the east bank of the Hudson River already contains a number of above-ground high tension lines, but even upgraded, these lines may be insufficient to meet needs in this heavily used corridor when new PASNY facilities and Con Ed's Cornwall facility are in operation. Con Ed is building an experimental direct current line in its Astoria facility to test the feasibility of DC transmission.

Table A2-10. Estimated Construction Expenditures for Electric System by Con Ed, 1976, 1986 and 1976-88 Period (in $ Millions)

Item	1976	1986	Total for 1976-88 Period[c]
Generating Facilities[a]	$ 42.2	$371.5	$1,564.7
Transmission	61.4	57.6	1,037.9
Distribution[b]	151.0	378.6	3,736.7
Total	$254.6	$807.7	$6,339.3

Source: Con Ed report to Federal Power Commission (March 1976).

[a]Includes $318.1 million for Cornwall in 1986 and $1,017 for Cornwall in thirteen-year 1976-88 period.

[b]Includes substations.

[c]These estimates include cost escalation at 7 percent per year until 1980 and 5 percent per year subsequently.

In addition to the new transmission line that PASNY is developing for Quebec hydro power, PASNY has other transmission plans related to its participation in the statewide electric grid (rather than to New York City).

Con Ed's Construction Expenditure Plan

Table A2-10 summarizes Con Ed's electric construction plans for the 1976-88 period. The company plans to spend over $6 billion for construction. Con Ed plans to increase the annual rate of construction expenditures for its electric system from an annual level of $255 million in 1976 to over $800 million in 1986.

In addition to the expenditures shown, Con Ed expects to benefit from construction expenditures of over $500 million per year by 1988 through activities of Empire State Power Resources, Inc. (ESPRI), an organization of all the private utility companies in New York State. Plans for ESPRI are still tentative; an application for its approval is pending before the Public Service Commission. A major ESPRI facility that might benefit Con Ed is a planned Hudson River nuclear complex capable of up to 4,000 MW; construction of this plant is scheduled after Cornwall; it is listed in Table A2-9 as the Mid-Hudson plant.

Another item not included in these estimates is construction of cooling towers to meet environmental standards for water temperature. Con Ed may have to invest on the order of $200 million to retrofit existing plants. Cooling towers would also add to the costs of new plants.

Generating and transmitting facilities are costly and complex, but they are only a part of the total electric energy system. The Con Ed construction plan indicates that in the next twelve years over half of all electric construction expenditures will be concentrated on the distribution system (including substations) within the utility's service area.

Con Ed spent $212 million on construction in 1965 and $316 million in 1975. Exclusive of the Cornwall plant, the company estimates its expenditures in 1985 at about $533 million.

Currently, PASNY's construction plans for the New York City area consist of the generating facilities listed in Table A2-9 and the high voltage transmission line for Quebec hydroelectric power.

Taken together, the costs of Con Ed's and PASNY's construction programs for the New York City area will come to about $9 billion between now and 1988.

Major Concerns and Problems

On its face, the New York Power Pool's plan for statewide electric energy needs represents a carefully thought out, detailed forecast of needs and resources planned nearly to the year 2000. But a number of significant contingencies (and a host of minor ones) call into question major aspects of the plan, especially as it affects New York City. Among the most significant contingent problems are:

1. *Forecast demand levels.* The sharp reductions in future demand in the 1976 plan from earlier Power Pool forecasts may represent an overreaction to the 1973-74 oil moratorium crisis. A return to anything near the precrisis demand level would require twice the planned amount of new generating capacity.
2. *Delays in the construction of major projects.* Especially in site and design approval stages, major energy construction projects tend to fall behind schedule. Environmental considerations are a significant, but not the only, source of such delays. Delays in the construction of PASNY facilities at Arthur Kill on Staten Island, at the pumped storage facility intended for New York City's Schoharie Reservoir, or at the nuclear facility planned for Greene County could result in serious shortages relative even to the low level of forecast demand. And in the eyes of many observers, Con Ed's pumped storage facility at Cornwall is a dubious starter.
3. *Funding constraints.* Of the $9 billion estimated cost of construction proposed by Con Ed's and PASNY's construction programs over the 1976-88 period, Con Ed should supply about a third out of its operating revenues; in the past, Con Ed has been able to finance $300-$400 million of construction per year internally. But both the company and PASNY will have to obtain most of the remainder from the bond market.

Con Ed's capacity to borrow large sums for new construction projects is unknown, but will probably be influenced by the outcome of the city's fiscal and economic crisis as well as by what the company does itself. Although PASNY's revenue bonds have done well in the tax-exempt market, even during a period of severe pressures on all New York securities, Internal Revenue Service (IRS) regulations have become increasingly restrictive as to the uses of tax-exempt revenue bonds. Effectively, only 10 percent of PASNY's new debt issues can finance generating facilities to serve private residences and industry; the other 90 percent must be used for public purposes (MTA, city agencies, etc.) or be held in reserve. These constraints do not require changes in the current plans for PASNY's role in the city's energy system, but if demand levels rise significantly or if Con Ed proves unable to finance or construct Cornwall, PASNY will face some difficult policy issues. At the moment, barring a change in IRS requirements PASNY's main alternative would seem to be reliance on higher cost taxable bonds. Given the long lead times in this field, planners should begin to address these three issues as soon as possible.

EDUCATION

During the past decade, the public education system of New York City has received the largest share of the city's construction funds. It appears unlikely to continue to do so in the coming decade because the most pressing space needs of the education system have been met and because enrollments in public schools and colleges are unlikely to increase.

Higher Education

In 1968, the New York City Board of Higher Education adopted a Master Plan, under which the City University of New York (CUNY) would eventually comprise ten senior colleges and ten community colleges located throughout the five boroughs. Under the Master Plan, the total student body would grow from 100,000 to an "open enrollment" level of about 164,000 by about 1976. The plan included a major construction program costing an estimated $1.7 billion.

In measuring enrollment, CUNY takes into account variations in individual programs; part-time, full-time, and evening programs involve varying demands on physical facilities. The term "student" as used here is based on estimates of "full-time equivalents" developed by CUNY's Office of the Master Plan.

The decision to initiate open enrollment for all New York City high school graduates in 1969, rather than on the slower schedule called for in the Master Plan, presented CUNY with an urgent need for additional physical facilities. The university undertook a massive program of leasing space, and now rents 2.6 million square feet of space at an annual cost of $16 million. The fiscal crisis forced CUNY to make enrollment cutbacks; thus, the university no longer uses all of the currently leased space and is seeking to sublet some of it.

With its current enrollment of 155,000 students (15 percent below the precrisis peak of 187,000 students in 1975), CUNY is still seriously overcrowded, compared to the State University of New York (SUNY). At present, CUNY has about 50 net assignable square feet (actually available for classroom use) per student; SUNY has 110 net square feet per student. Even if CUNY had carried out its Master Plan construction program, it would have only about 100 net assignable square feet per student.

The CUNY Construction Program. The City University Construction Fund (CUCF), a state-chartered "moral obligation" authority whose members are appointed by the mayor and governor, runs CUNY's campus design and construction program. The State Dormitory Authority (DA) issues bonds to finance the college construction program, and CUCF pays the debt service with funds provided in equal parts by the city and the state.

Through 1975, the university awarded and completed or substantially completed contracts for over $400 million worth of facilities, nearly one-fourth of the Master Plan target. Most of these were expansion facilities, but some replaced outmoded structures.

The fiscal crisis of 1975 caught CUNY's construction program in a badly exposed posture. Some $300 million in construction projects had been awarded for major projects at four campuses: City College, Lehman, and Hunter senior colleges, and the Borough of Manhattan community college. The state of the bond market prevented CUCF from authorizing or the DA from issuing bonds to finance these four projects fully, and work was suspended after only about one-third of it had been done. Unless it can obtain the additional funds, the university stands to lose the $100 million that has been invested, and may pay over $30 million in claims for broken contracts. The partially completed structures are wholly unusable in their present state.

Completing the Master Plan. To complete the 1968 Master Plan program would require an additional $1 billion.[7] The major projects financed by the additional funds would be new campuses for Baruch senior college and Hostos community college, as well as major additions at a number of colleges. Table A2-11 lists these facilities along with cost estimates.

Table A2-11. Status of City University Construction Program, 1976 (in $ Millions)

1. Projects currently in suspended status:

Campus	Expended to Date	Balance to Complete
City College	$31.9	$ 69.6
Hunter	16.8	67.1
Lehman	19.6	23.5
Boro of Manhattan CC	11.4	58.5
Total	$79.7	$218.7

2. Projects on which design is complete or nearly complete:

Campus	Total Project Cost
York	$ 72.3
Staten Island CC	65.2
New York CC	59.6
Queens (science bldg.)	29.9
Bronx CC (various items)	13.9
Hostos CC (alterations)	6.0
Total	$264.9

3. Major projects ready for design start:

Campus	Total Project Cost
Baruch (new campus)	$100

4. Major future projects in 1968 Master Plan:

Senior colleges:	Total Project Cost
City College (South Campus)	N/A
York College (Phase II)	$35.9

Community colleges:	
Bronx (Renovations)	$ 17.0
Kingsborough (Phase II)	25.4
Queensborough (Phase II)	12.0
Staten Island (Renovation)	N/A

Source: Memo from Donal Farley, Associate Administrator, Office of Campus Planning and Development, CUNY (March 1976).

Note: The above list does not include a number of planned alterations, renovations and individual new structures. It also omits permanent campuses for Medgar Evers, Richmond and La Guardia colleges (not called for in the 1968 Master Plan).

The Unclear Status of City University. Action on the remaining portions of the CUNY Master Plan is in suspension pending the resolution of major issues about the university's future role and status. The fiscal crisis has already brought about major changes in the underlying assumptions on which the Master Plan was based. Free tuition has ended; open enrollment is effectively suspended; Mayor Beame declared that the city would no longer help finance senior college operations, and the future roles of the city and the state in financing and administration of the university are under study by a commission appointed by Governor Carey.

Whatever the gubernatorial commission recommends, the Master Plan probably will not be completed in its original form. College enrollment for the entire State of New York is expected to level off in the 1980s or to drop below present levels. Substantially lower enrollments in the combined public and private systems in the state are a distinct possibility, barring a drastic change in the current pattern of college attendance among graduating high school seniors or a new pattern of college attendance by persons of middle age and older.

Thus, the future construction program for City University appears likely to range between the $200 million needed to complete current projects and the total of $1 billion needed to complete the Master Plan. Keeping to the lower end of this scale will require major rethinking of facility use and distribution among the various campuses of the university. In particular, insufficient funds may prevent those institutions that have not yet fully achieved permanent campus status from doing so prior to 1986—if ever. More established colleges may have to make do with rented or converted space for the indefinite future.

Elementary and Secondary Schools

New York City has just completed a decade of massive investment in the physical plant of its elementary and secondary school system. From 1966 to 1976, the city's school system had an effective first claim on the capital funds available to the city. Over one-fifth of all city construction dollars ($1.3 billion out of a total of $6.1 billion) went into the construction of new schools and into major modernization projects in existing schools. This heavy concentration of construction funds had a major positive impact on the school system. During this period, 135 new schools opened containing a total of 212,000 seats. These new schools represented 15 percent of all the schools in the city and 17 percent of school seats. Major renovations were completed in another 180 schools, 19 percent of the total, 21 percent of school seats. By 1976, 38 percent of the total capacity of the school system was located in newly constructed or recently renovated structures.

Table A2-12 depicts school enrollments from 1970 to (a projection for) 1980. Enrollments had risen rapidly during the 1960s. They peaked at 1,137,500 pupils in 1971; at present, they are just over 1,000,000, and they are projected to fall to 992,000 by 1980.[8]

Table A2-12. Elementary and Secondary School Enrollment, 1970-75 and Projection for 1980 (in Thousands of Students)

Year[a]	Elementary and Intermediate	High Schools	Total Enrollment
1970	847.6	285.2	1,132.8
1971	840.9	296.6	1,137.5
1972	815.9	303.2	1,119.1
1973	792.2	304.6	1,096.8
1974	780.4	308.0	1,088.4
1975	770.6	315.3	1,085.9
1980 (proj.)	691.5	300.6	992.1

Sources: 1970-75 from Board of Education; 1980 projection from Department of City Planning.

[a]As of October 31 of each year.

As a result, except in a few areas, the city's schools are no longer overcrowded. Once schools that are substantially complete are opened, only five of the city's thirty-one school districts will have any present or foreseeable needs for additional school capacity. These are the Fordham-Kingsbridge area in the Bronx, Middle Village-Glendale in Queens, the growing southern portion of Staten Island, Washington Heights in Manhattan, and Crown Heights in Brooklyn.

High school capacity appears adequate for the next ten years at least; localized needs can be met by converting excess capacity in elementary or junior high schools. A relatively small amount of additional construction—compared to the massive additions of the past decade—should meet all space needs in the next decade.

In fact, the Board of Education has already begun to reduce excess capacity; it has closed twenty obsolete buildings in the past year to save on operating costs, and plans to close another twenty this year.

Construction Needs in the Next Decade. A reasonable school construction program over the next decade might involve spending about $40 million per year. Such a program would finance major modernization in about ten schools per year at an average cost of about $1.5 million per building[9] or a total of about $15 million per year plus construction of two new schools per year at an average cost of about $12.5 million each.[10]

In the mid-1980s, school capacity may become strained again if birthrates rise, if the net out-migration of families with school-age children declines, or if enrollment shifts from parochial to public schools. None of these changes is currently foreseeable. By the mid-1980s, total enrollment may well drop to 900,000 pupils, roughly 20 percent below the 1971 peak.

Other Capital Needs. The city finances repair and minor rehabilitation of schools through a comprehensive repair program in the capital budget. Before 1976, this program operated at a level of about $50 million per year. Under the pressures of the city's fiscal crisis, the program has been cut to about $30 million in the current budget. But an annual expenditure of $50 million or more is needed to keep the school plant in a sound state of repair.

In addition, despite the improvements of the past decade, nearly 400 schools still burn coal, with serious pollution effects. The conversion of these city schools to pollution-controlled oil heating has been stalled by the fiscal crisis, the sharply rising cost of fuel oil, and the state's reluctance to provide its promised aid for the effort. At about $200,000 per school, this program will cost up to $80 million if and when it is resumed.

OTHER CONSTRUCTION NEEDS

Water Pollution Control

For the past decade, New York City has been engaged in a massive program of constructing water pollution control plants linked by interceptor sewers to the entire sanitary sewer system. The major uncompleted elements of this system are:

1. The North River plant in the upper West Side of Manhattan, whose superstructure will require another $500 million to complete.
2. The Red Hook plant in Brooklyn, which will cost $300 million plus another $400 million for interceptor sewers.

State and federal grants together will finance up to 87.5 percent of the cost of such facilities.

A further stage in the control of polluted discharges into the waters around the city would be an auxiliary treatment system to treat storm water overflow into waters such as Jamaica Bay. If and when such a system is undertaken, it will cost some $400 to $600 million.

In 1973, New York City began a ten-year program of installing sewers in the unserved or inadequately served areas of the city. Phase I, the first five years of the program, had an estimated cost of $800 million. Phase II, the next five years, would cost an estimated $700 million. The city had only begun to carry out the $150 million-per-year program when the fiscal crisis brought it to a virtual halt; sewer construction in 1971-75 averaged $41 million per year, more than triple the rate ($13 million per year) of the preceding five years but well below the planned annual rate.

The city needs to continue to repair and replace ancient sewers in many of the older sections of the city. The present rate of reconstruction is equivalent to more than a 300-year replacement cycle. Even modern sewers, built to far higher standards than many of the city's older sewers, are estimated to need replacement every 100 years. Replacement of existing sewers at a rate of 1 percent per year and an average cost of $1 million per mile would require investment on the order of $50 million per year, $500 million over the next decade.

Hospitals and Health Facilities

New York City has sufficient public and private hospital facilities to meet its foreseeable needs. In fact, the Health Systems Agency has estimated that there is a surplus of 5,000 beds. As a result, public hospital construction in the next decade should be limited to modernization and rehabilitation efforts in the older hospitals at only a small fraction of the public hospital construction rate ($100 million per year) in the peak years of 1971-73.

Other Public Buildings

The city also should be able to reduce the level of its investment in other public buildings below the past decade's level of $50 million per year. Recent construction has met virtually all of the urgent needs for police stations, fire stations, courts, and correction facilities. In the case of branch libraries, the construction program has so outpaced the operating budget that a number of new structures lie empty.

Parks and Museums

For a number of years prior to the financial crisis, city construction programs in parks, museums, and cultural institutions ran at a nearly constant $20-$25 million per year. This money paid for a number of important additions to facilities (museum buildings and swimming pools received major attention) but was insufficient also to keep pace with vandalism and deterioration.

The city seems highly unlikely to spend even $20 million per year on these facilities until the fiscal crisis is past. If funds were available, $25 to $35 million per year could be usefully invested in park and museum facilities. The major rehabilitation of Central Park that is long overdue could itself consume this amount for several years.

Economic Development

The City Planning Commission proposed a six-year economic development capital improvement program, involving wholesale markets, container ports, and industrial parks at a cost of $220 million, about $35 million per year, for the 1976-82 period. Extending the proposed program at the same level over the succeeding five years would bring the total expenditure for this program to $350 million over the 1977-86 period. The proposed Convention Center, stalled for lack of financing, is itself a $200 million project. The most recent projections indicate that little if any of this cost will be supported by direct revenues of the center.

Sanitation

The city is approaching a solid waste crisis. It scrapped earlier plans for "superincinerators" because of their extraordinarily high cost and pollution levels. The existing municipal incinerators can cope with only a declining fraction of the solid wastes generated within the city, and virtually all land fills except Fresh Kills on Staten Island are exhausted. Fresh Kills has already passed earlier estimates of its capacity.

In 1975, a mayoral task force recommended construction of eleven "resource recovery" plants throughout the city at a cost of $550 million. No funds are presently available for these facilities.

Other alternatives to solid waste disposal considered in the past—such as rail shipment of garbage to strip mine areas in Pennsylvania or Ohio—no longer appear to be under active consideration because they are expensive and controversial.

* * *

Table A2-13 depicts the city's estimated infrastructure needs, unconstrained by fiscal or other realities. They amount to about $24 billion, 140 percent more than the comparable infrastructure investment in the past decade.

The table assigns no priorities to needs and includes some needs that are not likely to be met even in part within the next decade. Such costly projects as completing City University's Master Plan, completion or extension of the Third City Water Tunnel, and a half-billion dollar program for solid waste treatment are not part of an agreed-on municipal capital construction program. And the city probably will not begin, in the foreseeable future, to reconstruct its water, sewer, and street systems at the recommended rate.

But none of the projects included is wholly speculative or lacking in merit. Even those that must by given low priority in a period of seriously limited finance—for example, the auxiliary pollution control system to treat storm water overflow—are of potential importance to a high quality urban environment.

Table A2-13. Summary of Capital Investment in Major Infrastructure Elements, Actual (1967-76) and Projected Needs (1977-86) (in $ Millions)

Functional Category	Capital Investment, 1967-76	Capital Needs, 1977-86
Mass transit:		
Queens trunk line		$1,200
Second Avenue line	$ 980	2,000
Existing subway system program		2,000[a]
Subtotal, mass transit	980	5,200
Streets and highways:		
Arterial highway system	N/A	2,000
Street system rehabilitation	209	600
Bridges and Structures	N/A	300
Subtotal, streets and highways	209+	2,900
Water supply and distribution:		
Croton Watershed Treatment System	—	200[b]
Hudson River Flood-Skimming	—	N/A
Third City Water Tunnel	220	1,200
Distribution system rehabilitation	105	250
Subtotal, water	325	1,650
Electrical supply:		
Generating and transmission	3,455[c]	4,400
Distribution system		2,600[d]
Subtotal, electrical supply	3,455	7,000

Table A2-13. *(continued)*

Functional Category	Capital Investment, 1967-76	Capital Needs, 1977-86
Education:		
Elementary and secondary	$1,187	$ 500
Higher education	492	1,200
Subtotal, education	1,679	1,700
Water pollution control:		
Treatment plants and interceptors	1,047	1,200
Auxiliary pollution control		500[b]
Sewer system extension	271	1,500
Sewer system rehabilitation		500
Subtotal, water pollution control	1,318	3,700
Public buildings:		
Health and Hospitals	458	200
Other public buildings	518	250
Subtotal, public buildings	976	450
Parks and Museums	199	300
Economic development:		
Convention center	—	200
Ports, terminals and industrial parks	113	350
Subtotal, economic development	113	550
Solid waste disposal	22	550
Total, above categories	$9,276+[e]	$24,000

Sources: City construction program (1967-76) from reports of the NYC Director of Construction; electrical supply system data (1966-76) from Con Ed. Data for 1977-86 projected as indicated in text of report.

[a]Estimated at $200 million/year (average of city and Tri-State rates).

[b]These programs have no city commitment at present.

[c]Data is for 1966-75 period.

[d]Estimate pro-rated from Con Ed 1966-88 forecast and PASNY estimates.

[e]Total does not include data on arterial highway system or site/planning expenditures on Convention Center.

Comparing Needs and Resources

Capital construction may be financed by:

1. City funds appropriated in the capital budget and raised through the sale of bonds.
2. State and federal aid provided to New York City through intergovernmental grants or invested directly through state or federal construction programs (such as the state's arterial highway program or the federal Gateway National Park program).
3. Revenue-supported bonds issued by public agencies, such as the State Power Authority, or private companies, such as Consolidated Edison, for construction of electric, gas, or steam facilities.

Capital projects can also be financed through charges against the annual operating budgets of public or private organizations. The federal government, for example, has no separate capital budget and makes no distinction in its borrowing between current expenses and long-term capital investments. In addition, much of the investment in maintenance of capital facilities is financed through operating budgets; the line between maintenance and reconstruction is not always distinct.

CITY CAPITAL BUDGET

New York City's authority to raise capital funds by borrowing is derived from the state constitution, which places two major constraints on the municipality:

1. The total amount that may be borrowed for most public purposes is equal to 10 percent of the fair market value of all taxable real property in the city. For this purpose, the value of taxable real property is "equalized" (the assessed value is divided by an equalization ratio set by the State Board of Equalization based on its study of actual sales). The amount is averaged over a five-year period to avoid sharp annual fluctuations in the limit.

At present, this limit on long-term borrowing by the city is about $7.6 billion. As of July 1976, debt outstanding or planned against the limit accounted for about $6.6 billion, leaving an unencumbered margin of about $1 billion.[1]

The constitution also authorizes the city to borrow an additional 2 percent of its assessed taxable property values for housing purposes. In practice, this amount can be added to the general debt limit, increasing it to the equivalent of about 11 percent of market value (with a current equalization ratio on the order of 0.5). Thus, the total limit is approximately $8.5 billion at present.

2. In addition, the constitution allows certain public activities to be financed by long-term borrowing outside the debt limit. The debt limit does not apply to water supply projects and revenue-supported projects (such as middle-income housing or parking garages) permanently; exemption for water pollution control projects is renewable, as it has been in the past for transit and hospital construction programs. The outstanding amount of debt excluded from the limit is about $3.6 billion at present.

Other constraints on city borrowing have been given increased prominence by the fiscal crisis.

The fundamental constraint is the city's ability to sell its bonds. Since the spring of 1975, the general securities market has been closed to New York City. The only sales of long-term bonds since that date have been negotiated sales to the municipal pension funds. At this writing, it is impossible to forecast when and under what limitations New York City will be able to reenter the general security market.

The pension funds are by no means an unlimited source of funds for New York City's long-term debt. In November 1975, the municipal pension funds committed themselves to purchase up to $2.5 billion of city debt; of this amount, only $0.5 billion remains available for the 1977-78 capital budget. At best, the pension funds probably can purchase up to $1 billion of city bonds per year.

A second important constraint is the state-mandated Emergency Financial Control Board (EFCB), which must approve all municipal expenditures, at least through fiscal 1978. The EFCB has set limits for city bond sales for the three years of the 1966-68 Financial Plan at about $1 billion per year.

Another important constraint on the city's use of capital funds for construction purposes is the past allocation of much of the city's capital budget to nonconstruction purposes. A major proportion of the $1 billion per year allowed by the EFCB as capital funding at present goes to finance wholly nonconstruction-related operating activities (such as manpower training, vocational education, and lease payments) and other activities that are only partially related to construction (such as repair programs and engineering staffs of city agencies). Together, these programs account for some three-fourths of the total capital funds available for each year. Additional significant amounts are needed for equipment (such as sanitation trucks). Hence, only about $200 million per year is now available for major rehabilitation projects and new construction. The city is committed, by both charter change and Municipal Assistance Corporation (MAC) mandate, to phasing out most of the nonconstruction activities in its capital budget over the next ten years at an annual rate of $50 to $75 million. At present rates, however, the phaseout will take until 1985.

As a result, it is impossible to predict with any precision what level of capital funds New York City will be able to allocate to new construction and major improvements over the next decade. But on the assumption that the recent level of about $1 billion per year for all capital funds will continue throughout the coming decade, that some source will be found for this amount (MAC, pension funds, or the securities market), and that the phaseout of nonconstruction-related activities continues, construction funds might be available as follows:

Fiscal Year	Available Construction Funds (in $ millions)
1977	$ 200
1978	250
1979	300
1980	350
1981	400
1982	450
1983	500
1984	550
1985	600
1986	650
Ten-year total	$4,250

Actual availability of capital funds may range from about $3 billion to about $6 billion.

STATE AND FEDERAL AID

New York City receives intergovernmental grants from both the State of New York and the federal government for capital construction. Table A3-1 summarizes state and federal aid listed in the city's capital budget in fiscal years 1970 through 1977. (The amounts are those budgeted by the city and not actual receipts of intergovernmental grants during the eight-year period.) The city has on occasion budgeted such grants on an optimistic basis; in addition, years often pass from the budgeting of aid to its actual receipt. The table does, however, provide a reasonably accurate indication of the allocation of intergovernmental aid.

State capital aid programs have been heavily concentrated in environmental protection (water pollution control plants and interceptor sewers) and in transit. The $522 million in state transit grants represents the bulk of the city's $600 million share of the 1968 state transportation bond issue.

Table A3-1. State and Federal Capital Grants Budgeted by New York City, 1970-77 (in $ Millions)

	State		Federal	
Environmental protection	$ 879.9	54.4%	$1,271.5	33.9%
Transit	522.7	32.3	1,862.6	29.8
Transportation	34.7	2.1	122.4	3.3
City University	94.3	5.8	—	—
All other	85.5	5.3	486.3	13.0
Total	$1,617.1	100.0%	$3,742.8	100.0%

Source: New York City Capital Budgets, fiscal years 1970-77.

Federal capital aid has been concentrated in the same two categories. The city also has received substantial amounts of federal aid for urban renewal and community development.

On an annualized basis, New York has budgeted about $200 million per year in state grants and $470 million per year in federal grants. Actual receipts have probably been somewhat lower.

The future level of intergovernmental capital grants will be influenced by known factors:

1. The city has finished constructing its planned major pollution control facilities, except for the North River plant in Manhattan

and the Red Hook plant in Brooklyn. Federal and state funds for these two projects will probably be available, but after their completion, the city will not be able to use these sources of aid even for related purposes, such as sewer construction.

2. The city's share of state transit bond funds will be exhausted with the completion of the Queens trunk line. Another statewide referendum is needed to generate additional funds for transit. Governor Carey recently proposed a referendum for a multiyear $750 million state general construction program; New York City's share would probably be about half of the total.

STATE AND FEDERAL PROJECTS

In addition to state and federal grants to New York City, the city's physical plant should benefit from construction undertaken directly by state and federal agencies at no cost to the city. For example:

1. The Interstate highway program is financed on a 90/10 basis by federal and state funds, with no city contribution required. Westway and other expressway projects will thus not be a drain on the city's scarce capital resources.
2. Both state and federal agencies now have park responsibilities within New York City. The federal government is expected to provide the funds for Gateway National Park.
3. State agencies, such as the Department of Mental Hygiene, maintain extensive physical plants within New York City.

PUBLIC AUTHORITY PROJECTS

A number of state and interstate public authorities have responsibility for major physical projects in and around New York City. These agencies finance many of their projects through tolls and user charges.

The Port Authority constructs and finances such toll facilities as cross-Hudson bridges and tunnels, regional airports, and port facilities. The Triborough Bridge and Tunnel Authority (TBTA) has constructed and operates a number of major toll tunnels and bridges whose surplus income is now used to help subsidize mass transit and commuter railroads. The MTA, TBTA's parent, has responsibility for the Kennedy Airport-to-Manhattan rail connection and presumably will have a similar responsibility for any LaGuardia-to-Manhattan link. These projects are likely to be built only when and if federal grants become available because they cannot be supported from fares.

PRIVATELY FINANCED PROJECTS

Improvements in privately owned utility systems, such as electricity, telephone, gas, and steam, will be financed from operating revenues or debt issued by Consolidated Edison, New York Telephone, and other private utility companies. The only serious construction finance issue that may arise in this regard concerns Con Ed's ability to invest adequately in its continuing program of distribution system upgrading and to raise the necessary capital for construction of new generating plants.

THE NEEDS-RESOURCES GAP IN
THE 1977-86 PERIOD

The troubled state of New York City's finances makes it difficult to estimate the size of the gap between the city's infrastructure investment needs and future resource availability. In addition, it is difficult to predict the availability of state and federal capital grants and direct construction programs, as well as the problems that private utilities, such as Consolidated Edison, may encounter in raising capital to accomplish their construction objectives.

Tables A3-2 and A3-3 summarize the forecast needs presented in Table A2-1 and divide them into groups by probable funding source.

The data in Table A3-2 must be used with considerable caution. The priority allocation is by broad functional groupings, and the estimation of urgency is based on only a rough approximation of the project-by-project analysis used in the capital budget decisionmaking process. And the definition of need used in the calculations encompasses what would be desirable, as well as what might be considered essential in the face of fiscal constraints.

The estimates in Tables A3-2 and A3-3 suggest a total capital investment need in the areas covered in this report of $24 billion over the next decade. Of this amount, city fund sources would have to provide just over $10 billion or 43 percent; the remaining $14 billion would come from state or federal grants or through private finance (in the case of the electricity system).

If the city could restore its access to the security market, it could

Table A3-2. Assessment of Infrastructure Priorities by Priority of Function and Urgency of Need for Major Projects or Programs, 1977-86 (in $ Millions)

Functional Category by Priority of System	Major Projects or Programs	Urgency of Need		
		Critical Need	Serious Need	Optional
High priority:				
Mass transit	Queens trunk line		$1,200	
	Second Avenue line			$2,000
	Existing subways	$1,000	1,000	
Streets and highways	Arterial highways		1,000	1,000
	Street system	300	300	
	Bridges and structures	100	200	
Water system	Croton treatment			200
	Third City Tunnel	600	600	
	Distribution system	125	125	
Electrical supply	Distribution system	2,000	600	
	Generating and transmission	4,400		
Subtotal, high priority	—	8,525	5,025	3,200
Medium Priority:				
Sanitation	Resource recovery centers		550	
Water pollution	Treatment facilities		1,200	
	Auxiliary treatment			500
	Sewer rehabilitation	200	300	
	Sewer construction	500	1,000	
Subtotal, medium priority	—	700	3,050	500
Low priority:				
Education	New school buildings			250
	Modernization		150	
	Heating plant conversion			100
	City University		200	1,000
Parks and museums	Construction and rehabilitation		100	200
Health and hospitals	Rehabilitation and modernization		200	
Public buildings	Construction and rehabilitation		150	100
Economic development	Convention Center,			200
	ports, terminals, etc.		200	150
Subtotal, low priority	—		1,000	2,000
Totals	—	$9,225	$9,075	$5,700

Source: Derived from data in Table A2-1 and assessment of urgency by D. Grossman.

raise $4 billion for construction purposes within the constitutional limit and an additional $3 billion outside the debt limit for water supply and water pollution control projects. But the city would then still be about $3 billion short of the forecast level of need.

During the past decade, New York City awarded contracts for $5.8 billion in municipal, state, and federal funds, plus about $1 billion in arterial highway projects not included in that figure and another $3.5 billion in Con Ed construction. This total of about $10

Table A3-3. Summary of Infrastructure Needs by Priority of Function, Urgency of Need and Type of Funds, 1977-86 (in $ Millions)

Priority of Function	Urgency of Need			
	Critical	Serious	Optional	Total
High	1,425 C	1,475 C	2,200 C	5,100 C
	100 S	425 S	100 S	625 S
	600 F	2,525 F	900 F	4,025 F
	6,400 P	600 P	—P	7,000 P
Medium	700 C	2,000 C	62.5 C	2,762.5 C
	— S	150 S	62.5 S	212.5 S
	— F	900 F	375 F	1,275 F
Low	— C	900 C	1,500C	2,400 C
	— S	100 S	500S	600 S
	— F	— F	—F	—F
All programs	2,125 C	4,375 C	3,762.5 C	10,262.5 C
	100 S	675 S	662.5 S	1,437.5 S
	600 F	3,425 F	1,275 F	5,300 F
	6,400 P	600 P	—P	7,000 P
Totals, all funds	$9,225	$9,075	$5,700	$24,000

Source: Derived from Table A3-2 in text and Assessment of Priorities.
Note: C = city funds
          S = state
          F = federal
          P = private (Con Ed and PASNY)

billion for the 1966-75 decade is substantially below the needs forecast of $24 billion for the coming decade.

Obtaining state and federal grant funds in the amount suggested in the table appears to be a much less difficult problem, at least in two of the four categories in which such funds would be anticipated. State and federal funds for the arterial highway and the primary water pollution control programs appear reasonably assured. The availability of sufficient federal funds for construction of mass transit facilities after the Queens trunk line (the Second Avenue subway, in particular) and continued state support of City University construction are much less certain.

Electric generating and transmission facilities listed under the "Other" funds category would be financed by the State Power Authority (through issuance of revenue bonds) and Con Ed.

Matching Needs and Resources

The city can try to bring its construction program in line with the fiscal resources it will have available over the next decade by obtaining additional aid from the state and federal governments or by cutting back on construction. Almost certainly, both strategies will be required.

The federal government seems a more likely source of additional aid than does the state. Recent federal action to finance public works programs as a means of stimulating the economy has already expanded the considerable existing federal construction aid programs. Particular targets for New York City to set in obtaining additional federal aid would be:

- job-generating projects in such areas as street repair and water pipe and sewer replacement;
- extension of federal aid for water pollution control construction, the auxiliary pollution control system, or the Third City water tunnel;
- aid for economic development projects, such as industrial parks.

In the absence of greatly expanded aid programs, New York City will be forced to allocate scarce fiscal resources among many desirable projects, and is likely to begin by cutting back the investments necessary to maintain the quality of the water, street, and sewer systems.

SUGGESTIONS FOR NEXT STEPS

The needs of the city's physical infrastructure require further consideration, including:

1. *More definitive analysis.* Given the limitations of time and funds available, this study has, of necessity, been largely bounded by information available in specific studies of particular functional areas (such as work by the Tri-State Regional Planning Commission, RPA, the Department of City Planning, and the New York Power Pool) and by information that could be obtained

through interviews. A more thorough analysis could refine these estimates of need considerably; in addition, attention could be focused on such important unresolved issues as:

- How adequate are present forecasts of electrical energy demand and generating station construction in relation to future city economic development goals?

- What standards are minimally acceptable for reconstruction and rehabilitation of critically important public utility systems, such as water and sewer lines?

- Is the Second Avenue subway still deserving of a place in the city's construction priorities in light of its enormous cost and small contribution to new transit ridership?

2. *A capital financing program.* The collapse of the city's capital budget under the pressure of the fiscal crisis, coupled with the near-collapse of the state's "moral obligation" public authority finance structure, leaves the issue of financing future infrastructure improvements wholly unresolved. Among the major alternative resources are state and federal capital grant programs and direct construction (e.g., Gateway Park). Alternatives such as increasing reliance on revenue-supported debt (e.g., for water and sewer line construction) also need to be explored.

3. *Exploration of additional subjects.* Important infrastructure elements not covered in this report include the telephone/telecommunications system, the commuter and freight rail systems, and the waterfront goods handling system. This report also does not address the serious physical and economic problems that affect the $60 billion worth of private residential, commercial, industrial, and institutional structures that the public infrastructure of New York City exists to support.

To a very great degree, the physical city of the mid-1980s already exists. In 1985, the city will be composed of most of the same streets, sewers, subways, and structures that comprise today's city. How well this physical system meets the needs of the New York City of a decade hence depends in substantial measure on investments in maintenance, rehabilitation, and new construction to be made during the years ahead.

Notes

CHAPTER A2

1. *1966-1977 Draft Capital Budget and Capital Improvement Plan for Ensuing Five Fiscal Years*, City Planning Commission, January 1976.
2. *Transportation Policy and Programs*, Mayor's Policy Committee, March 1975 (mimeo).
3. *Maintaining Mobility: The Plan and Program for Regional Transportation Through 2000*, Tri-State Regional Planning Commission, November 1976.
4. *Financing Public Transportation*, Regional Plan Association, March 1976.
5. *Main Report*, p. 37.
6. *Report of Member Electric Systems of the New York Power Pool (Pursuant to Article VIII, Section 149-b of the Public Service Law)*, 1976.
7. This figure includes an estimate for cost escalation to the time of contract award as planned in CUNY's 1971 construction program. The assumption was that costs would escalate by 60 percent from 1971 to 1978.
8. Parochial and other private schools enroll about three in every ten children of school age in New York City. Their enrollments have remained essentially constant in the past five years.
9. In current prices, major modernization costs about $750,000 per elementary school, $1.5 million for an intermediate school, and $2.5 million for a high school.
10. A 1,200-pupil elementary school costs about $10 million; an 1,800-pupil intermediate school costs about $14 million; and a 2,000-pupil high school costs about $15 million at present.

CHAPTER A3

1. *Report Pursuant to Section 212 of the Charter*, Office of the Comptroller, City of New York, October 15, 1976.